Raymond Aron and International Relations

At a time when the field of International Relations (IR) is diverting from grand theoretical debates, rediscovering the value of classical realism and exploring its own intellectual history, this book contributes to these debates by presenting a cohesive view of Raymond Aron's theory of IR. It explores how a careful reading of Aron can contribute to important current debates, in particular what a theory of IR can be (and thus, what is within or outside the scope of this theory), how to bridge the gap that emerged in the 1970s between a "normative" and a "scientific" theory of IR, and finally how multidisciplinarity is possible (and desirable) in the study of IR.

This edited collection offers a synthetic approach to Raymond Aron's theory of International Relations by bringing together some of the most prominent specialists on Raymond Aron, thus filling an important gap in the current market of books devoted to IR theories and the historiography of the field. The volume is divided into three parts: the first part explores Aron's intellectual contribution to the theoretical debates in IR, thus showing his originality and prescience; the second part traces Aron's influence and explores his relations with other prominent scholars of his time, thus contributing to the historiography of the field; and the third part analyses Aron's contemporary relevance. This comprehensive volume contributes to current debates in the field by showing the originality and breadth of Aron's thought.

This book will be of great interest to academics and students interested in IR theories, strategic studies and the historiography of the field.

Olivier Schmitt is Associate Professor of Political Science at the Center for War Studies, University of Southern Denmark, and the scientific director of the French Association for War and Strategic Studies (AEGES). His work focuses on International Relations theories, strategic studies and contemporary warfare.

The New International Relations
Edited by Richard Little
University of Bristol
Iver B. Neumann
Norwegian Institute of International Affairs (NUPI), Norway
and Jutta Weldes
University of Bristol

The field of international relations has changed dramatically in recent years. This new series will cover the major issues that have emerged and reflect the latest academic thinking in this particular dynamic area.

A full list of titles is available here: www.routledge.com/New-International-Relations/book-series/NEWIR

The Politics of Globality since 1945
Assembling the planet
Edited by Rens van Munster and Casper Sylvest

Evaluating Progress in International Relations
How do you know?
Edited by Annette Freyberg-Inan, Ewan Harrison and Patrick James

Russia and the Idea of Europe 2nd Edition
A study in identity and International Relations
Iver B. Neumann

Memories of Empire and Entry into International Society
Views from the European periphery
Edited by Filip Ejdus

Great Power Multilateralism and the Prevention of War
Debating a 21st century concert of powers
Edited by Harald Müller and Carsten Rauch

De-Constructing the Dynamics of World-Societal Order
The power of governmentality in Palestine
Jan Busse

Raymond Aron and International Relations
Edited by Olivier Schmitt

Raymond Aron and International Relations

Edited by Olivier Schmitt

LONDON AND NEW YORK

First published 2018
by Routledge
2 Park Square, Milton Park, Abingdon, Oxon OX14 4RN

and by Routledge
711 Third Avenue, New York, NY 10017

Routledge is an imprint of the Taylor & Francis Group, an informa business

© 2018 selection and editorial matter, Olivier Schmitt; individual chapters, the contributors

The right of Olivier Schmitt to be identified as the author of the editorial matter, and of the authors for their individual chapters, has been asserted in accordance with sections 77 and 78 of the Copyright, Designs and Patents Act 1988.

All rights reserved. No part of this book may be reprinted or reproduced or utilized in any form or by any electronic, mechanical, or other means, now known or hereafter invented, including photocopying and recording, or in any information storage or retrieval system, without permission in writing from the publishers.

Trademark notice: Product or corporate names may be trademarks or registered trademarks, and are used only for identification and explanation without intent to infringe.

British Library Cataloguing-in-Publication Data
A catalogue record for this book is available from the British Library

Library of Congress Cataloging-in-Publication Data
Names: Schmitt, Olivier, 1988– editor.
Title: Raymond Aron and international relations / edited by Olivier Schmitt.
Description: Abingdon, Oxon ; New York, NY : Routledge, 2018. | Series: The new international relations | Includes bibliographical references and index.
Identifiers: LCCN 2017054529| ISBN 9781138659575 (hardback) | ISBN 9781315620114 (ebook)
Subjects: LCSH: International relations–Philosophy. | Aron, Raymond, 1905–1983.
Classification: LCC JZ1305 .R4 2018 | DDC 327.101–dc23
LC record available at https://lccn.loc.gov/2017054529

ISBN: 978-1-138-65957-5 (hbk)
ISBN: 978-1-315-62011-4 (ebk)

Typeset in Times New Roman
by Wearset Ltd, Boldon, Tyne and Wear

Contents

Notes on contributors vii
Foreword x

Introduction 1
OLIVIER SCHMITT

1 **The classical foundations of Raymond Aron's theory of international relations** 14
BRYAN-PAUL FROST

2 **Pilgrims' progress: the disenchanted destinations of Raymond Aron and Georges Canguilhem** 33
REED M. DAVIS

3 **A theory of international relations or a theory of foreign policy? Reading *Peace and War among Nations*** 53
OLIVIER SCHMITT

4 **Aron's oxymorus international ethics** 70
JEAN-BAPTISTE JEANGÈNE VILMER

5 **Raymond Aron, war and nuclear weapons: the primacy of politics paradox** 93
CHRISTIAN MALIS†

6 **Raymond Aron and the idea of Europe** 111
JOËL MOURIC

7 **Beyond Soviet and American models of industrialization: Aron's third way approach to global development** 126
DANIEL STEINMETZ-JENKINS

8 **Raymond Aron's heritage for the International Relations discipline: the French school of sociological liberalism** 142
THOMAS MESZAROS AND ANTONY DABILA

9 **Raymond Aron and the ethics of current global affairs** 163
ARIANE CHEBEL D'APPOLLONIA

10 **The diplomat, the soldier, and the spy: toward a new taxonomy in International Relations** 179
OLIVIER CHOPIN

Index 195

Contributors

Ariane Chebel d'Appollonia, educated at Sciences Po (PhD, HDR), is a Professor in the School of Public Affairs and Administration (SPAA) and in the Division of Global Affairs (DGA) at Rutgers University. She is also Senior Researcher affiliated to the CEVIPOF (Sciences Po, Paris). Her research focuses on the politics of immigration, security issues, racism and xenophobia, administrative ethics, and ethics of global affairs. She has taught at universities both in France (Sciences Po, Paris III–Sorbonne) and in the United States (New York University, University of Pittsburgh). She was appointed as the Buffet Chair Professor at Northwestern University (2005) and was a visiting fellow at the European Center of Excellence at the University of Pittsburgh (2004–2006). She was awarded the EU–US Fulbright scholarship in 2006. She has published six books, 54 book chapters and articles, and two edited books. Her recent publications include *Les Frontières du Racisme* (Presses de Sciences Po, 2011), *Frontiers of Fears: Immigration and Insecurity in the United States and Europe* (Cornell University Press, 2012) and *Migrant Mobilization and Securitization in the US and Europe: How Does It Feel to Be a Threat?* (Palgrave Macmillan, NYU Series, 2015).

Olivier Chopin is Associate Researcher at the École des hautes études en sciences sociales (CESPRA-EHESS) and Adjunct Senior Lecturer at Sciences Po, Paris. His works include *Etudier le renseignement, état de l'art et perspectives de recherche* (Études de l'IRSEM no. 9, 2012), *Pourquoi l'Amérique nous espionne?* (Hikari, 2014) and, most recently, *Renseignement et Sécurité*, a textbook on intelligence studies (Armand Colin, 2016).

Antony Dabila has a PhD from Paris–Sorbonne University in political historical sociology. He is currently teaching at Lyon III–Jean Moulin University, in the Department of International Relations and Political Sciences. His work is focused on the conceptual framework of strategic decisions. He recently conducted a study on post-traumatic stress disorder and its influence on tactical decision and operational planning for the Strategic Research Institute of the Military School (IRSEM) of Paris. He has also started a study on the organizational consequences of cyber integration at the tactical level for the Lyon

Centre of International Security and Defence Studies (CLESID) and the Crisis Studies Institute (IEC).

Reed M. Davis is Professor of Political Science at Seattle Pacific University. His scholarship revolves primarily around exploring the work of Raymond Aron, and he is the author of *A Politics of Understanding: The International Thought of Raymond Aron* (LSU Press, 2009). In recent years, he has turned his attention to the influence of Darwinian evolution on the social sciences, especially in International Relations theory. His most recent article on Darwin and the social sciences, "Up from Nihilism: Classical Realism and the Case against a Darwinian Theory of International Relations," appears in the journal *Modern Age*. He also directs The Augustinian Fellowship, a study abroad program located in Honfleur and St. Maximin, France.

Bryan-Paul Frost is the Elias "Bo" Ackal, Jr./BORSF Endowed Professor of Political Science at the University of Louisiana at Lafayette. He is contributor and co-editor (with Timothy Burns) of *Philosophy, History, and Tyranny: Reexamining the Debate between Leo Strauss and Alexandre Kojève* (SUNY, 2016), co-editor (with Jeremy J. Mhire) of *The Political Theory of Aristophanes: Explorations in Poetic Wisdom* (SUNY, 2014), contributor, translator and co-editor (with Daniel J. Mahoney) of *Political Reason in the Age of Ideology: Essays in Honor of Raymond Aron* (Transaction, 2007), contributor and co-editor (with Jeffrey Sikkenga) of *History of American Political Thought* (Lexington Books, 2003) and editor and co-translator (with Robert Howse) of Alexandre Kojève's *Outline of a Phenomenology of Right* (Rowman & Littlefield, 2000). In addition to the above, Frost has also published articles on Aristotle, Cato the Younger, Cicero and Roman civic education, Rousseau, and Tocqueville and Emerson.

Jean-Baptiste Jeangène Vilmer has been the Director of the Institute for Strategic Studies (IRSEM, French Ministry for Armed Forces) since June 2016. Previously, he was a policy advisor on security issues at the French Ministry of Foreign Affairs Policy Planning Staff (2013–2016); a Banting postdoctoral fellow at McGill University's Faculty of Law (2011–2013); a Lecturer in International Relations at the Department of War Studies of King's College London (2010–2011); a postdoctoral fellow at the Ecole Normale Supérieure Ulm (2010); and a postgraduate fellow of the MacMillan Center for International and Area Studies at Yale University (2008–2009). Holding degrees in three different disciplines, philosophy (BA, MA, PhD), law (LLB, LLM) and political science (PhD), he conducts interdisciplinary research on the theory and ethics of international relations and on international public law. In particular, he studies the ethics and laws of war, international humanitarian law and international criminal law. He is the author of more than 15 books, including *Pas de paix sans justice? Le dilemme de la paix et de la justice en sortie de conflit armé* (Presses de Sciences Po, 2011), *Ethique des relations internationales* (PUF, 2013), *Erythrée, un naufrage totalitaire* (PUF, 2015),

La Responsabilité de protéger (PUF, 2015) and *La Guerre au nom de l'humanité: Tuer ou laisser mourir* (PUF, 2012).

Christian Malis† is a graduate of the Ecole Normale Superieure and an Associate Researcher with the St-Cyr military school. He is the author of several books on French strategic thought and contemporary security studies, including *Raymond Aron et le Débat Stratégique Français* (Economica, 2005), *Pierre-Marie Gallois: Géopolitique, Histoire et Stratégie* (L'Âge d'homme, 2009) and *Guerre et Stratégie au 21e Siècle* (Fayard, 2014).

Thomas Meszaros is currently Associate Professor of Political Science at the University of Lyon III (France). He is a member of the Lyon Centre of International Security and Defence Studies (CLESID) and of the Crisis Studies Institute (IEC). His research focuses particularly on the sociology and philosophy of International Relations, notably on the renewal of the Aronian research project, and Strategic Studies, in particular on crisis theory and modeling.

Joël Mouric is an *agrégé* and *docteur* (PhD) in history. He is an Associate Researcher at the University of Western Brittany in Brest, and winner of the 2011 Raymond Aron Prize. A contributor to *Commentaire* and the *Journal of Political Criticism* (Seoul), he has published *Raymond Aron et l'Europe* (Rennes University Press, 2013) and translated Hans Delbrück's *Die Stratégie des Perikles* (*La Stratégie oubliée*, Economica, 2015, with a foreword by Daniel J. Mahoney). He is co-editor, with Fabrice Bouthillon and Matthias Oppermann, of *Nationalisme, libéralisme, post-modernité, Raymond Aron et la défense de la liberté* (Bernard de Fallois, 2016).

Olivier Schmitt is an Associate Professor of International Relations at the Center for War Studies, University of Southern Denmark. He is the author of *Pourquoi Poutine est notre Allié? Anatomie d'une Passion Française* (Hikari, 2017) and *Allies That Count: Junior Partners in Coalition Warfare* (Georgetown University Press, 2018). His research focuses on multinational military cooperation, comparative defense policies and defense transformation in Europe, and French thought on international relations.

Daniel Steinmetz-Jenkins is a Presidential Visiting Assistant Professor in the Department of Religious Studies at Yale University. He is writing a book for Columbia University Press titled: *The Other Intellectuals: Raymond Aron and the United States*. He has published academic articles in *Modern Intellectual History*, *Journal of the History of Ideas* and the *Tocqueville Review*.

Foreword

Most International Relations (IR) scholars who are able to establish a legacy that outlasts their own lifetime have nonetheless remained largely unknown to the rest of the academic community. For Raymond Aron (1905–1983), the problem seems to be the opposite. Aron's place as an historian of social ideas is assured by dint of his work on sundry sociologists and also Carl von Clausewitz. As noted by a number of contributors to this volume, however, although his 1962 synthesis on IR, *Paix et Guerre entre les Nations* (English translation *Peace and War*, 1966), is still being read, Aron's standing as an IR theorist is tenuous. The most obvious reason for this remains Aron's own writing choices. Most of his IR writings were comments on contemporary affairs, be they in the form of newspaper columns or trade books. Meszaros and Dabila stress how what they call the Aronian tradition of sociological liberalism works on three levels of analysis: philosophical concepts, sociological regularities and historical inquiries. Regarding philosophy, Aron contributed little. It would be an overstatement to say that the best Aron produced regarding sociological regularities was his student Pierre Bourdieu, but it remains a fact that Aron solved no specific theoretical problem or coined no specific approach.

What is celebrated in Aron's volume is his "temperament" and his "wisdom", which seems to denote his willingness to take into consideration a wide array of factors. In addition to his interest in philosophy, sociology and history, particular stress is put on his insistence on keeping in mind both questions of ends and means when considering the ethical aspects of agency. If we pair this up with Aron's focus on agency and his insistence on privileging individuals generally and the statesman specifically in his analysis, we get the measure of a man who saw himself basically as a polyhistor who chose to be a sometimes critical advisor to the powers that be. Aron was what he called a *spectateur engagé*, or what an American would call a defence intellectual, who insisted on considering each event on its merits. The plying of such a trade cannot by definition be a theoretical one, for whatever definition one chooses for theory, it has to do with backgrounding certain aspects of a general phenomenon in order to foreground others. If one chooses to include everything that is potentially relevant, one may produce a well-rounded analysis of a specific event in time and space or, at least if one is Kant, a critique of the preconditions for a certain phenomenon. One would be hard put to theorise social form, however, for that would take abstraction, and abstraction would mean doing away with certain potentially relevant factors in order to highlight others. This is what Aron (as opposed to, say, Bourdieu) was unwilling to do, and so Aron stayed on the level of theoretically informed analysis of specific phenomena. The key possible exception is the analysis of the phenomenon of war that he produced in his Clausewitz book, and so it is no coincidence that this remains his best-remembered book on IR matters.

All this would be a problem were theory the only thing that mattered in social science, but it is not. The reason why this book appears in a series on The New International Relations lies elsewhere. As argued a quarter-of-a-century ago by Rob Walker, IR theory may be more interesting for what it tells us about ongoing politics than for its analytical purchase. As Aron himself would stress, ideas, or, more generally, knowledge production, is an integral part of policy formation. This book gives us a full-lit view of how French Cold War foreign policy emerged through the interventions of one particularly theoretically informed participant in its shaping, namely Raymond Aron. Particularly given its stress on security policy, it stands in this regard as a French companion volume to Rens van Munster and Casper Sylvest's *Nuclear Realism: Global Political Thought during the Thermonuclear Revolution*, which detailed the thinking and general impact of certain Anglo-Saxon and German thinkers on security policy in the post-war period. The New International Relations series is proud to contribute such hands-on analyses of the role of knowledge in foreign policy making and international relations, and hopes to expand the scope of these beyond the Western world in forthcoming volumes.

Iver B. Neumann

Introduction

Olivier Schmitt

Has another dead French thinker anything interesting to say about contemporary International Relations (IR)? With Bourdieu, Foucault and Derrida continuously referenced by critical scholars and international political sociologists, do we need to exhume Raymond Aron, entered IR's collective consciousness as a relatively outdated "Cold Warrior" classical realist? The answer is a resounding yes (as one could expect the editor of a volume on Raymond Aron would say). This book's ambition is to highlight the multiple ways Aron made an important, and under-appreciated, contribution to IR scholarship through an ambitious, pluri-disciplinary, intellectual agenda and an effort to weave together research and public debate.

In terms of topics covered throughout his career, Aron is one of the very few IR thinkers able to combine the study of power politics (including strategic and military issues), international economics, the long-term transformation of societies and ethical inquiry. Conceptually, Aron developed an original theory of history and a sociological approach that allowed him to give analytical clarity, rigour and cohesiveness to seemingly disparate social issues. In IR, his approach can be summarized in a number of key features:

- emphasizing concept development over structural theorizing;
- combining the study of regime types (comparative politics, a field to which he made several important contributions) and of the international system, thus exploring their mutual interactions;
- remembering the "primacy of politics" (and thus the possibility of war) in the study of international phenomena;
- exploring the ethical dimension of international activities, as human actions can only be interpreted, and assessed, through an appropriate ethical framework.

As such, an exploration of Aron's ideas and concepts is particularly interesting for contemporary IR scholarship, which emerges from the "inter-paradigmatic battle" between realism, liberalism and constructivism with a renewed attention to concept development and more complex thinking (or "analytical eclecticism"), and an appetite for social theorizing which explains the multiplicity of "turns" that the field is allegedly taking every two or three years. IR scholars are also more and more concerned with their place in public debates (Dyvik *et al.* 2017), as exemplified by the number of "bridging-the-gap" (between scholars and policy makers) contributions in various forms published every year. It just so happens that Aron has made several conceptual contributions to IR; his pluralist approach allowed him to be equally proficient in several interrelated subfields and his own life is a perpetual back and forth between scholarly thinking and political impact, upon which contemporary scholars could profitably ponder. In short, Aron is a complex thinker fit for our time.

This relevance of Aron's thinking is not limited to IR, as numerous recent publications illustrate. Recently, a *Companion to Raymond Aron* (Colen and Dutartre-Michaut 2015) usefully summarized the key aspects of Aron's thinking to an anglophone audience and illustrated the relevance of his intellectual contributions to several fields. For example, Serge Paugam (2005, 2014) uses Aron's sociological analysis of industrial societies to conceptualize the current transformations of class relations in a new economic era; Aron's complex relationship to Kant, Aristotle, Tocqueville and Machiavelli inspires contemporary thinkers on democracy and political theorists (Mesure 1984; Audier 2004; Manent 2010); and researchers of totalitarianism are inspired by his concept of "secular religion" (Gentile 2006; Maier 2004–2007).

In IR, success has been more modest. Despite *Peace and War among Nations* being recognized after its publication as a major work, the interest in Aron's scholarship faded with the emergence of structural realism as a major paradigm. Yet, several scholars made important contributions to the understanding of Aron's IR approach, and highlighted his importance. At Harvard, Stanley Hoffmann (who had personally known Aron) regularly referenced him and called *Peace and War* "the most comprehensive and convincing theory of interstate politics" in an obituary he wrote for the *New York Review of Books* (Hoffmann 1983a), later developing his argument on the importance of Raymond Aron for IR in an article published in English by *International Studies Quarterly* and in French by *Politique Étrangère* (Hoffmann 1983b, 1985). Hoffmann's important book *World Disorders* (2000) also makes numerous references to Aron, highlighting his differences with Hedley Bull and Kenneth Waltz, and using several of Aron's concepts in the analysis. Authors such as Bryan-Paul Frost (1997, 2006, 2013) and Daniel Mahoney (1992) have regularly called upon Aron's importance, and Reed M. Davis' *A Politics of Understanding: The International Thought of Raymond Aron* (2009) constitutes a primary resource to understand Aron's approach to international relations and the important role of his philosophy of history. In France, his student Pierre Hassner worked in Aron's tradition, but the local IR scholarship evolved in another, more Durkheim-inspired, tradition (Battistella 2013). It is nevertheless interesting to observe a new generation of French IR scholars explicitly using Aron's concepts to study international ethical issues (Jeangène Vilmer 2013; Châton 2012) or war and strategic studies (Holeindre 2012; Ramel 2013).

Despite these efforts, one could hardly say that Aron is a mainstream author in contemporary IR scholarship. This book's ambition is to help change that perception, by demonstrating how Aron's efforts are still relevant for contemporary debates in the field. The book understands the title *Raymond Aron and International Relations* in two ways. First, classically for IR scholars, the authors critically assess key aspects of Aron's work, emphasizing their originality and relevance. Second, the volume also shows how Aron contributed to the international politics debates of his time, for example on nuclear deterrence or Europe. The book therefore discusses Aron's contribution to both International Relations (as a scientific field) and international relations (as a political activity), by gathering a diverse group of internationalists, historians and political theorists. The remainder of this Introduction therefore briefly sketches out Aron's biography and his efforts to blend first-rate scholarship and policy debates, before emphasizing the peculiarity of his approach to social issues and presenting the various contributions to the volume.

Raymond Aron: a twentieth-century "committed spectator"

Raymond Aron's career is now well known, thanks to the publication of his own memoirs, as well as two important biographies (Colquhoun 1986; Baverez 1993) and a very apt summary (Châton 2017). Aron was born in 1905 into an intellectual, petit-bourgeois family. Both his parents were integrated Jewish: they supported the Republic, were patriotic and not religious, fitting the pattern of French Jews "passionate with the Republic" analysed by Birnbaum (1992). In 1924, he successfully passed the entrance exam of the Ecole Normale Supérieure (ENS), an elite literary school training the Parisian intellectual bourgeoisie, and openly acknowledged his left-leaning political sensitivity. While at the ENS, he met several future famous French intellectuals, including Jean-Paul Sartre, Paul Nizan and Georges Canguilhem. He was ranked first at the *agrégation* of philosophy in 1928, and started publishing pacifist articles, inspired by the star-philosopher of his time: Alain.

From March 1930 to August 1933, Aron travelled to Germany, teaching French in Cologne and researching in Berlin. This period had a strong influence on him, for two reasons. First, he vastly broadened his intellectual horizon by reading Marx (whose work was only partly translated into French at the time) and discovering new research in philosophy (notably phenomenology with Husserl and Heidegger, and the Frankfurt School through the work of Marcuse) and sociology (in particular historical sociology though his encounter with Max Weber, Karl Mannheim and Norbert Elias). For a young intellectual whose philosophical training was limited in France to the dominating neo-Kantianism and the sociological education that revolved around Durkheim's positivism, the German sojourn was an eye-opener. Second, Aron was the direct witness to the fall of the Weimar Republic and the rise of national socialism, which left a very profound impression on him as he understood that a new war with Germany was coming. When Aron came back to Paris, he was no longer a pacifist. His German experience, as an intellectual and a witness, thus deeply influenced his thinking as he devoted himself to a better understanding of both the philosophy of history and the importance of politics.

In 1938, Aron defended his PhD dissertation, entitled "Introduction to the Philosophy of History", which criticized the dominating positivist understanding of history (see below) and led to a rather heated public defence; he subsequently found his first academic job at the University of Toulouse in 1939. He was almost immediately mobilized in the French forces after the declaration of war, and spent the Phoney War reading Keynes and writing about Machiavelli. Taken aback by the surprising French defeat (Nord 2015), Aron sailed to the United Kingdom on June 23, 1940 (without having heard de Gaulle's famous BBC call of June 18) with the aim of joining the British forces to continue the fight. He was one of the few academics in London and was contacted by officers close to de Gaulle in order to take editorial responsibilities in the intellectual journal of the Free French, aptly named *La France Libre*. Although Aron had travelled to the UK to fight, he nevertheless accepted the offer after a few days of hesitation. Although the journal was initially conceived as a very "Gaullist" publication, it quickly acquired editorial independence from the core of the Gaullist movement, and Aron was one of the authors participating in this intellectual emancipation: he was never a hard-core Gaullist, being instinctively resistant to the cult of personality that surrounded de Gaulle.

After the war, Aron went back to Paris as a journalist. In particular, between 1946 and 1947, he worked for *Combat*, one of the most prestigious left-wing intellectual newspapers that emerged from the French resistance, joining authors such as Albert Camus, Jean-Paul Sartre, André Malraux and Emmanuel Mounier. He later worked for *Le Figaro*, a surprising move for an author coming from the Left, with the explicit aim of shaking the beliefs of the French bourgeoisie. In 1947, he joined the Rassemblement du Peuple Français (RPF), a political movement founded by de Gaulle, with the hope of influencing the party toward a more pro-American and pro-parliament line. Aron left the movement in 1953, observing the RPF's failure to transform French politics, and his own failure to deeply influence the party line. In 1955, he published an important book, *L'Opium des Intellectuels* (translated into English in 1957), in which he criticized left-wing intellectuals (particularly Sartre and Merleau-Ponty) for their adulation of the communist movement based on three "myths": the myth of the Left, the myth of Revolution and the myth of the Proletariat. From that moment on, he was definitely perceived by left-wing circles as a core member of the conservative bourgeoisie.

Aron went back to university in 1955, being elected the chair of sociology at Sorbonne University. He thus started a thirty-year-long dual career as an academic and a political commentator. His overarching intellectual effort was an attempt to study in depth the sociological transformation of modern societies, in particular through the double influence of industrialization and competing ideologies. He published a number of important books on those topics, including *Dix-Huit Leçons sur la Société Industrielle* (1962), *Démocratie et Totalitarisme* (1965), *Trois Essais sur l'Âge Industriel* (1966) and *Les Désillusions du Progrès* (1969). International relations are the general context in which he studied the transformation of modern societies from a sociological perspective, and he could not leave this important aspect aside. His intellectual contributions to the topic notably include a general intellectual framework to think about IR (*Paix et Guerre entre les Nations*, 1962), an analysis of nuclear strategies in relation to the French debate (*Le Grand Débat*, 1963), an analysis of the US foreign policy (*La République Impériale*, 1973) and a critical discussion of the epistemology of war based on a close reading of Clausewitz (*Penser la Guerre, Clausewitz*, 1976). Aron was thus a prolific writer, contributing to several important academic debates of his time. He was also a driving force behind the institutionalization of sociology as an independent academic discipline in the French landscape, creating the Centre de Sociologie Européenne in which, notably, he trained Pierre Bourdieu. He finished his academic career by being elected to the Collège de France in 1970. While highly influential in the academic circles of the time, Aron's work is now rarely quoted, which sociologist Peter Baehr (2013) attributes to a failure on Aron's side to "brand" his scholarship around a few buzzwords ready for easy consumption by students and academics alike.

Simultaneously, Aron kept engaging with the public debates of his time. In 1957 and 1958, he published two books on the Algerian war, in which he calls for decolonization and explains why there could be no other conclusion to the conflict than independence (*La Tragédie Algérienne* and *L'Algérie et la République*). The right-wing parties, who thought that Aron was "one of them" after he had criticized the fascination for communism in his *L'Opium des Intellectuels*, were taken aback and vigorously counter-attacked. As Aron was writing in his typical dispassionate tone, logically parsing the arguments and concluding with a defence of Algerian independence, his opponents accused him of "ice-cold realism": if he defended independence, surely, he must have no heart and no feelings (Winock 2017: 1194–1202). A few years later, Aron was an important actor in the major strategic debate taking place in France concerning the proper nuclear strategy to adopt. In *Le Grand Débat* (1963), Aron became the proponent of an approach according to which the French nuclear deterrent should be aimed at reinforcing the American deterrence capabilities: while France could be in competition with some allies on several issues, competition should not be confused with hostility. The enemy was to the East. This ties in with Aron's long-term engagement against communism and his constant reminder of the ideological challenge that the Soviet Union was posing to liberal democracies. Through his numerous op-eds and journalistic articles, Aron was strongly engaged in the defence of Western countries, which led him to be identified as being to the right in the French political field.

In 1981, interviews with sociologists Jean-Louis Missika and Thierry Wolton were published under the title *Le Spectateur Engagé* (the committed spectator), which stuck as Aron's nickname, since it captured so well the difficult balance between scholarship and political debate he had tried to achieve. In 1983, Aron published his *Mémoires* with great success, just before passing away on October 17 of the same year.

Aron's approach to the social world

Aron's understanding of the social world (including International Relations) is based on two important premises: the philosophy of history he developed, as well as a critical engagement with Max Weber. Discussing those two aspects, which constitute his broader meta-theoretical approach, is therefore important in order to fully appreciate his contribution to IR scholarship.

In his PhD dissertation, "*Introduction à la Philosophie de l'Histoire*", Aron tackles the issue of the epistemological basis for a historical science. He particularly rejects two tendencies: on the one hand, the analyses postulating a unicity of human history; on the other, the approach emphasizing the multiplicity and incommensurability of human experiences. Historical materialism is a good example of the former tendency, while Spengler's philosophy (inspired by Nietzsche) illustrates the latter. Aron shows that there are two intertwined problems related to the study of historical knowledge. First, to what extent can historical knowledge be constituted as a specific science? Aron discusses here the famous opposition between *explaining* and *understanding* and argues that the unicity/multiplicity tendencies he is battling against are each a radicalization of one of those approaches to historical knowledge: the "unicity" tendency puts an over-emphasis on explanation, while the "multiplicity" tendency is an exaggeration of understanding. Second, what relationship can be established between the particular and the general, or between the micro and the macro levels of analysis?

Aron proposes an integrated solution to those two issues. He considers that all human phenomena are social (as they happen among social groups) but hold a degree of uniqueness: collective forces cannot explain everything. For Aron, there is no single element determining the course of societies, whether religious, political or economic. This understanding leads him to criticize both psychologists unwilling to recognize macro-level data, and sociologists who are prisoners of their research on "regularities", and to call for an integration of both. In contemporary terms, one could say that he notices the co-constitution of the agent and the structure but gives none of them ontological priority in the explanation of an event. Therefore, it is necessary for historical research to explore two directions simultaneously: the event (and the roles of actors' strategies in it) and the regularities of some phenomena. Patterns only appear in the social order at the macro level, and provide the context in which to understand the micro level, which must be studied with all its specificities. Historical research must then both explore the conjuncture, which makes a situation *possible* (and can be the subject of research on the regularities of the occurrence of such situations), and the specific unfolding of the *event*, which is by definition exceptional, taking into account the actors' motivations and strategies. Aron therefore calls for a "hermeneutic circle" between *explaining* and *understanding*, challenging both the positivist accounts underlying the research of general "causes" and a relativism over-emphasizing the uniqueness of each event. Before studying the macro level (where social patterns can be *explained*), one must attempt to *understand* a specific event through the use of appropriate concepts, an effort that Aron calls "deterministic probabilism": the attempt to uncover patterns of regularities can only go so far and actors' decisions must be interpreted in context. Aron then particularly opposed the "events happened as they did because they had to happen" or the "I could have told you so" types of scholarship.

Aron bases this philosophy of history on a critical engagement with Max Weber (Breiner 2011). Aron's discovery of Weber was enlightening for the young French scholar, as the German sociologist's interpretivist approach dovetails neatly with his reluctance regarding the positivist abstract research of general causes, epitomized in France by Emile Durkheim. He was also seduced by the importance Weber grants to politics, and the importance of the concept of *domination* in the chapter 4 of *Economics and Society*. However, although he was initially interested in Weberian concepts such as the ideal-type or the difference between the ethics of conviction and the ethics of responsibility, Aron distances himself from Weber in a number ways. Famously, Weber creates the methodological tool of the ideal-type, an intellectual construct exaggerating social features that serves the investigator as a measuring rod to ascertain similarities as well as deviations in concrete cases. Aron is generally favourable to the ideal-types, albeit with certain reservations, which reveal a deeper disagreement on the interaction between analysis and values. Aron observes that the logic of the ideal-type implies that each researcher tries to answer a self-defined question and, once the question is established, one only has to harvest the facts to find an answer. Therefore, because the question is self-asked and the methodological tool self-constructed, there is a risk that the answer will only represent a viewpoint. This might seem surprising, as Weber is famous for establishing the "axiological neutrality": the idea that science and value should be neatly separated, which has the alleged double advantage of guaranteeing objectivity in the conduct of research while preserving the plurality of value. But Aron notices that this position also risks removing any rational basis for the choice of scientific enquiries, as if research were ultimately a voluntary, quasi-Nietzschean act. For Aron, the scientific inquiry has to be related to value choices:

> a historian or sociologist incapable of distinguishing between a true prophet and a charlatan would, by the same token, be incapable of genuine understanding. An art historian unable to distinguish between the painting of Leonardo da Vinci and those of its imitators could not grasp the specific meaning of the historical object – in other words, the quality of the work. A sociologist who put Hitler and Washington, or Boulanger and Charles de Gaulle, a politician whose sole interest was power and a statesman impassioned with the sense of his nation's greatness, all in the same basket would throw everything into confusion on the pretext of not taking sides.
>
> (Aron 1985a: 353)

Aron recognizes that science and values belong to two different orders, but a difference is not necessarily an antinomy. For Aron, value choices must have a basis grounded in reason, even if nobody can know the result of an action before it is engaged, and even if rational choices can lead to greater evils. But it is precisely this unpredictability which makes an ethics of prudence even more necessary. Moreover, there are rules of morality that are not reducible to their contingent historical construct, but hold a universal value. For example, "thou shall not kill" or "don't do to others what you don't want done to you" are values not up for choice (just like one prefers blue to red), but can be grounded in reason. As Aron explains in his introduction to the French translation of Weber's *Politics as a Vocation*, "if everything which is not a scientific truth were arbitrary, scientific truth would also be nothing more than a preference, as little grounded as the opposite preference for myths" (Aron 1959: 43). Aron therefore refuses Weber's contention that modern culture is ultimately a never-ending "war of gods" as there would be no way to choose between competing values. Since there *are* values which can be grounded in reason, there is no logical explanation for Weber's apparent relativism. For Aron, Weber transformed a factual observation (humans have different and competing values) into an ultimately contradictory philosophy of the human condition (all values are neither true nor false). Therefore, the artificial antinomy created by Weber between science and values leads not only to an irrational selection of values, but also to a rootless science. Thus, normative thinking is not for Aron an afterthought which can be considered once the scientific analysis of the social world has been conducted: values are the very condition of the possibility of a scientific analysis. One can observe the influence of his Kantian training in this insistence on the possibilities of establishing universal values grounded in reason.

As such, Weber's epistemology is for Aron ultimately based on an assumption of science and reality as being ontologically different: Weber's understanding of scientific research has therefore little to do with reality. Weber understands reality as an accumulation of dispersed facts to which the sociologist tries to give a degree of cohesiveness through the use of theoretical constructs (ideal-types). Instead, for Aron, reality pre-exists the theoretical constructs: it is therefore necessary to empirically analyse its structures instead of being limited by abstract reconstitution: the sociologist

> avoids bias and attains fairness only by denying himself the liberty that Max Weber permitted in the construction of ideal-types, and by elaborating an analytical theory that would at least indicate the principal determining factors and allow for a reconstruction of the whole.
> (Aron 1985b: 219)

Therefore, while Weber thought that objectivity would be achieved through a strict respect of the axiological neutrality, Aron thought that objectivity can be grounded in reality itself, something he may have gathered from Canguilhem, as Reed M. Davis discusses in Chapter 3. To borrow Patrick Thaddeus Jackson's (2012) typology, Weber is an "analyticist" while Aron is a scientific realist. This difference with Weber explains Aron's emphasis on the necessity to use proper concepts (and not ideal-types) in order to study the social world.

As discussed above, Aron's approach does not accept a strong dichotomy between normative and scientific inquiry. One should therefore explore the normative tradition to which Aron belongs. Three different interpretations are possible (Châton 2017). For some, Aron is a neo-Kantian, an interpretation defended, for example, by Sylvie Mesure (1984). This interpretation is based on the fact that one can find multiple references to an "idea of reason" in Aron's writing. Aron's scholarship would then be a continuation of Kant's *Critique of Pure Reason*. Another reading separates Aron from the moderns (Kant and Weber) and instead defines him as a neo-Aristotelian (Mahoney 1992; Manent 2010). In that reading, Aron would not be a modern, intellectual heir to the nineteenth-century liberals, but would instead be a classic, defending liberal values as they, in context, are the ones furnishing a satisfying social life. Aron's concerns for the "common good" or "civic virtue", and his limited trust in the idea of progress, would be examples of his deep Aristotelian temper hidden under the veil of his liberal preferences. Finally, a third reading understands Aron's scholarship as the bridge between Tocqueville and Machiavelli (Audier 2008): Aron would in fact be a "liberal republican", renewing this tradition by adding to the liberal concern for independence and the republican concern for national liberty a socialist concern for the capability to act and social justice. Aron's commitment to liberty would then have simultaneously a liberal, republican and socialist undertone, a tension explored by Jeangène Vilmer in his chapter.

Aron's approach is then interesting for sociologists and political theorists. But how does it contribute to our understanding of International Relations?

Organization of the book

This volume is organized in three different sections. The first section discusses Aron's approach, scrutinizing his intellectual influences and contributions. It comprises chapters by Bryan-Paul Frost on the classical foundations of Aron's IR theory, Reed M. Davis on the intellectual dialogue between Aron and Canguilhem, Olivier Schmitt on a reading of *Peace and War among Nations* as a theory of foreign policy and Jean-Baptiste Jeangène Vilmer on Aron's international ethics. The second section explores the ways Aron contributed to major debates of his time. Christian Malis examines his contribution to the French debate on nuclear strategy, Joël Mouric discusses his perception of the European construction and Daniel Steinmetz-Jenkins explores his engagement with economic debates on global development. Finally, the third section uses Aron's concepts to engage with contemporary issues. Thomas Meszaros and Antony Dabila analyse how Aron's approach could contribute to current debates in IR theories, Ariane Chebel d'Appollonia examines how his "praxeology" is helpful to tackle current ethical problems in global affairs and Olivier Chopin introduces a new figure ("the Spy") to complement Aron's dialectic between the "Diplomat" and the "Soldier".

It must be mentioned that this separation is quite blurred: several contributions complement each other in important ways. For example, several authors

(Frost, Schmitt, Meszaros and Dabila, and Chebel d'Appollonia) offer their own reading of *Peace and War*, which illustrates how this masterpiece can be used for a multiplicity of purposes. Not all contributors also agree on each aspect of Aron's interpretation and the reader will encounter sometimes diverging views in the following chapters. However, several common themes emerge, related to Aron's understanding of the social world.

First, the relationship between the micro and the macro levels is mentioned by several contributors to the volume. In IR, two major distinct but connected debates deal with the interaction between micro and macro levels of analysis. The first debate is related to the proper "level of analysis", or the famous "three images" (individual, state, system) described by Waltz. The second debate (similar to those happening in other fields of the social sciences) explores the interactions between the agent and the structure. As discussed above, Aron's approach to the social world calls for a "hermeneutic circle" between understanding and explaining, which immediately highlights the limits of the various attempts to find regularities and patterns in IR. Bryan-Paul Frost illustrates how the contextual determinants that Aron identifies in *Peace and War* (space, population, resources) would not qualify in mainstream methodological textbooks as yielding "parsimonious, demonstrable, and falsifiable propositions". While they provide a context for understanding decisions, they are not deterministic. Aron's approach thus has consequences for the choice of a proper level of analysis: Schmitt's chapter illustrates how *Peace and War* can ultimately be read as an attempt to identify the scope for agency, and thus that the three "images" all matter in varying proportions depending on the context. Meszaros and Dabila also explore the consequences of this approach for a truly sociological contribution to IR theories. But Aron's hermeneutic circle also implies a degree of dialogue between two traditionally separated fields: comparative politics and IR. If the attempt to find regularities is ontologically limited by the ultimate need to interpret decisions in context (and at their appropriate analytical level), then the study of the international system (the level at which one could identify regularities) must be coupled with the comparative study of political regimes, which provide the context necessary to understand events. Frost shows how Aron's emphasis on political regimes stems from Aristotle's (and Montesquieu's) influence, and Steinmetz-Jenkins illustrates how this concern led Aron to be critical of his American colleagues' enthusiasm for the "transfer" of Western political values.

The second important contribution Aron made to IR scholarship is his use of concepts. Frost shows how Aron turned to Clausewitz for his conceptualization of aspects of international relations, since in his understanding concepts aided asking the right questions, which is the role of a good theory. Davis also insists on Aron's interaction with Canguilhem and their shared understanding that experience is important to create concepts. Schmitt and Meszaros and Dabila also illustrate how a number of Aron's concepts are worth exploring in order to enrich contemporary discussions in IR. Schmitt discusses how Aron's distinctions between power and strength, permanent and temporary allies, homogeneous and heterogeneous systems or traditional and revolutionary states hold important insights, while Meszaros and Dabila elaborate on the concepts of "oligopolarity" and "polypolarity" to go further than the "unipolar/multipolar" binary discussion so prevalent in IR scholarship. Malis and Mouric exemplify how Aron operated with concepts through his contribution to the French strategic debate and the European construction.

Several authors also mention Aron's emphasis on "the primacy of politics". Frost shows the intellectual origins of such a preference, while Jeangène Vilmer discusses how Aron reconciled the notion of the primacy of politics with an ethical enquiry. This notion of the primacy of politics is also central to Aron's understanding of Europe (as Mouric illustrates) or economic development (Steinmetz-Jenkins). However, Malis illustrates how Aron became an unexpected victim of this primacy of politics, by succumbing to his desire for policy influence, thus overstating his opposition to the French nuclear deterrent. One can therefore recognize that politics matters strongly in the understanding of human societies, while misreading a political situation. This is important food for thought for political scientists longing for "policy relevance".

Finally, Aron's rejection of the artificial separation between scientific and normative theory is explored in three contributions. First, Jeangène Vilmer lays out Aron's ethical thinking while Chebel d'Appollonia discusses the consequences for today's global affairs. This discussion is important, as it locates Aron within the "pluralist/communitarian" debate, but also offers interesting insights into other ethical debates such as humanitarian intervention. Again, Aron does not provide definitive answers, but he gives the necessary tools to ask the right questions. Finally, Chopin also explores the ethical issues related to intelligence through his discussion of the spy as a new "figure" of international relations. Those chapters also contribute to (although they do not settle) the debate on Aron's intellectual forefathers, Jeangène Vilmer dubbing him a "post-Kantian machiavellist".

Together, these contributions illustrate the multiple ways a reading of Aron could contribute to current IR scholarship, by enriching numerous debates. However, one should also refrain from finding in Aron a new prophet encompassing all aspects of international relations. As he himself acknowledges, he does not have much to say on transnational movements (such as migrations or economic flows) which are, to a limited degree, shaping the international system. He is also unfairly critical of International Law and exaggerates its alleged weakness compared to politics. But those very limitations justify a close and serious reading of Aron, as it is only through a critical engagement that his manifold contributions can emerge. However, Aron's scholarship is unfortunately difficult to access for English speakers. First, his masterpiece *Peace and War* suffers from a clumsy translation (as Jeangène Vilmer and Chopin note in their chapters), which can sometimes obscure its meaning. Second, Aron's numerous contributions to IR thinking (op-eds, journal articles, book chapters) are scattered across several volumes, and many of them are only available in French. This unfortunate situation complicates access to Aron's scholarship, and this volume can also be considered as an invitation to explore his contribution in more detail. More immediately, we hope that this volume will help change Aron's image of a "realist Cold Warrior", thus contributing to the more nuanced reading of realism that has already been accomplished with Morgenthau and Carr.

This volume started out as a panel at the International Studies Association annual meeting in Toronto, in 2014. It was followed up by a workshop in Paris in May 2016, generously funded by the Chair in War Studies of the Fondation Maison des Sciences de l'Homme, thanks to the support of the chair holder, Jean-Baptiste Jeangène Vilmer. Those exchanges brought together scholars from both sides of the Atlantic and from various disciplines, which we hope is true to Aron's spirit of plurality and truth-seeking.

References

Aron, R. (1959), "Introduction", in Weber, M., *Le Savant et le Politique*. Paris: Plon, 5–51.

Aron, R. (1985a), "Max Weber and Modern Social Science", in Draus, F. (ed.), *History, Truth, Liberty: Selected Writings of Raymond Aron*. Chicago: University of Chicago Press, 335–373.

Aron, R. (1985b), "Science and Conscience of Society", in Draus, F. (ed.), *History, Truth, Liberty: Selected Writings of Raymond Aron*. Chicago: University of Chicago Press, 208–233.

Audier, S. (2004), *Raymond Aron: La démocratie conflictuelle*. Paris: Michalon.

Audier, S. (2008), "Raymond Aron entre libéralisme, républicanisme et socialisme", in Audier, S., Baruch, M.O. and Simon-Nahum, P. (eds), *Raymond Aron, la philosophie et l'histoire: Armer la sagesse*. Paris: Éditions de Fallois.

Baehr, P. (2013), "The Honored Outsider: Raymond Aron as Sociologist", *Sociological Theory*, 31:2, 93–115.

Battistella, D. (2013), "La France", in Balzacq, T. and Ramel, F. (eds), *Traité de Relations Internationales*. Paris: Presses de Sciences Po, 157–180.

Baverez, N. (1993), *Raymond Aron: Un Moraliste au temps des idéologies*. Paris: Flammarion.

Birnbaum, P. (1992), *Les fous de la République: Histoire politique des Juifs d'État de Gambetta à Vichy*. Paris: Seuil.

Breiner, P. (2011), "Raymond Aron's Engagement with Weber: Recovery or Retreat?", *Journal of Classical Sociology*, 11:2, 99–121.

Châton, G. (2012), "Pour un 'Machiavélisme Post-Kantien': Raymond Aron, théoricien réaliste hétérodoxe", *Études Internationales*, 43:3, 389–403.

Châton, G. (2017), *Introduction à Raymond Aron*. Paris: La Découverte.

Colen, J. and Dutartre-Michaut, E. (eds) (2015), *The Companion to Raymond Aron*. Basingstoke: Palgrave Macmillan.

Colquhoun, R. (1986), *Raymond Aron*. London: Sage Publications (2 vols).

Davis, R.M. (2009), *A Politics of Understanding: The International Thought of Raymond Aron*. Baton Rouge, LA: Louisiana State University Press.

Dyvik, S.L., Selby, J. and Wilkinson, R. (eds) (2017), *What's the Point of International Relations?* Abingdon: Routledge.

Frost, B.P. (1997), "Resurrecting a Neglected Theorist: The Philosophical Foundations of Raymond Aron's Theory of International Relations", *Review of International Studies*, 23:4, 143–166.
Frost, B.P. (2006), "Better Late than Never: Raymond Aron's Theory of International Relations and Its Prospects in the 21st Century", *Politics and Policy*, 34:3, 506–531.
Frost, B.P. (2013), "Realism Meets Historical Sociology: Raymond Aron's Peace and War", in Bliddal, H., Sylvest, C. and Wilson, P.C. (eds), *Classics of International Relations*. Abingdon: Routledge, 99–108.
Gentile, E. (2006), *Politics as Religion*. Princeton, NJ: Princeton University Press.
Hoffmann, S. (1983a), "Raymond Aron (1905–1983)", *New York Review of Books*, 30:19.
Hoffmann, S. (1983b), "Raymond Aron et la Théorie des Relations Internationales", *Politique Étrangère*, 39:4, 723–734.
Hoffmann, S. (1985), "Raymond Aron and the Theory of International Relations", *International Studies Quarterly*, 29:1, 13–27.
Hoffmann, S. (2000), *World Disorders: Troubled Peace in the Post-Cold War Era*. Lanham, MD: Rowman & Littlefield.
Holeindre, J.V. (2012), "Survivre, c'est vaincre? La pensée stratégique de Raymond Aron à l'épreuve des guerres de notre temps", *Études Internationales*, 43:3, 439–457.
Jackson, P.T. (2012), *The Conduct of Inquiry in International Relations: Philosophy of Science and Its Implications for World Politics*. Abingdon: Routledge.
Jeangène Vilmer, J.B. (2013), "Pour un réalisme libéral en Relations Internationales", *Commentaire*, 141, 13–20.
Mahoney, D. (1992), *The Liberal Political Science of Raymond Aron*. Lanham, MD: Rowman & Littlefield.
Maier, H. (ed.) (2004–2007), *Totalitarianism and Political Religions*. Abingdon: Routledge (3 vols).
Manent, P. (2010), *Le Regard politique*. Paris: Flammarion.
Mesure, S. (1984), *Raymond Aron et la raison historique*. Paris: Vrin.
Nord, P. (2015), *France 1940: Defending the Republic*. New Haven, CT: Yale University Press.
Paugam, S. (2005), *Les Formes élémentaires de la pauvreté*. Paris: Presses Universitaires de France.
Paugam, S. (ed.) (2014), *L'Intégration inégale: Force, fragilité et rupture des liens sociaux*. Paris: Presses Universitaires de France.
Ramel, F. (2013), "De la Puissance militaire: Aron revisité", *Ceriscope*, online.
Winock, M. (2017), *La France Républicaine*. Paris: Robert Laffont.

1 The classical foundations of Raymond Aron's theory of international relations

Bryan-Paul Frost

Although Raymond Aron is considered by many to be a towering figure in International Relations theory in the twentieth century, it must be recalled that this is not how many individuals would have predicted his intellectual trajectory: given his background and accomplishments, many if not most of his friends, colleagues, and admirers would have claimed that he was to become one of France's leading *philosophical* intellectuals of his generation. After graduating first in his class from the Ecole Normale Supérieure, Aron went on to write a highly original and provocative dissertation that broke decisively with the neo-Kantianism (and passivism) of his teachers. Indeed, during a sojourn in Germany before the completion of his dissertation, Aron also wrote two books that many claim introduced the French intellectual community to the emerging theories of German historicism, sociology, and historical philosophy. Of course, this sojourn in Germany did more than acquaint Aron with modern German philosophy – it also, and perhaps most decisively, allowed him to observe the rise of Hitler and fascism in the 1930s, and to surmise accurately what this might portend for the future of Europe, in particular, and the world, in general. Aron's philosophical trajectory was now merging with a decidedly political one as well. After World War II, the political trajectory tended to trump the philosophical one, although Aron never abandoned philosophy in any real sense. It would be most accurate to state that Aron always brought philosophy to bear in all of his writings, but that the issues and events that France faced in the post-World War II era more or less forced Aron, as one of the leading liberal and conservative thinkers of his time, to turn to politics, as his numerous books, articles, and editorials attest. Aron was, in the best sense of the words, a genuinely public or civic intellectual, educating and thus trying to guide the French to its best and therefore true interests (Aron 1938, 1961, 1964).[1]

The purpose of this chapter is to attempt to limn some of the philosophical sources and influences that underlie *Peace and War: A Theory of International Relations* – in other words, to highlight some of the great thinkers and learning that is contained in this book. It should go without saying that there can be no question of doing justice to all of Aron's philosophical references: to do this would require a book in itself, which would in many ways be a history of political philosophy (the index to *Peace and War* amply supports this idea)! Nor will this chapter discuss how Aron deepened his reflections on some of these thinkers over the course of his lifetime: this too would require a separate book (especially considering the fact that *Peace and War* was originally published in 1962, and that Aron still had two decades of productive scholarship ahead of him). Instead, we will examine *Peace and War* on its own terms, a book that Aron had thought about for some ten years as he tried to concretize his understanding of international relations and the new emerging international order. Finally, it should be emphasized that we use the term "classical" in the broadest possible sense, namely to identify the many philosophers, historians, and scholars (both ancient, modern, and contemporary) from which Aron drew in his exhaustive analysis of international politics, and how he managed to weave them together into a coherent whole. In sum, this chapter hopes to demonstrate how and why Aron rejected a narrow or even parochial approach to IR theory, even at the risk of writing a book whose conclusions, as more than one scholar has pointed out, were disappointingly modest (Aron 2003).[2]

In the style and substance of Montesquieu

Aron begins *Peace and War* with an often quoted passage from Montesquieu's *The Spirit of the Laws* (I, 3): "International law is based by nature upon this principle: that the various nations ought to do, in peace, the most good to each other, and, in war, the least harm possible, without detriment to their genuine interests." Critics of Aron might argue that he begins with this quotation because his book is similar to Montesquieu's: both are massive, sprawling, and ultimately disorganized works that lack internal coherency. But just as Montesquieu cautioned readers against making such a hasty judgment about his book, so readers of Aron's great tome should do the same. What might appear as bedlam at first glance is a carefully constructed and organized synthesis of all the major aspects of international relations: theory, sociology, history, and practice (or praxeology). One may disagree with whether Aron's book is orderly (as many have done with Montesquieu), but one cannot deny his ultimate intention.

More to the point, why does Aron begin the book with this quotation from Montesquieu? Three overlapping reasons suggest themselves. First, and perhaps ironically, one might claim that Aron's book is fundamentally about peace, and not war. Of course, Aron could hardly have called the book *War and Peace* unless he wanted to tread upon a previous, illustrious title; but even if Tolstoy had not written that magisterial novel, one might suspect that Aron would have entitled his book just as he had. There is no doubt – absolutely no doubt – that Aron understands that war has been, is, and probably will remain, an inherent aspect of human relations; but Aron's concern, like Montesquieu's, is how to mitigate that often inevitable catastrophe. Peace is the proper relation between states; but understanding how and why war occurs might help to bring about more peaceful relations (the last line of the above quotation suggests this very idea). At the very least, war-like nations should be as peaceful as possible in war. Aron is fully aware of the sometimes horrible extremes to which war ultimately leads, especially in the twentieth century. Second, in stark contrast to modern-day positivists and behavioralists, Aron denied that there could be a value-free social science. Indeed, at the beginning of Part Four of *Peace and War*, Aron forthrightly admits that all theories in the social sciences have inherent normative implications, and Aron spells out his own over the course of some 200 pages in the section titled "Praxeology" (Aron 2003: 575). And finally, third, the character of these normative implications betray a Montesquieuian moderation in both thought and practice. To take but one example – and one that might be quite discordant to American sensibilities – Aron argued that the demand for unconditional surrender by the Germans during World War II betrayed a disjunction between "strategy and policy," in that (among other reasons) it "incited the German people to a desperate resistance" (Aron 2003: 27). Whatever one might think of Aron's conclusion here, the humanity and compassion of Montesquieu is on full display throughout the book – although this never prevents Aron from making some very hard-headed judgments. In short, philosophy can never be divorced from theory or history or practice. Montesquieu helps us to see this key insight.

In addition to the above reasons, we can recognize a further affinity with Montesquieu when we turn to Part Two of *Peace and War*, "Sociology." Aron claims that sociology investigates two kinds of causes or determinants: "the material or physical causes on the one side, the moral or social causes on the other, to use Montesquieu's vocabulary." The material or physical causes are space (geography), population (demography), and resources (economy); moral or social determinants are "the *nation*, the *civilization, humanity*" (Aron 2003: 179). These are hardly the typical or ordinary variables that one encounters as the hallmarks of modern social science – in other words, variables that are at once readily quantifiable, easily defined, discreet, narrow, and specific, and that yield parsimonious, demonstrable, and falsifiable propositions. It should be emphasized that Aron is not at all against such kinds of propositions or theories, and he often offers his own throughout *Peace and War*; rather, it is to say that Aron categorically rejected unilateral or unidimensional explanations of international relations: just as Aron rejected Marx's singular explanation of the historical process, so too did he reject singular explanations for the cause(s) of peace and war. The variables that he examined might better be described as "eternal" or "permanent" causes or determinants, all of which contribute something to understanding the complex tapestry of international relations, but none of which explain those relations fully. The seemingly sprawling nature of Aron's analysis is similar to Montesquieu's in that both canvassed an array of ideas for understanding their subject matter. In Aron's case, although none of the variables discussed in Part Two succeeded in giving a comprehensive explanation of international relations, each one of them certainly illuminated enduring characteristics of those relations that must be seriously considered by thinkers at all times and places.

It is also worth mentioning that the section on "Sociology" further illuminates and reveals Aron's classical foundations – for almost every chapter in Part Two is a detailed examination not only of a particular variable but also of an author(s) closely associated with promoting or exploring it. For example, in chapter 7, Aron turns to (not surprisingly) Montesquieu's discussion of the influence of geography and climate; in chapter 8, he highlights Gaston Bouthoul's "demographic theory of war"; and in chapter 9, he offers a trenchant critique of the Marxist–Leninist economic theory of imperialism and colonialism. Such discursive explorations occur repeatedly throughout *Peace and War* (for example, see the discussions of Heinrich von Treitschke, Hans Morgenthau, and Pierre-Joseph Proudhon in chapter 19 alone). Aron's approach is sometimes critical, sometimes appreciative, and sometimes combative – but it is always informative as these discussions help to frame the enormous task Aron has set for himself, namely to understand the "implicit logic" of international relations.

Let us restate all of the above observations in this section in the following way. The style and substance of Montesquieu was a clear corrective to the prevailing trend among so many academics, pundits, and even politicians as to how to comprehend international relations. Theirs was an attempt to *explain* international relations in the hopes of making it a *predictive* science akin to economics in character and scope. But Aron rejected both this approach and ideal – his was an attempt to *understand* international relations and thereafter to suggest *normative* principles that were at once both moderate and prudent (Davis 2009).[3] There could be no *theory* of international relations in any strict sense. As Aron concluded early on in *Peace and War*:

> The *diplomaticus* of theory, who would have as his goal the maximization of resources, of actual forces, or of power, would not be an idealized portrait of the diplomats of all ages, he would be a caricatured simplification of certain diplomatic personages at certain periods...
>
> If diplomatic behavior is never determined by the relation of forces alone, if power does not serve the same function in diplomacy as utility in economy, then we may legitimately conclude that *there is no general theory of international relations comparable to the general theory of economy*. The theory we are sketching here tends to analyze the meaning of diplomatic behavior, to trace its fundamental notions, to specify the variables that must be reviewed in order to understand any one constellation. But it does not suggest an "eternal diplomacy," it does not claim to be the reconstruction of a closed system.
>
> (Aron 2003: 91, 93)

One might suggest that the more social or political scientists strive in the direction of explaining, the more the desire for predictive outcomes will dominate their scholarship; by contrast, a theory of understanding will tend in the opposite direction, rejecting grand theories, oversimplified paradigms, and unidimensional explanations in favor of partial, complex, and provisional conclusions. Aron did not limit himself or subscribe to the trademarks of contemporary, positivistic social science. Aron will not offer easy solutions; but by the same token, he will help us to see the right philosophical questions to ask.

Vulgar Machiavellianism, naive Kantianism, and Aristotelian prudence

As suggested above, Montesquieu's influence extends throughout the book, and in particular into Part Four, titled "Praxeology." Aron here begins to delineate his understanding of the principles of true statesmanship.

> [T]he moment one shifts from observation to precept, the paradox of international relations is clearly revealed: relations between states are social relations controlled by the *possible and legitimate* recourse to force. Now, the use of force is not in itself immoral (might in the service of right has always been considered moral). But each of the actors, if he be the judge, and the sole judge, of the legitimacy of his cause, must feel threatened by the others, and the international game becomes a struggle in which the player who abides by the rules runs the risk of being victimized by his (relative) morality. At this point two sorts of questions arise: Is foreign policy in and of itself diabolical? What means may be legitimately employed, it is being understood that the states are jealous of their independence? Further, is it conceivable, and if so is it practicable, to go beyond foreign policy? To subject states to one law, that of collective security or of a universal empire? Can we put an end to what we call international anarchy, that is, the claim of states to take law into their own hands? In other words, the essence of inter-state relations raises two praxeological problems that I will call the *Machiavellian problem* and the *Kantian problem*: that of legitimate means and that of universal peace.
>
> (Aron 2003: 577)

Aron eschews such stark, Manichean distinctions, and instead advocates what he calls a morality of "*prudence*."

> To be prudent is to act in accordance with the particular situation and the concrete data, and not in accordance with some system or out of passive obedience to a norm or pseudo-norm; it is to prefer the limitation of violence to the punishment of the presumably guilty party or to a so-called absolute justice; it is to establish concrete accessible objectives conforming to the secular law of international relations and not to limitless and perhaps meaningless objectives, such as "a world safe for democracy" or "a world from which power politics will have disappeared."
>
> (Aron 2003: 585)

It is tempting to assume that Aron views Machiavellianism as worse than Kantianism, especially given the time in which Aron lived and his repeated reflections on totalitarianism, both from the Left and the Right. But the quotation above seems to suggest the opposite in some ways, as both examples are from, or refer to, the modern Kantian par excellence, namely Woodrow Wilson and his disciples. It may be that a morality and diplomacy of avowed purity and good intentions is the greater threat to peace in the Cold War era, and not its opposite (although Aron, of course, saw both as a threat fundamentally). The self-conscious and self-proclaimed Kantian, it is assumed, cannot be evil or have any ulterior motives; the dastardly Machiavellian is wholly the opposite. But what Aron may have seen, especially in light of the inter-war period, is that Wilsonianism can raise expectations, inflate hopes, and create impossible dreams that will never be realized, at least in this lifetime. And when these expectations, hopes, and dreams are deflated and destroyed, then people may begin to look for different, and more ugly, solutions, especially from those who might promise the same but who are not at all afraid to use methods Wilson and others abhorred. Machiavellians, as Aron well knew, can cloak their intentions in melodic Kantian verses.

To see the fears that Aron may have envisioned, one can turn to his critique of a certain advocacy and/or understanding of nuclear weapons policy, namely the categorical rejection of the use of nuclear weapons.

> The original aspect of our age of thermonuclear bombs is the propensity to give an air of responsibility to decisions made for motives of conscience and without calculating the risks and advantages. For that matter, why should this be so surprising? Never has the statement "none of the evils men claim to avoid by war is as great an evil as war itself" seemed so true as it does today: and yet it is not true. Thermonuclear weapons make it possible to exterminate the enemy population in the course of hostilities. But extermination after capitulation has always been one of the possible expressions of victory. The capitulation of one of the duopolists would not necessarily mark the end of the danger. This capitulation being out of the question, it is futile to transfigure a partial measure which may be opportune or which may be more dangerous than useful, and to pretend that it alone opens a path to salvation.
>
> (Aron 2003: 634–665)

Although it is certainly more comforting to deny in this era the necessity or use of (nuclear) force in politics than its continued existence, Aron argues that the former belief would likely lead to the opposite – a possible increase in the use of force, precisely because aggressors will use such moral scruples or naivety against those who profess them. As states have not renounced being the final arbiters in the use of force when it might be in their perceived interest, a prudential diplomat must consider the balance of force and the survival of the state. In other words, a prudential diplomat must renounce all "Christian virtues" that condemn or are in tension with the actions required to protect their state in the bellicose international arena (Aron 2003: 579–580). As long as states remain what they are, Aron does not believe that the Machiavellian and Kantian antinomy can ever be fully overcome. On the one hand, even though states share certain norms of behavior, they reserve the right to use force as they see fit, and diplomats who neglect to calculate the balance of forces fail in their duty; on the other hand, states have rarely considered every recourse to arms legitimate, and they have often sincerely aimed at promoting and defending higher goals and values. Aron is neither a cynic nor an idealist, and he is able to avoid both a vulgar Machiavellianism (or a "morality of struggle") and a naive Kantianism (or a "morality of law") (Aron 2003: 608–610). The bellicose character of international politics cannot be transcended, only moderated, but such moderation can come neither from opportunism divorced from reflection upon higher principles nor from the single-minded pursuit of heartfelt convictions divorced from considerations of the consequences of those actions. We will discuss briefly below Aron's conclusions concerning the use of nuclear weapons; let us for now return to his Aristotelianism.

It should go without saying that Aron's morality of prudence cannot give any positive, concrete answers or imperatives to future problems in international relations: a morality of prudence can only urge a diplomat to look at the entire concurrence of forces and events and to act accordingly. But perhaps this is also why Aron advocated such a morality. The problem with Wilson (and like-minded Kantians) is precisely that they did give answers, make predictions, and issue demands – and sometimes demonized those who did not agree, often to disastrous effect. The morality of prudence is the studied avoidance of extremes and thus false hopes.

Yet another similarity between Aron and Aristotle is their categorical rejection of determinism in international relations and theory. Although it is fashionable in some circles to claim that the character of the international system determines (more or less) the actions of states, Aron rejected such a pronouncement. Aron was fully aware that the "structure of international systems is always *oligopolistic*," and that there is an important if not decisive difference between a bipolar and multipolar system. States will certainly be influenced by the character of the system in which they find themselves. But Aron averred that it is the study of regimes that can sometimes be determinative – or in modern parlance, that the unit (and even individual) level of analysis can sometimes be primary over the systemic level.

> In each period the principal actors have determined the system more than they have been determined by it. A change of regime within one of the chief powers suffices to change the style and sometimes the course of international relations.
>
> (Aron 2003: 95)

Aron therefore pays great attention to what he describes as "homogenous" and "heterogenous" systems: the former obtains when the major powers share similar regimes and conceptions of policy and justice, the latter when the regimes are "*organized according to different principles and appeal to contradictory values*." Because states in a homogeneous international system share the same general principles of legitimacy, such systems *tend* to display greater stability; to limit violence when it does occur; to be more predictable in their political traditions and diplomatic codes of conduct; and to engage in competitive and even hostile behavior that does not degenerate into hatred of the rival or adversary. "Heterogeneity of the system produces the opposite": instability, an increase in violence, uncertainty, and hatred between the enemy states (Aron 2003: 100–101). The configuration of the relation of forces, while certainly an essential variable in understanding any international system, cannot be divorced from the ends or goals sought by the major powers, and these latter depend decisively on the character of the state's regime (Aron 2003: 147–149). Maintenance of the system or the system's "equilibrium" is not the exclusive or primary goal of the powers within that system. This may be a prudential consideration for sure, but the goal of the "maintenance" or "safeguarding or functioning of the system is to return, by a devious route, to the error of certain theoreticians of power politics: to confuse the calculation of means or the context of the decision with the goal itself" (Aron 2003: 130–131). Regardless of the system – whether bipolar or multipolar – both can lead to hostilities and war, and both are capable of equilibrium. Aron does not deny that each system tends to display specific characteristics, but neither system is inherently more bellicose or peaceful than another, and therefore the dynamics of a particular system cannot be rigidly determined by a theorist in advance. The critical importance of the regime (or the unit level of analysis) clearly makes Aron's theory of international relations much more akin to the classical political thought of Aristotle than it does to many contemporary theorists. Aron, like Aristotle and the classical philosophers in general, does not believe that the two supposedly distinct political science sub-fields of international relations and comparative politics can be separated: indeed, Aron seems to privilege the study of domestic regimes over the international system. Is it any wonder that the "Introduction" to *Peace and War* begins with a tip-of-the-hat to Plato and Aristotle (among others)?

Alexandre Kojève and the end of history?

The final two chapters of *Peace and War* read, in many ways, like a commentary on Alexandre Kojève's "end of history" thesis, most recently popularized by Francis Fukuyama. This should not come as a surprise: not only did Aron attend some of Kojève's lectures on Hegel's *Phenomenology of Spirit* in the 1930s, but in his *Memoirs*, Aron admitted that Kojève was one of the most brilliant men he had ever met. And in the final two chapters of the book, Aron does indeed ask what the conditions are and the likelihood for the end of power politics altogether. To be sure, Kojève is never mentioned by name in chapters 23 and 24 – but it could very well be that Kojève's end of history thesis was in the back of Aron's mind throughout (Aron 1990: 65, 465–466; Kojève 1980; Fukuyama 1992).[4]

As international relations involve the alternatives of war and peace between distinct political units, should the alternative of war become obsolete or impossible, or should political units themselves disappear, then the history of international relations would effectively come to an end. At the beginning of chapter 23, Aron acknowledges that this question or problem is especially poignant for his readers.

> The horrors of twentieth-century war and the thermonuclear threat have given the rejection of power politics not only an actuality and an urgency, but also a kind of obviousness. *History must no longer be* a succession of bloody conflicts if humanity is to pursue its adventure. Never has the disproportion appeared so striking, so tragic, between the possible catastrophe and the stakes of inter-state rivalries. All classical strategy ... appears lamentably inadequate, measured by the demands of peace and the dangers of war. It leads to an acknowledgement of impotence, a kind of resignation to the absurd. I do not protest against these sentiments; I share them. Men aspire to a historical transformation of states and their relations.
> (Aron 2003: 703)

In order to see how such a transformation could occur, Aron breaks up his discussion into two parts: first, what political, economic, and social conditions must exist for international relations to stop being characterized as power politics; and second, how likely are these conditions to be realized in the foreseeable future. In answering the former question, Aron begins by arguing that there are, in general, two ways in which theorists explain the cause of war. Either states go to war in order to obtain something for themselves (e.g., land or wealth) or because they are so constituted as to be subject to certain internal or external pressures (e.g., capitalist countries go to war because they are competing for new markets or raw materials in underdeveloped countries). In other words, certain *stakes* prompt nations to go to war, or there is something peculiar about the *state itself* which causes it to be subject to certain bellicose pressures, whether from within or without (Aron 2003: 703–706).

If what Aron says is true, then one way that peace would reign in the international system would be if there were a sudden conversion in the *character* of *both* the stakes and the actors. We could expect an end to international relations only if the traditional stakes in war had suddenly lost all their meaning or value *and* if the actors themselves suddenly lost the desire to dominate one another or the fear of being dominated. Aron, however, doubts that any such conversion will take place in the foreseeable future. While he admits that "industrial society effectively attenuates the economic causes of wars," even if all states shared the same type of regime, the most that could realistically be expected would be the unlikelihood of a "major war between the principal actors of the international system": it would not eliminate the possibility of conflict altogether, for population pressures, limited resources, territorial constraints, economic stagnation, and other such factors can lead to conflict and violence. Rather than hold out for such a radical change in the stakes and the actors, the more likely chance for universal peace would be if states relinquished their right to be the final dispenser of justice. In other words, Aron sees the chance of universal peace to be much greater if the "Hobbesian situation" (or state of nature) between states was attenuated – if states could somehow be made or compelled to renounce the right of using force in their own affairs (Aron 2003: 707–709).

Certainly Aron is aware that relinquishing the right to use force to settle disputes would require a change – and a very large one – in the behavior of states; but at the very beginning of chapter 23 at least, he argues that it would require a much smaller change than asking them to stop dominating one another or to stop desiring things such as land and wealth. In the scenario that Aron envisions, there could still be disputes between states in the international system, but those disputes would be settled in one of two ways: states would either have to agree to settle their differences through arbitration, or they would have to allow a superior force to impose a solution. Aron calls these two possibilities peace by law and peace by empire: either one can hope that states will submit their grievances to international tribunals and voluntarily follow the decisions of those tribunals, or one can establish an international power that is strong enough to make binding decisions upon states in the midst of a conflict.

Aron begins with peace through law. Now Aron points out several "essential imperfection[s]" in international law, two of the most significant being a logical or theoretical tension within international law itself, and the other being a political problem of applying that law in the real world. He notes that every theory of international law that "takes as its point of departure the sovereignty of states and, in one way or another, relates law to this sovereignty, robs international law of certain constituent characteristics of law." Two of the most salient characteristics are "a tribunal to express the law" and "an irresistible force to impose it" (Aron 2003: 722, 720). According to Aron, the principle of sovereignty necessarily undermines the obligatory character of international law *as law*, a law which is supposed to be superior to the state and to which states are to be held accountable. Without an acknowledged arbiter or tribunal to render a definitive interpretation of the law, and without the means to enforce that decision, international law falls short of the very concept of law: at most, international law would be an exhortation or warning or moral precept that sovereign states could accept or reject as they saw fit. Even if states occasionally submitted to the decisions of international tribunals, the theoretical problem would still remain; for weak or spotty compliance makes a mockery of law as such, and even good international laws become contemptible when they are haphazardly enforced. It is little wonder, then, that few states have confidence in the integrity and efficacy of international law, and in the tribunals that are supposed to interpret that law.

A third "imperfection" of international law stems from its content, or lack thereof: Aron asks what is to be the "fundamental" or "originating norm," or set of "normative facts," that is to be posited when constructing a system of international law comparable to the norms and facts that govern a state's internal laws? To say nothing of the fact that international law is by and large "*jus Europaeum*," a fact that would most likely limit its appeal if it were made compulsory upon all nations, Aron can discover no principle "that is not itself a rule of thumb" that could govern the international system. Certainly the principle *pacta sunt servanda* is "indispensable to international order," but Aron rightly wonders how this rather formulaic injunction could yield a concrete set of normative directions and obligations for all states. As for basing international law on tradition and custom, Aron muses: "Which custom must states respect? The recourse to force constitutes part of the age-old behavior of states: how condemn it in a juridical system which is supposed to be the outcome of custom?" At the end of the day, the "determination of facts and the interpretation of norms" is at the discretion of separate states, and we once again return to a self-enforcing (and therefore ineffective) system of international law. As Aron rather wryly concludes: "When the [international] jurist asserts that 'the will of the international community must be obeyed,' it is too easy to reply that the will common to the sovereign states exists only in the imagination of the theoretician." Rules of thumb are no substitute for agreed upon foundational principles that guide the entire system (Aron 2003: 718–720, 733).

Notwithstanding these difficulties, Aron does not yet give up hope of finding the conditions whereby states would submit to the rule of law. If the problems associated with the principle of state sovereignty are greatly exacerbated in a heterogeneous international system, then perhaps these problems could be overcome if the system were rigorously homogeneous. In other words, if the leaders of states were subject to similar political controls and norms (e.g., majority rule, and free and fair elections); if all states had republican constitutions with similar principles of legitimacy (e.g., consent of the governed and rule by law); and, in general, if all states espoused similar goals and aspirations for their people (e.g., economic development and the exercise of basic rights and freedom), then it is at least conceivable that states could create and abide by a detailed body of international law. But while Aron sees these are the necessary conditions for the rule of law, they are still not sufficient: in addition, each and every state would have to agree to a renunciation of violence. States would have to stop suspecting one another of the "worst intentions," and they would have to subordinate their desire to exercise their will to power to their desire to see the universal reign of the rule of law, even when judgments went against their perceived vital interests. In the broadest possible terms, what Aron is trying to get us to see is that the successful operation of international law is always a side-effect of a pre-existing state of international harmony and stability, and not a cause of it: international law is always the outgrowth of some underlying, near unanimous agreement between states, and without that prior agreement, then the mere profusion of rules and regulations will have little if any effect on global stability. International law, therefore, will not make a substantial contribution to peace unless *states themselves* have more or less completely overcome their distrust and fear of one another (Aron 2003: 733–736).

At all events, by the very end of chapter 23, Aron wonders whether the conditions for peace by law would not inevitably lead to a global federation or empire: after all, if the international system were rigorously homogeneous, and if states did in fact renounce their right to take up arms, then what would prevent them from granting to some supra-national regime the authority to enforce the rule of law? Aron seems to suggest that the conditions for the existence of peace by law ultimately boil down to the conditions for peace by empire: to require states to comply with the decisions of an international tribunal is, in essence, to ask them to transfer some of their sovereignty to a supra-national regime, thereby giving international law its obligatory character as law (Aron 2003: 713, 716–717, 724, 736).

Now Aron believes that one of the first examples his readers (in the 1960s) will conjure up to illustrate the general idea of peace through empire is the Common Market (or European Union): the Common Market has the right to make certain decisions which the member states are obliged to follow, although this does not erase the sovereignty of the states as such. But while Aron admits that there is some truth to this example, it would be wrong to imagine that the simple establishment of a transitional regime will on its own lead to the type of regime which could effectively eliminate the possibility of war altogether. "[T]he formation of a Common Market does not lead, either by juridical necessity or by historical necessity, to an authentic federation." Aron sees as one of the "great illusion[s] of our times" that technological and economic integration will inevitably lead to political unification; that states will renounce having separate foreign policies and standing armies; and that a common political will or consciousness might arise between them. Aron does not categorically rule out this possibility, but it would have to be desired by the peoples and leaders themselves and would not emerge as a kind of natural outgrowth of integration pure and simple. Politics or the political have a primacy in international relations that cannot be reduced to economic considerations: economic integration may help shape political decisions but it certainly does not determine them. Aron, then, takes issue with one of the predominant themes of our time, namely that situations of complex economic interdependence necessarily create expected patterns of behavior between states that ultimately influence and constrain their political actions. Similar to the successful application of international law, situations of integration and interdependence are the result and not the cause of prior, political actions on the part of the states involved (Aron 2003: 745–748).

But there is a deeper reason why it is highly unlikely that states would be willing to sacrifice their political sovereignty (as opposed to some of their economic sovereignty) at the altar of a universal empire of states: nations respond to and are an outgrowth of a people's desire to express their unique and autonomous culture or character. "[T]he modern nation in Europe consists precisely of the conjunction of a community of culture and a desire for autonomy." Aron readily acknowledged that not every political unit in the world today could claim to be a nation in this sense, and he was equally aware that the community of culture was "never entirely one and homogenous" and that it contained disparate elements within it. Nonetheless, through centuries of "force" and "bloodshed," certain nations had coalesced in order to achieve an (admittedly "never perfect") "singular grouping of beliefs and behavior" – "a union of culture and politics, history and reason."

The nation has its language and its law, which it has received from the past and which express a unique calling. Citizens seek to live together, to establish their own laws in order to make a contribution to the human enterprise which, without them, would not exist.

For Aron, a universal empire would necessarily efface this wondrous multiplicity, where each nation, as in a fine tapestry, "express[es] the wealth of human possibilities. The diversity of cultures is not a curse to be exorcized but a heritage to be safeguarded." This is not to deny that human beings also think of themselves in universal terms and that they can feel connected to and obligated toward others in ways that transcend national borders: indeed, Aron suggests that in certain areas (e.g., resource conservation and allocation, or population control) it might be better if the human race approached these problems as if they were a "single collectivity." But this desire for universalism is much weaker than attachment to the nation precisely because consciousness of the community of all human beings is much weaker than the consciousness of our national society. In fact, the possibility of the former is based upon the latter, and it is thereby more diluted in its intensity because it is more general (Aron 2003: 748, 750–753).

With these thoughts in mind, Aron argues that a better chance to achieve peace by empire while still preserving the communities of culture would be through a global federation along the lines of the Swiss Confederation: it is the Confederation, and not the separate cantons, that has a standing army and an independent foreign policy, and it is to the Confederation that the cantons look when they have disputes among themselves. Aron ends his discussion in chapter 24 by asking two questions: first, what conditions would have to be met in order for such a global federation to come into existence; and second, would such a federation be contrary to nature (Aron 2003: 752–753)? To establish a universal federation would more or less require the same conditions required by peace through law. First and foremost, states would have to renounce the recourse to arms. This, in turn, would require the rigorous homogeneity of the international system; similar governments and goals between all the states involved; and the creation of a supra-national political and military regime which would settle disputes and enforce compliance. In essence, this form of peace by empire would require depriving states of their "external sovereignty" – "the state's right of determining justice without appeal" – while at the same time not depriving them of the management of their internal affairs as separate states. And this is precisely the crux of the problem, according to Aron. One the one hand, if states were deprived of military and a significant amount of political sovereignty – of their ability to be the final arbiter in cases of justice – then what would the state be reduced to, and would it retain enough dignity to be called a (sovereign) state at all? On the other hand, if one does not strip political and military sovereignty from states, then how is peace by empire ever to be achieved (Aron 2003: 753–754, 758–759)?

At the end of the day, if the chance for realizing peace by empire boils down to the chance of realizing peace by law, then neither event is ever likely to occur, nor the end of the history of international relations. What Aron's analysis helps to put in perspective is the following idea: even if we begin with the most optimistic assumptions about bringing about universal peace – namely, asking states to forgo the use of force by submitting to international law or empire – the conditions by which this could be realized would require a radical change in the very nature of *states* and the meaning of the *stakes* for which they fight. We simply cannot hope to attenuate the state of nature without inevitably asking for the conversions of the actors and the stakes; and as Aron had remarked in the beginning of chapter 23, this is almost too fanciful to imagine, requiring as it would a fundamental change in human nature (Aron 2003: 708–709, 756). Of course, this means that Aron believes that international relations, or the alternatives of war and peace, will remain a permanent fixture of human history as long as states remain what they are.

Aron as philosopher: how to understand the character of the twentieth century

Although Aron relied on many other thinkers of the past to guide his analysis, he more or less guided himself when it came to understanding the unique features of the twentieth century. Part Three of *Peace and War* therefore tries to delineate those unique features of the emerging Cold War. According to Aron,

> the circumstances of 1960 [are] dominated by two major facts: the *technological revolution*, origin of both the enormous capacity to destroy (thermonuclear weapons) and to produce (the futility of conquests), [and] the *global extension of the diplomatic field*, origin of both real heterogeneity (diversity of the principles of state legitimacy, dimensions of the political units) and of juridical homogeneity (United Nations, equality and sovereignty of states).
> (Aron 2003: 371)

It is important to note that although there are two "major facts" of the twentieth century (i.e., technology and extension), each of these facts has two additional aspects: the technological revolution has yielded both an incredible destructive *and* productive capacity while the extension of the diplomatic field has resulted in both political heterogeneity *and* juridical homogeneity. There are then four distinctive characteristics of the new post-World War II system, each of which is fundamentally independent of the others; for it is perfectly conceivable that the technological revolution could have yielded destructive *and not* productive capacity while the extension of the diplomatic field could have resulted in political heterogeneity *and not* juridical homogeneity (and vice versa). Of course, while these four aspects are independent of one another, they are also elaborately interconnected, and Aron unpacks the internal dynamics of each as well as how each one affects the other aspects of the international system.

Admittedly, Aron spends much less time in Part Three speaking about the new productive capacity of the world (perhaps because he had already discussed these themes in what is called his Sorbonne Trilogy [1955–1958]) (Aron 1964, 1967, 1969). Nonetheless, we begin to get a glimpse of the new complexity of the Cold War when looking at economics and how it interacts with diplomatic extension (Aron 2003: 506–536). Because all political units now have political and juridical sovereignty and equality with all others, all states collectively belong to humanity or the international community as a whole: there is thus no apparently valid moral reason why some states should be richer than others, or to say nearly the same thing, every economically advanced state has a duty to help its more impoverished brethren (Aron 2003: 373–381). Economic assistance and humanitarian aid are now central issues in global politics – indeed, these issues have been transformed from considerations of generosity (on the part of the rich) and thankfulness (on the part of the poor) into issues of obligation (on the part of the rich) and right (on the part of the poor) (Aron 2003: 506–507, 513). But while some states and leaders may genuinely believe they have either a duty or a right to humanitarian aid and economic assistance, Aron is keenly aware that political heterogeneity complicates global politics even further: poor states can cynically demand aid and assistance even when the leaders are the ones who have impoverished the nation, or they can play one superpower off against the other in order to get the best economic deal for their country. And in the zero-sum game of the Cold War, the superpowers themselves are often more than willing to give such aid and assistance (even when knowing better) in the hopes of increasing the power of their alliance structure and/or of creating a more "just" and "caring" image internationally (Aron 2003: 513–522). Smaller states, whose power is exponentially eclipsed by the two superpowers, are thus able to enjoy and even to flaunt in various forms of neutrality, neutralism, and/or non-alignment an unreal or virtual independence, using their newfound juridical homogeneity to bolster their importance and influence in a starkly heterogeneous political environment (Aron 2003: 507–513). There would now seem to be three kinds of aid and assistance in the world: genuine, cynical, and that by extortion.

But as unprecedented as the world's new productive capacity is, as well as the worldwide extension of the diplomatic field, Aron considers that the "most truly revolutionary" feature of the twentieth century is thermonuclear weapons: "For the first time, men are preparing a war they do not want, a war they hope not to wage" (Aron 2003: 371). Indeed, for the first time in human history, a traditional notion of defense has been rendered obsolete: there exists the ability to annihilate opponents without first disarming them (Aron 2003: 396, 435). Now it is simply impossible to do justice to Aron's description of nuclear strategy in Part Three as it would require us merely to repeat the multiple scenarios and complicated layers that he can envision in the heterogeneous, bipolar world of the superpowers. What is therefore essential to emphasize are two underlying principles that animate his analysis. First, despite the unprecedented destructive capacity of nuclear weapons, Aron never rules out their use in extreme circumstances (e.g., a Soviet invasion of Western Europe); and second, he does not believe that the first- (or second-) strike use of these weapons would necessarily lead to an all-out conflict. While thermonuclear bombs seem to be weapons unlike any other in history, they are still weapons: Aron can consequently imagine (and he believes the superpowers can as well, under extreme circumstances) the possibility of a *limited nuclear* war (Aron 2003: 404–440, 476, 494, 641). It should go without saying that Aron repeatedly deplores (and is indeed sickened by) such a thought; nevertheless, he never lets his emotions get in the way of his reason. He famously observed as early as 1948 in *Le Grand Schisme* that the emerging diplomatic constellation between the superpowers was a "bellicose peace," and that while peace between the blocs was impossible, war was highly improbable – but it was improbable and not impossible (Aron 1948: 1–31). In other words, the improbability (or unattractiveness) of nuclear war had the effect of making the Soviets and Americans *les frères ennemis*, and their collective interest in avoiding nuclear war overrode and to some extent moderated their ideological antagonism (Aron 2003: 389, 407, 428, 536, 546, 564). Of course, this dynamic tension between the blocs also had repercussions within the blocs (as well as outside them): *les frères ennemis* then became *les grands frères* within their respective alliance structures, the particular internal diplomatic relations of which were strongly influenced by the different internal regimes of the Soviets, Americans, and their various allies (Aron 2003: 441–475). Nevertheless, despite these complicated, worldwide dynamics, Aron maintains that the strategy of deterrence has not been rendered obsolete with the introduction of nuclear weapons, and a diplomat's decision-making process in the nuclear age remains "formally" the same as in any other age (Aron 2003: 404–408, 435–436, 636). As Aron sees it, the global extension (and juridical homogeneity) of the diplomatic field in the post-world war era has not eclipsed the necessarily "*oligopolistic*" nature of the international system and its various sub-systems (Aron 2003: 95, 389–394). Indeed, it has only accentuated it.

The conclusion of this massive case study is announced in the opening pages of Part Three and demonstrated throughout: "What are called weapons of mass destruction have changed *something* in the course of relations between what are called sovereign states. They have changed neither the nature of men nor that of political units." In fact, Aron goes even further in restricting the revolutionary character of these weapons: "The formation of blocs owes little or nothing to the introduction of atomic weapons. It has been a mechanical effect of the situation created by the Second World War. Two states had emerged reinforced from the turmoil." Despite the horrendous devastation incurred by the Soviet Union, it alone possessed a massive army in the heart of central Europe, while the United States, having been spared a destructive invasion on its mainland, possessed great industrial capacity as well as (at least for a short time) the sole possession of nuclear weapons. Therefore, the

> constitution of a Soviet zone of influence in Eastern Europe provoked a regrouping in the West which, in its turn, provoked a reply in the form of a tightening of the links between the People's Democracies and the Soviet Union.

Aron concludes: "The dialectic of the blocs is, as such, classical, in accord with the predictable logic of a bipolar equilibrium" (Aron 2003: 371–372, 476). What we now see is a "permanent combination of *deterrence, persuasion* and *subversion*," which, while new, does not change the essentially Clausewitzian character of international politics: "war is the continuation of policy by other means" (Aron 2003: 369, 382, 398, 439–440, 506–535). The twentieth century is certainly novel, but it is not fundamentally unique.

In conclusion: Clausewitz and conceptualization

As should be clear at this point, Aron did not subscribe to a modern or contemporary understanding of international relations theory. And Aron himself was acutely aware of this. Writing a few years after the publication of *Peace and War*, Aron asked whether or not his analysis should be classified as a "*theory*" or a "*conceptualization.*"

> It all depends on what we expect of a theory, of the model of a theory (in physics or in economics) to which we refer. Such a conceptual analysis seems to me to fulfill some of the functions that we can expect from a theory: it defines the essential features of a sub-system; it provides a list of the main variables; it suggests certain hypotheses about the operation of the sub-system, depending on whether it is bipolar or multipolar, homogeneous or heterogeneous.
>
> (Aron 1967a)

It would seem that Aron thought it more important to make certain that his analytical framework helped to elicit the right questions about international relations – that it allowed individuals to see the plurality of factors animating international politics. Perhaps this is why he turned to Clausewitz to help him to frame his theoretical conceptualizations.

After initially claiming that "inter-state relations" revolve around two "symbolic" individuals, namely "the *diplomat* [or *ambassador*] and the *soldier*," the first quotation from Clausewitz emphasizes that peace and war do not belong

> to the province of Arts and Sciences, but to the province of social life … It would be better, instead of comparing it with any Art, to liken it to business competition, which is also a conflict of human interests and activities.

Aron continues in his own words: "Thus we can readily understand why international relations afford a focus of interest to a particular discipline and why they escape any precise delimitation" (Aron 2003: 5–6). Indeed, Aron goes on to highlight that Clausewitz, perhaps more than any other theoretician, emphasized the role of chance and uncertainty in war, both in theory and practice. War can be conceptualized but it remains unpredictable and perhaps indeterminate (Aron 2003: 53–54).

Admittedly, the preponderance of quotations from and references to Clausewitz occur in the opening three chapters of *Peace and War*, and the majority of these refer to the dynamics of warfare. But the singular quotation that Aron reminds us of throughout the book is also Clausewitz's most famous, namely that "war is a continuation of policy by other means": the purpose of war is the imposition of our will over our adversary's (and vice versa) (Aron 2003: 21, 71, 160). To understand war and peace properly, therefore, requires understanding the multitudinous array of factors that define or determine our own will and the will of our adversary – the character of the regime, motivations both moral and otherwise (real and professed), the historical and sociological context, and so on. To put it baldly, one must begin to understand the soul or conscience of the diplomats and soldiers involved in the potential conflict. But it was precisely this aspect of understanding that was in danger of being lost by contemporary social scientists; or to say the same thing, the diplomat's and soldier's perspective (which was essentially Clausewitz's *political* perspective) was being eclipsed by decidedly new models of explanation. One reason has been mentioned in the previous section: many theorists argued that nuclear weapons had fundamentally changed the nature of international politics in the modern world. But another reason, which Aron alerts us to at the very beginning of the book, was the loss or rejection of the historical (or political) perspective, in all its complexity and contingency.

> Historians did not wait for the accession of the United States to world primacy to study "international relations," but they described or related more than they analyzed or explained. No science, however, limits itself to describing or relating. Further, what profit can statesmen or diplomats derive from the historical knowledge of past centuries? The weapons of mass destruction, the techniques of subversion, the ubiquity of military force because of aviation and electronics, introduce new human and material factors which render the lessons of the past equivocal at best. Or, at least, such lessons cannot be used unless they are assimilated into a theory that includes the like and the unlike, and separates constants in order to elaborate, and not to eliminate, the part played by the unknown. This was the decisive question. Specialists in international relations were unwilling merely to follow the historians; like all scholars, they wanted to establish axioms, create a body of doctrine.
>
> (Aron 2003: 2, 768)

Aron needed to make certain that his audience – and his audience included informed citizens, academics, and politicians of various persuasions and ranks – understood that the dynamics of peace and war had not changed in any fundamental sense. Every age tends to imagine that theirs is so unique that it cannot be grasped without absolutely new concepts and paradigms and theories. Aron wanted to prevent this potentially dangerous tendency, in some sense, by returning to the familiar and sober conceptualizations of Clausewitz, in particular, and the history of political philosophy, in general.

Notes

1 The best place to begin to understand Aron's intellectual trajectory is with Aron himself: Raymond Aron (1990 [1983]), *Memoirs: Fifty Years of Political Reflection*. New York: Holmes & Meier. For an exceedingly useful secondary source that describes and summarizes the aforementioned writings, as well as providing the original French bibliographical citations (and English translations, when available), see R. Colquhoun (1986), *Raymond Aron: The Philosopher in History, 1905–1955* and *Raymond Aron: The Sociologist in Society, 1955–1983*, London: SAGE Publications.
2 Unless otherwise noted, all emphasized words in quotations are contained in the original. For Aron's own estimation of the book, see Aron, *Memoirs*, pp. 301–312. Colquhoun, *Raymond Aron: The Sociologist in Society*, pp. 163–201, provides a very useful schematic diagram of the overall structure of the work, summarizes its contents, and chronicles its scholarly reception in both France and the United States.
3 On this point, see, for example, Davis (2009), *A Politics of Understanding: The International Thought of Raymond Aron*, Baton Rouge, LA: Louisiana State University Press.
4 This might not be the first time Aron engaged in a covert dialogue with other thinkers (in this case Carl Schmitt): see P. Raynaud (1989), "Raymond Aron et le droit international", *Cahiers de philosophie politique et juridique*, 15: 115–128.

References

Aron, R. (1938), *Essai sur la théorie de l'histoire dans l'Allemagne contemporaine: la philosophie critique de l'histoire*. Paris: Vrin.
Aron, R. (1948), *Le grand schisme*. Paris: Gallimard.
Aron, R. (1961 [1938]), *Introduction to the Philosophy of History: An Essay on the Limits of Historical Objectivity*. Boston: Beacon Press.
Aron, R. (1964 [1935]), *German Sociology*. New York: Free Press of Glencoe.
Aron, R. (1964 [1957]), *La lutte de classes: Nouvelles leçons sur les sociétés industrielles*. Paris: Gallimard.
Aron, R. (1967a), "What Is a Theory of International Relations?" *Journal of International Affairs*, 21:2.
Aron, R. (1967b [1956]), *18 Lectures on Industrial Society*. London: Weidenfeld & Nicolson.
Aron, R. (1969 [1958]), *Democracy and Totalitarianism*. New York: Praeger.
Aron, R. (1990 [1983]), *Memoirs: Fifty Years of Political Reflection*. New York: Holmes & Meier.
Aron, R. (2003 [1962]), *Peace and War: A Theory of International Relations*. New Brunswick, NJ: Transaction Publishers.
Colquhoun, R. (1986), *Raymond Aron: The Philosopher in History, 1905–1955* and *Raymond Aron: The Sociologist in Society, 1955–1983*. London: SAGE Publications.
Davis, R.M. (2009), *A Politics of Understanding: The International Thought of Raymond Aron*. Baton Rouge, LA: Louisiana State University Press.
Fukuyama, F. (1992), *The End of History and the Last Man*. New York: Free Press.
Kojève, A. (1980 [1947]), *Introduction to the Reading of Hegel: Lectures on the "Phenomenology of Spirt,"* Ithaca, NY: Cornell University Press.
Raynaud, P. (1989), "Raymond Aron et la droit international," *Cahiers de philosophie politique et juridique*, 15: 115–128.

2 Pilgrims' progress
The disenchanted destinations of Raymond Aron and Georges Canguilhem

Reed M. Davis

At first glance, mapping out the philosophical influences on Raymond Aron seems to be a relatively straightforward exercise. Virtually all of Aron's commentators agree that Max Weber exerted the earliest and most decisive influence on Aron. Indeed, Aron's encounter with Weber hit him with all the force of a conversion experience. In Weber, Aron once declared,

> I discovered what I was looking for: in him was to be found a combination of historical experience, political understanding, a striving for truth, and, ultimately, decision and action. The decision to grasp truth and reality and at the same time to act in the world seem to me to be the two imperatives which I have tried to follow throughout my life – and I found these two imperatives in Max Weber.
>
> (Colquhoun 1986: 45)

Nevertheless, Aron became increasingly uncomfortable with Weber's single-minded preoccupation with power and the contingencies of history. Consequently, he cast about for a thinker who could soften the sharper edges of Weber's nominalism and political realism. Here, however, the challenge of mining for intellectual influences becomes more difficult, as Aron never clearly identified a philosophical school or an individual thinker who could serve as a counterweight to Weber. In fact, Aron's idealism is so diffuse that some argue that it is of little or no consequence. Pierre Manent, for example, has argued that Aron should be approached as "a perfect gentleman who experienced no need for transcendence" (Hancock 2010).

Aron's idealism may be loose-fitting but it is not non-existent. The difficulty commentators have had in charting the boundaries of Aron's idealism derives from the fact that Aron explored a wide range of philosophies in the course of his rather restless search for the truth of human existence. Consequently, commentators find themselves in the same predicament with Aron as do the proverbial blind men and their elephant: Sylvie Mesure argues that Aron stands squarely in the tradition of neo-Kantianism, while Iain Stewart identifies Wilhelm Dilthey's *lebensphilosophie* – a very different philosophy indeed – as a major influence on his intellectual development. For our part, we argued that

Edmund Husserl's phenomenology needs to be reckoned with in assessing the fundamental character of Aron's philosophical orientation (Mesure 1984; Davis 2003; Stewart 2011).

No assessment of the origins of Aron's philosophical attitude would be complete without a discussion of Aron's relationship to his close friend Georges Canguilhem. Both met as students at the Ecole Normale Supérieure and remained in close contact for the rest of their lives. (In fact, Canguilhem delivered the eulogy at Aron's funeral.) Aron once described Canguilhem – who was a physician, a philosopher, and a historian of science – as a thinker of rank who influenced not only several generations of students, including the likes of Michel Foucault and Gilles Deleuze, but his own thinking as well. Canguilhem's reach was extensive indeed: he was not only a professor at the Sorbonne but a member of the French national *agrégation* committee, which meant that he had considerable influence over French doctoral exams in philosophy.

Locating the points of contact between Canguilhem and Aron, however, is difficult for two reasons. First, in his memoirs, Aron discreetly drew a veil over his relationship with Canguilhem. Canguilhem would be angry with him, Aron wrote, if he "attempted a literary portrait," an exercise that would "hardly [be] compatible with a half-century of friendship" (Aron 1990: 33). Consequently, if one searches for more than fleeting words of appreciation between Aron and Canguilhem, one searches in vain. Second, Canguilhem and Aron inhabited two dramatically different worlds: Canguilhem was a physician and a historian of medicine, Aron a philosopher. How much influence *could* Canguilhem have exercised, especially on Aron's idealism of all things?

Despite these challenges, we believe that the connection between Aron and Canguilhem is significant. More specifically, we believe that points of contact can be made at the level of "categorial frameworks," a phrase we have taken from Stephan Körner (1970). A categorial framework describes those all-inclusive interpretations of the human condition that establish the basic distinctions and logical relations that are believed to obtain in reality. What makes the relationship between Aron and Canguilhem of particular interest is that Canguilhem seemed to be open to the insights of the social sciences to advance his rather novel biological ideas, while Aron seems to have imported some of Canguilhem's ideas to overcome the shortcomings of Weber's nominalism. In the end, it may have been Canguilhem's self-professed "vitalism," ironically enough, that left Aron more receptive to the possibilities of transcendence than some commentators have suspected. The categorial similarities between the two, then, are such that the ideas that Canguilhem wrestled with cast light on the ones that preoccupied Aron as well.

We begin at the Ecole Normale Supérieure in 1926. It was there that Aron discovered not only philosophy but biology. This prompts an unanswerable question: to what degree was Aron's discovery of biology owed to Georges Canguilhem?

The half-turn to biology

Aron's discovery of philosophy at the Ecole Normale Supérieure ("Before the class of *philosophie* darkness, thereafter, light") must not obscure the fact that he was interested in biology for a considerable time too. In fact, it was to biology that Aron turned after his undergraduate years, devoting a year to reading genetics in preparation for a dissertation in the philosophy of science. Although Aron recounted little of those years (his papers and syllabi had all been destroyed during the war), he recalled that he spent a good deal of time in the laboratories at the Ecole Normale Supérieure which were then under the direction of Etienne Rabaud. Rabaud was a hugely consequential figure in French science. As Aron explained, Rabaud "had declared war, once and for all, on Mendelism, genetics, and experiments on the fruit fly that had permitted mapping genes on the four chromosomes" (Aron 1990: 38). Why? Because "the structure of chromosomes, of hereditary matter, the atoms of heredity that constitute the genes, did not fit with Etienne Rabaud's paradigm, a paradigm of a living totality, of the harmony between organism and milieu." Rabaud was not alone: most of the "general biology" in Aron's time was dominated by a rather virulent strain of anti-Mendelianism (Burian *et al.* 1988: 357–402). Even Lucien Cuévot, a French pioneer in experimental genetics, turned against the Mendelianism of his early years. This hostility toward Mendelianism was particularly acute in the social sciences. As Aron related in his memoirs, Marcel Mauss, a sociologist who fancied himself a scientist, told Aron while both were waiting for a train that he flatly rejected Mendelianism.

At root, the fight revolved around the reductionist tendencies of the new genetics: Mendelians believed that genes could be resolved into their physiological and biochemical components (molecular genetics), while Mendelian critics like Rabaud insisted that "living totalities" exhibited a complexity that could not be accounted for simply by referring to the material parts of a living organism. Although some historians have been tempted to label the anti-Mendelians as "anti-scientific," this is much too narrow an interpretation; many biologists grudgingly admitted that the anti-Mendelians advanced a rather substantive scientific agenda of their own, while leveling scientific criticisms of the Mendelian enterprise along the way that Mendelians had difficulty in rebutting.

This biological dispute over parts and wholes seemed to mirror the philosophical dispute beginning to boil over in France at that time. As Aron explained it, the problem with the philosophy of his day was that it "taught us nothing about the real world in which we lived" (Aron 1990: 20). Utterly indifferent to the harsh realities of political life, members of the French academia occupied themselves with theoretical abstractions far removed from the non-academic concerns of their country, a turn of mind that scandalized the younger generation of students under their tutelage. This monumental indifference sparked a revolt in French thought that profoundly affected the course of Continental philosophy. As if to compensate for their predecessors' apparent historical ignorance, members of the French intelligentsia, inspired by the vast, syncretic systems of

Hegel and Marx, rushed to follow Sartre's lead in searching for a method of total historical knowledge. Starting from the assumption that history "is not a simple sum of juxtaposed facts," this historico-philosophical quest generated countless studies on the problem of historical understanding which, despite their diversity, had one thing in common – the desire to see history whole. Aron was thus tempted to represent this movement as a half-conscious "return to Hegel" in opposition to the "return to Kant" of the previous generation. For his part, however, Aron deplored this trend and turned back, as we will see, to somewhat less elevated ambitions for his hope and inspiration.

This, then, was the supercharged scientific and philosophical atmosphere in which Aron and Canguilhem found themselves as graduate students. Canguilhem plunged ahead with his medical and biological studies, while Aron, after much soul-searching, abandoned biology to concentrate on the philosophy of history, reasoning that no philosopher of science could understand the procedures of a geneticist better than a geneticist. Moreover, adopting the attitude of a scientist in a laboratory left Aron "unsatisfied." The person that we are at our most profound level of existence "is not a scientist." Consequently, Aron searched for a field of inquiry "that would demand an attempt at scientific rigor and, at the same time, would engage me entirely in my research." In other words, Aron was struggling to find "a subject of investigation that would simultaneously interest the heart and the mind" (Aron 1990: 39). That subject would be the philosophy of history, or a philosophical study of the formation of historical concepts. In choosing the philosophy of history, Aron may have left biology behind, but his exposure to the early battles of Mendelian genetics had marked him forever: by the time of his dissertation, Aron's resistance to reductionism had permanently congealed and his turn to transcendence had begun.

History, biology, and the problem of freedom

Interestingly enough, both Canguilhem and Aron wrote dissertations dedicated to the process of concept formation. While Aron was preoccupied with locating the boundaries of objectivity in the creation of historical concepts, Canguilhem was searching for the boundaries of objectivity in biological ones, particularly those devoted to ideas of the normal and the pathological. Although their subjects were obviously quite different, Aron and Canguilhem grounded their studies in a remarkably similar set of first principles.

More specifically, both Aron and Canguilhem insisted that the process of concept formation reckons with the facts of contingency. In searching for the limits of historical objectivity, Aron restored a significant measure of indeterminacy to history and human action, a move that greatly agitated his elders at the Ecole Normale Supérieure. Utterly oblivious to the tragic dimensions of history, many of Aron's instructors professed what Aron and his classmates took to be a rather simple scientism, one that assured both actors and observers that moral progress was inevitable. Aron, however, eventually fashioned a philosophy of history that stressed the lacunae of history, a turn of mind that scandalized the older generation. What his teachers found so unsettling about Aron's conceptual universe was how little it promised. Concepts such as "reason" and "progress" were little more than abstract possibilities to Aron, ideals that in themselves did nothing to dispel the specter of tragedy from history or, conversely, assure the moral progress of human beings. Aron never ruled out the possibility that human behavior could progress; he simply insisted that given the reality of human freedom and historical contingency, there was no way to know that it *would*.

Although Aron defended his dissertation to much acclaim, he had to contend with a jury that was openly hostile to his somewhat melancholic approach to history. Paul Fauconnet, for example, wrapped up his cross-examination with these words: "I conclude with an act of charity, faith, and hope: charity by repeating to you my admiration and my sympathy; faith in the ideas that you condemn; hope that the students will not follow you" (Aron 1990: 76). In fact, speaking for several members of the jury, Fauconnet declared that Aron's dissertation was so pessimistic that he judged Aron to be either possessed by the devil or in the grip of a pathological despair. Aron later wrote that he was "neither Satanic nor desperate [but] was experiencing in advance the world war that my judges did not see coming" (Aron 1990: 90).

If Aron's insistence on freedom was unsettling, Canguilhem's was nothing short of revolutionary, as it flew directly in the face of Darwinian orthodoxy. The neo-Darwinian understanding of natural selection rests on the premise that the costs and benefits of genetic mutations are judged exclusively by a cold, unforgiving environment: after a genetic mutation occurs, all organisms simply stand mute before the forces of biological necessity, passively awaiting nature's verdict. As Jerry Fodor put it, "the phenomena of evolution ... are very largely the effects of environmental causes" (Fodor and Piattelli-Palmarini 2010: 6; Canguilhem 2008: 105). Living organisms, in other words, can do nothing to alter the externally imposed conventions of natural selection.

Canguilhem, however, insisted that organisms "debated" or "negotiated" with their environments, both internally and externally. As Kurt Goldstein – whom Canguilhem greatly admired – explained, "Biology ... has to do with individuals that exist and tend to exist, that is to say, seek to realize their capacities as best they can in a given environment." The biological study of nourishment, for example,

> does not consist solely in establishing a [biochemical] balance sheet, but in seeking, within the organism itself, *the sense of the organism's choice* – when free in its milieu – to seek sustenance in such and such a species or essences while excluding others that could ... procure it equivalent energetic provisions for its maintenance and growth.
>
> (Canguilhem 2008: xix)

This, of course, is biological heresy. Declaring that organisms possess "choice" or develop "capacities" capable of bending the forces of nature is altogether too teleological for most biologists: current-day Darwinians begin from the premise that natural necessity, acting on random genetic variations, is the motor force driving selection and behavior, not an organism's purpose or intention.

It needs to be noted that neither Aron nor Canguilhem believed that freedom was absolute; both accepted the fact that freedom, however real, was limited. As historical actors or biological creatures, human beings simply do not have the ability to shape their environments however they please. For both men, then, freedom was neither absolute nor non-existent but variable: freedom changed according to the situation or according to the nature of the object at hand.

In order to bring the connecting threads between Aron and Canguilhem into sharper relief, we need to understand how these first principles were brought to bear on the objects of their respective sciences and on the methods they fabricated to know them. ("Ever since Vico," Aron explained, "all those who have reflected on history have in one way or another upheld a sort of kinship between the nature of that reality and the mode in which reality is appropriated by consciousness" (Aron 1976: 92)). In the end, we will see that the structure of the historical self and the stuff of life – as well as the cognitive processes by which we come to understand them – are remarkably similar. And in noting these similarities we take our measure of Aron's turn toward transcendence.

The indeterminacies of life and human action

In the introduction to the second edition of Canguilhem's most important book, *The Normal and the Pathological*, Michel Foucault underscored the fact that the formation of concepts lies at the heart of Canguilhem's work in biology and medicine. The particular challenge that biologists face in fabricating concepts, Foucault observed, is that "the role of a strictly biological concept is to cut out from the ensemble of the phenomena 'of life' those which allow one, without reducing, to analyze the process proper to living beings" (Canguilhem 1989: 19). Like Aron, Canguilhem accepted the Kantian premise that knowledge is obtained through the creation of concepts. However, Kant had his limits: both Aron and Canguilhem rebelled against the notion that a priori knowledge gives us a sufficient knowledge of life and human action. "Transcendental logic," Canguilhem argued, "which constitutes nature *a priori* as a system of physical laws, does not in fact succeed in constituting nature as the theater of living organisms" (Canguilhem 1994: 311). Kant's critique of pure reason may have advanced "a better understanding of the concept of causality" but this does not mean that we "understand the causality of the concept" (Canguilhem 1994: 310).

Indeed, "life" resists conceptualization. Why? Because life has the capacity for "self-creation." We here approach the heart of Canguilhem's self-professed vitalism, expressed in his notion of "thematic conservation." An organized being, Canguilhem declared, "is one that is both its own cause and its own effect; it organizes itself and reproduces its organization; it forms itself and creates its own replica in accordance with a type" (Canguilhem 1994: 310).

This idea of biological "forms" connects Canguilhem to the great nineteenth-century biologist, Claude Bernard, whom Canguilhem criticized at times but nevertheless held in the highest regard. Both Canguilhem and Bernard pushed back against the mechanistic reductionisms of modern biology, whereby functioning organisms were believed to be reducible exclusively to their physiochemical components. Unlike many of his contemporaries, Bernard was convinced that "the organized living thing is the temporary manifestation of an *idée directrice*," or some sort of guiding life principle. The need for a governing idea emerges when one considers the relation between biological parts and wholes. To take but one example, if the body is really nothing more than the sum of independent cells, "how do we explain the fact that it forms a whole that functions in a uniform manner? If cells are closed systems, how can the organism live and act as a whole?" (Canguilhem 2008: 52). In other words, Bernard argued that the laws of chemistry or physics contain in themselves absolutely no directive explaining how they are to be applied in the creation of complex organisms. The question that mechanists have most difficulty in answering, then, is "in what sense is an organism organized?" (Canguilhem 1994: 312).

Bernard believed that the life was somehow housed in protoplasm, which for him was not a purely chemical substance. As Canguilhem explained it, Bernard intuited that protoplasm had a peculiar structure and that this structure was in some way hereditary. To Bernard's way of thinking, protoplasmic structure was "the manifestation here and now of a primitive impulse, a primitive action and message, which nature repeats according to a pattern determined in advance" (Canguilhem 1994: 314). Remarkably enough, Bernard had sensed that biological inheritance involves the transmission of what we now think of as "information," information that bears a striking similarity to the genetic code, utterly unknown in Bernard's time. To Bernard's way of thinking, vital phenomena are therefore subject not only to physical and chemical factors, but to "an immanent design, a plan, a regularity, which is responsible for its harmony, persistence, and, if need be, its restoration" (Canguilhem 1994: 313). All of this, Canguilhem declared, has been given "retroactive legitimacy" by the discovery of a program encoded in a sequence of nucleotides. In short, life should now be understood as "meaning inscribed in matter," not simply as the grim, forward march of natural necessity.

If this is true, then all life is both casual *and* intentional. In other words, biological organisms do not simply float passively on the currents of natural necessity, but exhibit the capacity to learn and manage information and, in so doing, survive and perhaps even flourish. Living systems are thus "open, non-equilibrium systems that maintain their organization both *because* they are open to the external world and *in spite of* being open to the external world" (Canguilhem 1988: 141). Biological organisms at all levels of complexity are thus now described by a proliferation of terms that deploy the prefix *auto-* to describe the workings of organized systems: auto-organization, auto-reproduction, auto-regulation, and so on. Self-preservation, in other words, presupposes a certain capacity for self-knowledge.

If life is understood to be an indissoluble connection of meaning and matter, or of matter and form, then the chief challenge for the biologist is, as Foucault suggested, to tease out biological individualities from within the complex welter of biological systems. This is a problem of immense scope and concern to Canguilhem; consequently, a thorough treatment of the topic is beyond the limits of this chapter. However, having isolated the basic components of life from Canguilhem's biology, meaning and matter, we offer two brief observations about their relationship.

First, the relationship between materiality and form is both continuous and discontinuous. Here Canguilhem again appeals to Bernard because Bernard's formulation "is so up-to-date" (Canguilhem 1988: 139). On the one hand, Bernard declared that "vital phenomena are subject only to physical and chemical causes," a statement that plainly testifies to Bernard's belief in the indissoluble continuity between biological and physico-chemical phenomena. Indeed, Bernard "has the indisputable merit of having denied the antithesis admitted until then between the organic and the mineral, plant and animal, [and] of having affirmed the universal applicability of all physico-chemical phenomena regardless of their setting and appearance." In fact, Bernard's great discovery of the glycogenic function of the liver was "one of the most beautiful results" of the determination to "recognize everywhere the continuity of phenomena" (Canguilhem 1989: 73). On the other hand, Bernard also accepted the originality of biological phenomena. "Today," Canguilhem wrote,

> one would have to be quite uninformed of the methodological tendencies of biologists – even those biologists least inclined to mysticism – to believe that anyone can honestly boast of having discovered, by physico-chemical methods, anything more than the physico-chemical content of phenomena, whose biological meaning escapes all techniques of reduction.
> (Canguilhem 2008: 16)

Thus the paradox of biology: forms and meanings are *at one and the same time* conditioned by and independent of physico-chemical forces. However, it is precisely this paradox that guarantees the irreducibility of life to natural necessity.

Second, the relationship between form and matter is interactive and reciprocal. As Canguilhem explains, "the biological relationship between [a] being and its milieu is a functional relationship, and thereby a mobile one; *its terms successively exchange roles*" (Canguilhem 2008: 111). In other words, materiality can affect intentionality and form, while intentionality can mold or shape materiality. As an example, Canguilhem offers up the case of aphasia, or brain damage, whereby the brain is able to rewire itself to compensate for a loss of functionality sustained in injury. Indeed, the polyvalence of organs, or the fact that one organ can assume the function of another – researchers can now equip patients who are blind to see with the assistance of their tongues – testifies to an organ's ability to relearn and even relocate functionality. This is why Canguilhem insists that biological organisms "debate" with their environment rather than passively submit to them. "What is essential in Lamarck's ideas," Canguilhem declared, is that the organism's adaptation to its milieu is attributed to the initiative of the organism's needs, efforts and continual reactions. The milieu provokes the organism to orient its becoming by itself. Biological response far exceeds physical stimulation By rooting the phenomena of adaptation in need, which is at once pain and impatience, Lamarck centered the indivisible totality of the organism and the milieu on the point where life coincides with its own sense, where, through its own sensibility, the living situates itself absolutely, either positively or negatively, within existence.

(Canguilhem 2008: 115–116)

The capacity of all living organisms to learn and create means that life will forever extend beyond the reach of theoretical thought. "Transposing the dialectical process of thought onto the real," Canguilhem wrote,

one can maintain that it is life, the object of study itself, which is the dialectical essence, whose structure thought must espouse. The oppositions of Mechanism and Vitalism, Preformation and Epigenesis are thus transcended by life itself as it extends into a theory of life.

(Canguilhem 2008: 61)

Compare now Canguilhem's description of biological individuality with Aron's discussion of the self and self-knowledge. The most significant development in Aron's thought, and especially his philosophy of historical knowledge, was his description of the intelligible structure of the self. Like Canguilhem, Aron stressed the limits of theoretical thought, emphasizing that we can never know a theoretical object – in this case, a part of our past – in all its fullness. To Aron's way of thinking, there is always a gap between the "memory" of an action and the "moment" of action: even if every possible nuance of a past episode were somehow relived in our present consciousness, "this miracle of resurrection would make our knowledge in the proper sense useless, for we would again *be* the same self we had been" (Aron 1961a: 51).

Because the past cannot be relived, it must be reconstructed. Accordingly, there are two ways to reconstruct one's own past. The first is "to rediscover the goal or goals which motivated the action and seemed to justify it." Aron labeled the ideas that prompted an action *motifs*. The second is to track "states of consciousness in order to follow the formation of this motif itself" (Aron 1961a: 53). These states of consciousness – *mobiles* in Aron's terminology – are psychological antecedents that may be said to have "caused" our behavior or motivating ideas. Both approaches are legitimate but, considered singly, each fails to account for a part of reality. However, even when taken together, both alternatives are equally parts of a whole, the totality of which exceeds the sum of its parts. Aron argued that self-knowledge

attains neither the whole nor the unity – or at least our self is a constructed unity, situated in infinity, like the unity of all objects. We perceive a series of inclinations which are ours: the self would be the fictive source of them. The more we extend our inquiry the closer we get to the totality without ever reaching it.

(Aron 1961a: 56)

Because the essence of all things, including human beings, is located at a point situated in infinity, there is a "gap" or a "break" between the intentional and the psychological components of behavior that guarantees the irreducibility of one to the other. But there is at the same time a marked degree of interaction between the two. All self-knowledge, Aron declared, implies a certain idea of oneself. "And this idea is animated by certain assertions of value. Even those who claim to discover themselves passively choose themselves." In other words,

the knowledge of self develops according to a dialectic: between the ever-incomplete discovery and a never triumphant decision, the individual defines himself by a double effort at lucidity and creation. Always menaced by Pharisaism or resignation, he can relax neither of the two tensions.

(Aron 1961a: 57)

The structure of the self is now complete. Aron, like Canguilhem, presented the self as a unified totality within which two different elements – the intentional and the causal (or psychological) – emerge from a common, unknowable source. The relation between these two modes of experience is ambiguous and complex: the will does not create itself *ex nihilo* but "emerges gradually from the process of experience which it is capable of influencing because it is the expression of it as well as the judge" (Aron 1961a: 57). Intentionality is thus at one and the same time directed by and independent of causal factors, a state of affairs which suggests that self-knowledge leads to the discovery of a riddle or paradox that reason can recognize but never resolve.

It should be noted that Aron did not judge historical reality to be simply a "buzzing booming confusion" as Weber did. Consequently, he ascribed the same structure of intelligibility to history as he did to human nature. In history, Aron wrote, "the real distinction is between ideal entities and real entities rather than between categories of behavior" (Aron 1962: 141). This distinction – which Aron elsewhere presented as a series of "works" and a series of "events" – clearly has its origins in the distinction between motifs and mobiles. Moreover, the unity of history, as with the unity of the self, is located at a point situated in infinity:

In spite of the massing of evidence, total understanding ... emphasizes the role played by decision. For the unity towards which we strive, the unity of an epoch or culture, is nothing but the fictive source of works and actions which is all that is directly accessible.

(Aron 1961a: 118)[1]

For this reason, history is "ambiguous and inexhaustible but not incoherent."

The structure of life and the historical self, then, are remarkably similar. In both cases, intentionality and causality originate from a common, unknowable center, are inextricably intertwined, and exercise a mutual influence one over the other. Fashioning an ontology was but half of the problem facing Aron and Canguilhem; the other was creating the epistemological tools by which intelligible structures are known or understood.

The structure of knowledge

Given the materiality of life and human nature, both Aron and Canguilhem accepted the necessity of causal reasoning. In other words, both accepted the fact that there are causal laws that govern biological and historical development. Because causal analysis attempts to subsume the diversity of phenomena under general laws, placing a biological or historical event in its context here means integrating it into the framework of a broader causal network. Given the importance both ascribed to contingency, however, both Canguilhem and Aron argued that causal analysis must distinguish between sociological causality, which searches for general laws, and historical causality, which seeks to narrate singular events. As Aron put it, "historical research sticks to the antecedents of a singular fact, sociological research to the causes of a fact which may be repeated" (Aron 1961a: 220).

This distinction is accepted largely as a matter of course in the social sciences, not so much in the life sciences. "Too often," Canguilhem explained, "scientists hold the laws of nature to be essentially invariant." From this perspective, singular phenomena are "failures" of a sort: they fall short of reproducing "these laws' supposed lawful reality in its entirety" (Canguilhem 2008: 123). Rather than conceiving a living being as a "system of laws," Canguilhem preferred to treat living beings as an "organization of properties." The difference revolved around his understanding of biological anomalies and singularities. As an order of properties, living things are regarded as "an organization of forces and a hierarchy of functions whose stability is necessarily precarious, for it is the solution to a problem of equilibrium, compensation and compromise between different and competing powers" (Canguilhem 2008: 125). As Canguilhem liked to remind his readers, "at all levels ... biologists have identified ordering structures that while generally reliable sometimes fail" (Canguilhem 1988: 142). Viewed from this angle, living things experience irregularities and anomalies not as accidents or imperfections "but as its very existence" (Canguilhem 2008: 125).

Here Canguilhem's thought takes a remarkable turn, one that is perhaps best captured by his provocative idea that all biological organisms have a "normative" relation to life. "The new science of living things," he explained, "has not only *not* eliminated the contrast between normal and abnormal but it has actually grounded that contrast in the structure of living things" (Canguilhem 1994: 214). In other words, organisms care about the conditions of their life, both internally with regard to health and disease, and externally, with regard to the natural and social environments with which they interact. And this care or "sense," as Canguilhem occasionally called it, "is an appreciation of values in relation to a need. And for the one who experiences and lives it, a need is an irreducible, and thereby absolute, system of reference" (Canguilhem 2008: 120).

However, in acknowledging the importance of "sense" or "need" in establishing the boundaries of the normal and the pathological, Canguilhem has staked out the limits of causal explanations. Statistical norms are of limited utility in defining the normal and the pathological for the simple reason that they shed no light on how subjects feel about their health or sickness. And that feeling, Canguilhem insists, is just as constitutive of health or sickness as are the causal data.

Like Aron, Canguilhem is anxious to thread the needle here between the extremes of relativism and dogmatism. On the one hand, having introduced a subject's sense into the definition of health and disease, Canguilhem insisted that "normal" has no absolute, essential meaning. On the other hand, it made no sense to him to believe that just because the concepts of normal and pathological were variable, definitions of the normal and the pathological were completely arbitrary. "If what is normal here can be pathological there," he argued, "it is tempting to conclude that there is no boundary between the normal and pathological." But, he warned,

> this does not mean that for a given individual the distinction is not absolute. When an individual begins to feel sick, to call himself sick, to comport himself as a sick man, he has passed into a different universe and become a different man. The relativity of the normal must in no way encourage the physician, in confusion, to nullify the distinction between the normal and the pathological.
>
> (Canguilhem 2008: 130–131)

Given the import of subjective sense and the reality of choice, Canguilhem argued that causal biological explanation needs to be supplemented by "understanding" or "comprehension," a modality of knowing that seeks to retrieve or uncover the intentional determinants of behavior. Understanding, Aron wrote, is the knowledge of life and action that we acquire "as long as [they] remain intelligible without the elaboration of causal regularities" (Aron 1961a: 47). This is notoriously difficult epistemological terrain to navigate. The problem is that understanding has no univocal method. Do we "understand" by relating means to ends, as Karl Jaspers believed, or by relating parts to wholes as Wilhelm Dilthey insisted? In the end, both Aron and Canguilhem seemed to agree that we understand by creating "global structures," or by relating parts to wholes. Relating actions to intentions as means to ends, Aron explained, "usually turns out to be too simple" because historians are inevitably drawn toward "other considerations that set the framework within which the act is reduced to a choice of means" (Aron 1978: 48). We can understand the behavior of a general in battle, for example, only if we know something about the organization of his army, the techniques and quality of his armaments, the rules of battle, and so on.

Comprehension, then, by its very nature, seeks out ever larger wholes and contexts in which to situate decisions and behaviors.

Because Canguilhem defined life as meaning inscribed within matter, he repeatedly argued that comprehension was a legitimate mode of biological knowledge. "Once one recognizes the originality of life," Canguilhem declared, "one must '*comprehend*' matter within life, and the sciences of matter – which is science itself – within the activity of the living" (Canguilhem 2008: 70). Indeed, "the world is intelligible and in particular, living things are intelligible because the intelligible is in the world" (Canguilhem 1994: 304). Consequently, Canguilhem reasoned, if life is indeed the formation of forms, then

> [i]t is normal that an analysis could never explain a formation and that one loses sight of the originality of forms when one sees them only as results whose causes or components are to be determined. Because they are totalities whose sense resides in their tendency to realize themselves as such in the course of their confrontation with their milieu, living forms can be grasped in a vision, never by a division.
> (Canguilhem 2008: xix)

Parts, then, are known (at least partly) in relation to wholes: cells to organs, organs to bodies, bodies to environments.

By declaring that science frequently requires a "vision," or some sort of intuitive apprehension of systemic wholes, Canguilhem was forced to confront the problem of what he called, "scientific ideologies," which for him was an intermediate concept pulling both scientific and non-scientific thinking into the same loose orbit. For Canguilhem, a theory is scientific insofar as it fashions itself after a widely accepted scientific theory, Herbert Spencer's social Darwinism being a case in point. Such science-minded ambitions degenerate into ideology, however, when a theory advances ideas that far outstrip what a given scientific theory is able to confirm. Although scientific ideologies often retard the advance of science, Canguilhem saw a fruitful role for them. As Gary Gutting points out, the overly ambitious ideas advanced by scientific ideologies often provide a necessary, if somewhat reckless, boost to the intellectual imagination without which a good number of scientific discoveries would not have occurred (Gutting 2001: 231): Aron agreed. Even in physics or biology, Aron argued, "there always exists, in every age, laws or explanations which are admitted as true without our ever being certain of their truth or able to demonstrate them" (Aron 1961b: 106). Neither Aron nor Canguilhem, then, was willing to draw a clear line of demarcation between science and non-science.

But if this is true, what guarantees the objectivity of the concepts that Aron and Canguilhem deployed in order to understand the objects within their respective fields of discourse? At this point, Aron's solution to the problem of objective knowledge reveals its dependence on what Sylvie Mesure recognized as the "fundamental philosophical option," namely, "the Kantian thesis, according to which it is a certain representation of the end of history as the *idea* of reason which orients, in a regulatory fashion, historical knowledge" (Mesure 1984: 95). "There is in Kant," Aron once declared in an interview near the end of his life, "a concept to which I still subscribe: it is the idea of Reason, an image of a society that would be truly humanized" (Aron *et al.* 1983: 267). Despite the senseless turmoil of the twentieth century, Aron never ceased "to think, or dream, or hope – in the light of the idea of Reason – for a humanized society" (Aron *et al.* 1983: 269). For Aron, as for Kant, a truly humanized society is one that recognizes the freedom of the individual to enhance his or her moral worth under laws hypothetically of his or her own making. The universal reign of law and the establishment of perpetual peace thus constitute "two representations of the Idea as the goal of history and as the realization of a rational humanity" (Mesure 1984: 118). From this vantage point, a historical reconstruction can be objective to the degree that it interprets the sequence of events as so many steps leading toward the fulfillment of this idea. Or, as Mesure puts it, "An interpretation will be more objective when it is oriented by values capable of being shared by the whole community" (Mesure 1984: 116).

What saved Aron from the revolutionary optimism of the Marxists – and the non-revolutionary optimism of nineteenth-century liberals such as Auguste Comte and Herbert Spencer, for that matter – was his unshakeable conviction that the idea of the end of history was just that, an *idea*. As an idea, the end of history is simply an assumption or working hypothesis that is necessary for history and historical science to make any sense at all. As Mesure explains this point, a historian's effort

> would be an absurd enterprise if the historian did not suppose ... that the successive moments have between them a relationship of continuity which makes so many steps in a univocal direction readable in their succession itself: this direction without which the very will to separate the meaning of events would be aberrant, is only in its turn thinkable ... from the idea of a virtual outcome, thus a goal of history from which each event would appear as a step toward this accomplishment.
>
> (Mesure 1984: 116–117)

History and historical knowledge, then, require an "inaccessible paradise" or a "disenchanted destination" in order to be possible. Canguilhem's discussion of objectivity echoes Aron's. A living organism, Canguilhem declared,

> is one that is both its own cause and its own effect; it organizes itself and reproduces its organization; it forms itself and creates its own replica in accordance with a type. Its teleological structure, in which the interrelation of the parts is regulated by the whole, exemplifies a nonmechanical causality of the causality of the concept. We have no *a priori* knowledge of this type of causality. Forces that are also forms and forms that are also forces are indeed a part of nature and in nature, but we do not know this through the understanding; we perceive it, rather, in experience.
>
> (Canguilhem 1994: 310–311)

Given the importance of experience for constructing concepts, the idea of a "natural end" in biology – or the idea of a self-constructing organism – "is not a category in Kant but a regulative idea," one which can be applied "only in the forms of maxims" (Canguilhem 1994: 311).

Thus it is that epistemology recapitulates ontology: the contrast between the causal and the intentional finds its epistemological correlate in explanation – which is resolved into sociological and historical causalities – and understanding or comprehension for both thinkers.

Max Weber and Georges Canguilhem: the love of power versus the power of love

As we noted earlier, it is impossible to recover or reconstruct an exact history of the intellectual connections between Aron and Canguilhem. Accordingly, we make no claim here as to the precise influence one may have exercised over the other. But both thinkers agreed that both disciplines could learn from one other. In other words, Canguilhem clearly believed that biology had something to learn from political science, while Aron similarly believed that political science could freely profit from the insights of biology. Canguilhem's essay on the history of cell theory is perhaps the best case in point. In this essay, Canguilhem is interested in discovering the origins of cell theory. The microscope played a role, to be sure, but Canguilhem was intrigued by the fact that there were ideas about the cell – as the sole component of all living beings – that were beginning to congeal before microscopes existed. Where, he wondered, did those ideas come from? He concluded that they originated, at least in part, from the world of political ideas. "The history of the concept of the cell," Canguilhem maintained, "is inseparable from the history of concept of the individual." And this, he declared, "has allowed us to maintain that social and affective values hover above the development of cell theory" (Canguilhem 2008: 128).

Canguilhem also locates another point of contact between biology and politics. If environments and milieus play a decisive role in biological development, as biological research currently indicates, then social and political values clearly have a bearing on how organisms develop. If it is true, Canguilhem argues,

> that anomaly, an individual variation on a specific theme, becomes pathological only in relation to a milieu of life and a kind of life, then the problem of the pathological in man cannot remain strictly biological, for human activity, work and culture have the immediate effect of constantly altering the milieu of human life.

In a very real sense, then, Canguilhem mused, there is no longer any natural selection of the human species "to the extent that man can create new milieus instead of passively submitting to the old ones" (Canguilhem 2008: 42).

Aron also reflected on what modern-day science, especially biology, has to offer social science. These thoughts were collected and presented in an essay dedicated to Michael Polanyi on the occasion of Polanyi's seventieth birthday. We will sidestep the ongoing debate over exactly how we should understand Polanyi's vitalism and simply note that Polanyi shares Canguilhem's core convictions, especially as presented by Aron. Indeed, the similarities between Canguilhem and Polanyi are so striking that one cannot help but wonder if Aron's salute to Polanyi is actually a tribute to Canguilhem.

Significantly, Aron chose to highlight the key features of Polanyi's thought by contrasting him with Max Weber. This conjunction may surprise some readers, Aron noted rather drily: after all, not only did Weber and Polanyi not know or write about one another, they were intellectually quite different. Indeed, Aron presented them as polar opposites. Weber was a "philosopher of contradiction" committed to science "but in suffering, with the covert sorrow of being excluded by the progress of science from the paradise of faith." Polanyi, however, "was a philosopher of reconciliation, convinced that it is only through a misunderstanding of its true nature that science disenchants the universe." In short, "between the knowledge of the verifiable and the intuition of the inexpressible, the former establishes a radical break and the latter a continuous progression" (Aron 1961b: 99).

Aron's summary of Weber here zeroed in on his theory of knowledge. Weber's chief mistake, Aron argued, was to posit an iron-clad distinction between facts and values. Weber insisted that although the questions social scientists asked – or the concepts they deployed – were purely subjective, the answers they received were purely objective, informed as they were by a rigorous logic of historical and sociological verification. As Aron explained,

> Every causal relation ... is partial and analytic; it results from cutting up reality into fragments; it does not apply to the sequence of totalities. But this process of dissection is inseparable from our way of asking questions and hence from our concepts. Causal relations are not arbitrary, but they are dependent on an arbitrary choice of values or of questions.
> (Aron 1961b: 103)

Ironically, Aron declared, Weber's theory of knowledge dissolved the very truth it set out to secure:

> Faithful to the absolute separation of facts and values, to the postulate of a univocal reality, Weber would have demanded what at bottom is paradoxical – that the historian disregard, in past beings, the will for value or truth, without which the historian himself would not exist or the contemporary student would become unintelligible.
> (Aron 1961a: 95)

In the end, then, "the role of universal truth in a science founded on many and contradictory questions remains indeterminable and evanescent" (Aron 1961b: 103).

Weber was driven to this point because he believed that the human world was utterly unintelligible. His world was one in which the irrational, subterranean forces of power and conflict held sway. Intelligibility, then, was for Weber something that had to be created and not discovered. Given that human will – and not reason – is the driving force of history, order must be imposed on human action by way of conceptual constructs, not immediately intuited or grasped by an act of the understanding.

Polanyi, however, like Canguilhem, lived in a vastly different universe. For him, the world was rational, meaningful, and coherent, which accounts for its immediate intelligibility. For that reason, both human culture and biological phenomena can be "understood" as well as "explained." Polanyi, Aron wrote, agreed that understanding is the proper end of the cultural sciences, "but he uses the same word for the intelligibility achieved by the sciences of nature" (Aron 1961b: 113). In other words, "Polanyi shows that the biologist starts from complex, living realities ... the interpretation of which is impossible apart from reference to the finality of functions and, even before this, the distinction between the normal and the pathological" (Aron 1961b: 107). Thus, the same logic governing the relationship between parts and wholes that marked Canguilhem's thought also marked Polanyi's.

Because the complex, living realities that biologists study have a teleological or normative structure, they must be understood the same way. This is, in fact, the area of Polanyi's greatest contribution to the sciences, namely, his notion of personal knowledge. Polanyi's notion of personal or tacit knowledge paralleled Canguilhem's understanding of the role of "vision" in understanding systemic, biological wholes. In every scientific endeavor, natural as well as cultural, there are "trans-empirical beliefs" at work that belie what Aron called "the objectivist superstition," or the idea that acts of knowing can be completely stripped of subjective beliefs. Even acts of verification are unable to eliminate subjective penumbras: even in a discipline as rigorous as physics, Aron argued, verifications "are always imperfect, subject to doubt and revision." Although critical or empiricist thought erected a difference of kind between positive, demonstrated knowledge and moral or even religious knowledge, Polanyi was "determined to re-establish the continuity between them by discovering once more the presence of the person, the fiduciary commitment even in the first steps in the acquisition of knowledge, in *learning*" (Aron 1961b: 110). And so Polanyi, again like Canguilhem, refused to make a clear distinction between scientific and non-scientific knowledge.

Does this formula not, however, infect objective, scientific knowledge with the relativity that plagued Weber's theory of knowledge? Here a familiar motif returns. The concepts fabricated by social scientists, Aron argued, should reflect "what we may call the *dialogue* or the *dialectic* which constitutes the authentic experience of social science and social scientists" (Aron 1961b: 108). Both the subjectivism of Weber and the objectivism of Marx (in which concepts are presumed simply to reflect structures inscribed in reality itself) falsify that experience. "The sciences of man," Aron declared, are simply the elaboration, empirical and conceptual at once, of what is given in the universe experienced by men [and women]. There is no one single conceptual system implied by the existence of a society or a civilization, nor are there an unlimited number; still less is there a total freedom of choice.

(Aron 1961b: 110)

Knowledge of human worlds must start from the meaning given to them by those who have "made their homes in them." In other words, the awareness of other human worlds "is an element in a dialogue comparable to that which scientists have with one another or scientists with artists or priests" (Aron 1961b: 111). Human beings, like all living things, thus engage in ongoing, never-ending "debates."

In sum, Weber accepted his peculiar form of objectivism, inspired as it was by a mechanistic understanding of science, "before revolting against it." But it is utterly impossible, Aron maintained, to live in a universe that lacks all intrinsic meaning or sense: if science eliminates religion and strips human life of purpose, then all political and metaphysical convictions become, in their very irrationality, the manifestation of a condition presented to human beings "by the knowledge which explains the facts but strips the totality of meaning." In making our commitments, we escape necessity "only to be lost in arbitrariness" (Aron 1961b: 115).

Polanyi, however, rose above Weber's "painful contradictions." In a passage worth quoting in full, Aron explained that Polanyi believed that the "commitment of faith" is present

from the first stage of knowledge and the hierarchy of spiritual worlds is ordered towards ultimate goal. The existentialism of Polanyi issues in reconciliation because it moves towards religion. Thus the confrontation between Max Weber and Michael Polanyi over and above the epistemological problem, illustrates the dialogue of two persons: *the man of tragedy* and *the man of reconciliation*. The science of Polanyi leads without a break to faith; the science of Max Weber keeps a space for the faith it condemns and which it denies.

(Aron 1961b: 115)

Aron and Canguilhem thus struck out in an entirely different direction than Weber, seeking a path illuminated not by science but by *wisdom*. Practical wisdom straddles the middle ground between abstract theory and concrete experience. That there is such a middle ground is evidenced by the fact that theoretical concepts simply cannot capture the fullness of life and lived experience; conceptual abstractions, by definition, provide only a partial look at the "durational flux" from which they are abstracted. Aron and Canguilhem thus underscored the priority of a living vitality over conceptual abstraction and in so doing transformed what Weber had treated as polar opposites into partial truths.

In *Peace and War*, Aron's taste for biological dialectics is particularly evident in his discussion of the role that biological drives play in human aggression, a topic he raises in connection with our propensity for war. At first glance, he seems to suggest that biological determinants are indeed decisive in the development of human behavior. In fact, Aron here sounds downright Darwinian: "Whether spontaneous or the result of learning," he intoned, "combative behavior, to the human observer, often seems adaptive" (Aron 1966: 342). After a lengthy discussion of frustration and aggression, Aron then concluded his chapter "The Roots of War as an Institution," by observing that "the human animal is aggressive, but does not fight by instinct, and war is an expression, it is not a *necessary* expression of human combativity." Thus it is that

> the difficulty of peace has more to do with man's humanity than his animality. The mouse which has received a beating yields to the stronger, and the hierarchy of domination is stable. The wolf that bares its throat is spared by its victor. Man is a being capable of preferring revolt to humiliation and his own truth to life itself. The hierarchy of master and slave will never be stable. Tomorrow the masters will no longer have need of servants and they will have the power to exterminate.
>
> (Aron 1966: 365–366)

Biology, then, is a necessary condition of human action, but as an explanatory factor, its reach is limited indeed.

So what must we make of Aron's turn toward transcendence? Manent, we confess, was partly right: Aron's idealism certainly did not usher him straightaway into Kant's kingdom of ends. But surely Aron's turn is not for nothing. In order to blunt the more damaging manifestations of materialism and determinism that savaged Europe in his own lifetime, for example, Aron urged statesmen and philosophers "to begin from the idea of the presence, in each individual, of a soul or a spirit, upon which is founded human dignity and the right to respect." Indeed, human beings must now use the "consciousness" they have of themselves "to better accomplish [the] task of civilization and not debase or lower [themselves] to the level of an animal species" (Aron 1944: 178). It may be, then, that Manent was also partly wrong: we prefer to think of Aron not as a perfect gentleman with no need of transcendence, but as someone who was a perfect gentleman precisely because he sensed its possibility.

Note

1 Canguilhem also appeals to the concept of infinity in explaining the coherence of living things. Descartes, Canguilhem observed, tried to efface teleology from life but failed to do so.

> The model of the living machine [for Descartes] is the living itself ... And just as a regular polygon is inscribed within a circle, and in order to derive the circle from it, it is necessary to pass through infinity, so the mechanical artifice is inscribed within life, and to derive one from the other it is necessary to pass through infinity – that is to say, God.

References

Aron, R. (1944), *L'homme contre les tyrans*. Paris: Éditions de la Maison française.
Aron, R. (1961a), *Introduction to the Philosophy of History*. Trans. Irwin, G.J. Boston, MA: Greenwood Publishing Group.
Aron, R. (1961b), "Max Weber and Michael Polanyi," in *The Logic of Personal Knowledge: Essays Presented to Michael Polanyi on His Seventieth Birthday*, 1st edn. London: Routledge & Kegan Paul, 99–115.
Aron, R. (1962), *Opium of the Intellectuals*. Trans. Kilmartin, T. New York: W.W. Norton & Company.
Aron, R. (1966), *Peace and War: A Theory of International Relations*. Trans. Howard, R. and Baker, A. Garden City, NY: Doubleday & Company.
Aron, R. (1976), *History and the Dialectic of Violence: Analysis of Sartre's Critique de la Raison Dialectique*. New York: Harper & Row.
Aron, R. (1978), "Three Forms of Intelligibility," in Conant, M.B. (ed.), *Politics and History: Selected Essays by Raymond Aron*. London: Transaction Book, 48.
Aron, R. (1990), *Memoirs: Fifty Years of Political Reflection*. New York: Holmes & Meier.
Aron, R., Missika, J.L., and Wolton, D. (1983), *The Committed Observer: Interviews With Jean-Louis Missika and Dominique Wolton*. Trans. McIntosh, J. and McIntosh, M. Chicago: Regnery Publishing.
Burian, R.M., Gayon, J., and Zallen, D. (1988), "The Singular Fate of Genetics in the History of French Biology, 1900–1940," *Journal of the History of Biology*, 21:3, 357–402.
Canguilhem, G. (1988), *Ideology and Rationality in the History of the Life Sciences*. Trans. Goldhammer, A. Cambridge, MA: MIT Press.
Canguilhem, G. (1989), *The Normal and the Pathological*. Trans. Fawcett, C.R. and Cohen, R.S. New York: Zone Books.
Canguilhem, G. (1994), *A Vital Rationalist: Selected Writings from Georges Canguilhem*. Ed. Delaporte, F., trans. Goldhammer, A. New York: Zone Books.
Canguilhem, G. (2008), *Knowledge of Life*. New York: Fordham University Press.
Colquhoun, R. (1986), *Raymond Aron: The Philosopher in History, 1905–1955*. London: Sage Publications.
Davis, R. (2003), "The Phenomenology of Raymond Aron," *European Journal of Political Theory*, 2:4, 401–413.
Fodor, J., and Piattelli-Palmarini, M. (2010), *What Darwin Got Wrong*. New York: Farrar, Straus and Giroux.
Gutting, G. (2001), *French Philosophy in the Twentieth Century*. Cambridge: Cambridge University Press.
Hancock, R. (2010), "Pierre Manent on Raymond Aron and Leo Strauss," *First Things*, 207, 88.
Körner, S. (1970), *Categorial Frameworks*. Oxford: Basil Blackwell.
Mesure, S. (1984), *Raymond Aron et la raison historique*. Paris: Vrin.
Stewart, I. (2011), "Sartre, Aron and the Contested Legacy of the Anti-Positivist Turn in French Thought, 1938–1960," *Sartre Studies International*, 17:1, 41–60.

3 A theory of international relations or a theory of foreign policy?

Reading *Peace and War among Nations*

Olivier Schmitt

The popularity of Raymond Aron' international thought has varied since the first publication of *Paix et Guerre entre les Nations* (*Peace and War among Nations*) in 1962. Although the book was praised by Hans Morgenthau and Robert C. Tucker, Hedley Bull used Aron's definition of the international system (Bull 1977) and the American Political Science Association ranked it as the third most important book on international relations in the 1970s after *Politics amongst Nations* by Morgenthau and *System and Process in International Politics* by Kaplan (Battistella 2013), Bryan-Paul Frost could rightly argue 20 years later that Aron was a "neglected theorist", and that "it is doubtful whether more than a handful of students seriously study this monumental work at all" (Frost 1997: 143). It is true that reading Aron is difficult, but rewarding work. In the United States, the ultimately unsuccessful quest for finding a systemic grand theory of International Relations (IR)[1] certainly diverted from studying the complex and nuanced approach developed by Aron in his work. Yet, as Stanley Hoffmann explains, Aron's originality and interest are obvious, especially compared with the US-based IR specialists: "his view is larger, his intellectual constructs are more flexible (for which he was sometimes blamed by spirits eager for false certainties), and his analyses have sometimes preceded those developed in the US" (Hoffmann 2006: 724). His fate is no better in France, where he has sometimes been instrumentalized as the defender of a "sociology of International Relations" devoid of any theoretical attempt which he would not recognize or could not agree with (Battistella 2013).

Many observers agree that Aron is an "uneasy realist". His approach consists of defining features of what is usually considered a "realist" school such as Groupism, Egoism and Power Politics (Wohlforth 2008: 132), but adds many insights that ultimately puzzle many readers: his distinction between a sociological and a historical approach or his "praxeology" are surprising elements that clearly distinguish him from other mainstream realists.

In this chapter, I argue that Aron has much to offer now that IR theories have moved away from the fake battle of "isms" opposing neo-realism, neo-liberalism and constructivism. I reconstruct Aron's theory of IR in light of some contemporary debates, and illustrate how his analysis echoes, precedes and enriches current research. In particular, I make the claim that *Peace and War* can be fruitfully understood as a theory of foreign policy, particularly relevant for the current international system. I read Aron in light of the "realist-constructivist" synthesis defined by J. Samuel Barkin, and show that rediscovering his approach can bring numerous elements to the study of foreign policy and of the international system.

This chapter is organized as follows: I first summarize the main features of realist-constructivism as defined by Barkin, and four core elements that are necessary for a realist-constructivist approach: that it is a theory of foreign policy, that it cannot theorize agency but identifies scope for agency, that it pays attention to the historical context and reflexivity and that it studies morality in a way that avoids both pure messianism and pure cynicism. The first three dimensions serve as guidelines to reconstruct Aron's approach and illuminate contemporary challenges, the normative dimension being explored by Ariane Chebel d'Appollonia and Jean-Baptiste Jeangène Vilmer in their respective chapters.

Some core features of realist-constructivism

The traditional narrative about IR theories is that the discipline is regularly subject to a number of "debates" on theoretical, methodological or ontological issues. Although the historiography and sociology of the field have done much in recent years to debunk these partially mythologized narratives (Bell 2001; Navon 2001; Ashworth 2002; Guilhot 2008; Bell 2009; Schmidt 2012), the influence of such thinking is still pervasive in the way IR theories are taught at the undergraduate level or presented in textbooks. In particular, it is common to present realism and its variants, liberalism and its variants and constructivism as competing paradigms. However, such presentation has attracted criticism from several scholars arguing that realism and constructivism are in fact compatible, and probably more compatible with each other than the mix of liberal values and constructivist ontology often found in constructivist research (Sterling-Folker 2002; Jackson and Nexon 2004), and innovative empirical work combining insights from both approaches were published (Krebs and Jackson 2007; Goddard 2008/2009). The most articulated presentation of such a research agenda to date is the book by J. Samuel Barkin (2010), soberly and appropriately entitled *Realist Constructivism*.

In this book, Barkin develops the main features of a potential realist-constructivist synthesis, showing the points of convergence, but also the point of divergences. Not all realist research has to incorporate constructivist features, and not all constructivist research needs to focus on power the way realists do. But it is possible to find convergences and a realist-constructivist research agenda is by no means an oxymoron. The remainder of this section maps the main features of such a realist-constructivist synthesis as presented by Barkin, and offers the key elements that will be used to assess Aron's own theory of IR.

Barkin's first step is to define the core elements of both realism and constructivism. The main concepts underlying constructivism and realism are intersubjectivity and power politics, respectively. However, not all forms of realism are compatible with constructivism. Barkin is explicit in referring to classical realism, as opposed to the structural versions of realism that followed Waltz's own theoretical contribution to the field. Classical realism is, in essence, a theory of foreign policy instead of a systematic theory of international relations. This derives from a conception of power, understood as relative and relational, which is partially endogenous. It is impossible to know how much power one has before exercising it: power is not a predictor of outcomes but a defining feature of international politics (and, realists would argue, politics itself). As such, realist thinking cannot be predictive, as this would contradict its own understanding of power.

Constructivism brings an important aspect to the study of politics, which is a distinctive set of methods to study intersubjectivity and the co-constitution of structures and agents. Constructivist research does not give any ontological priority to either the agents or the structure: they are in a permanent state of co-constitution.

The combination of constructivism and realism would then be particularly fruitful, because "the former tells us about how to study politics, but little about how politics works. The latter tells us about how politics works, but not how to study them" (Barkin 2010: 4).

This rapprochement of realism and constructivism is possible because both approaches share a foundation in a logic of the social rather than a logic of the individual. When looking at the holism/individualism debate, classical realism is in fact more on the holist than on the individualist side, mostly because

> its key unit of analysis, the state, is a social aggregate. Its logic is therefore based on the assumption that people will act in the interests of the social aggregate, even when this requires action that is not in their immediate individual self-interest.
>
> (Barkin 2010: 10)

This grounding in the logic of the social obviously relates to constructivism's core mechanism that socially constructed (instead of exogenously given) preferences have an impact on actors' behaviour. Because both approaches share a grounding in the logic of the social, they share an interest in the construction of the public, or national, interest and emphasize the need for reflexivity. As such, realism and constructivism are more orthogonal to each other than antagonistic, and a realist-constructivist approach is possible.

There are several consequences of such a realist-constructivist synthesis. First, realist-constructivism is, and must be, a theory of foreign policy instead of a systemic theory of international politics. This derives from the impossibility of granting ontological priority to either the structure (the international system) or the agents (the state). The international system influences the behaviour of actors, but at the same time those actors reshape the structure of the international system itself, an issue commonly referred to as the "agent–structure problem". This ontological agnosticism is combined with the previous observation based on the classical realist insight that power is relative and relational: it cannot be used to predict outcomes. As such, it is impossible for a realist-constructivist approach to be a general theory of international politics: it must be a theory of foreign policy that combines observations about the co-constitution of structure and agents with insights about the use of power in the relations between states.

Second, and linked to the above, it is impossible to theorize agency, which in fact would be denying that such agency exists: if by theorizing agency we could predict how agents would behave, the very meaning of agency would be void. However, it is possible to theorize *space* for agency, which means identifying the structural conditions in which agents have more or less capability to act and shape their environment. This derives from both the realist and the constructivist understanding of human nature as being inherently social, which generates in-group and out-group dynamics translated into political outcomes. A realist-constructivist research agenda, focusing on foreign policy, can then attempt to understand the normative and power politics influences constraining the action of agents and explain how their combination vary depending on the situation (and thus leave more or less room for agency), but this type of research cannot predict the agents' behaviour.

Third, realist-constructivism pays attention to the historical context and reflexivity, in opposition to transhistorical approaches such as neo-realism. National and international normative contexts change over time, and it is then important to understand the specifics of each time period in order to properly understand international relations. Moreover, reflexivity is needed because scholars and policy makers "need to recognize that political activity will be seen elsewhere through a different normative lens than by those who undertake it" (Barkin 2010: 10). This observation on the need of reflexivity, which derives from the realist and constructivist grounding in the social, is also consistent with the fact that realist-constructivism is a theory of foreign policy: recognizing that others have a different understanding of actions based on different socialization mechanisms is an important recommendation for the conduct of foreign policy. As Barkin explains: "a realist constructivism is well placed to see that, however much we believe in a political morality, to see that morality in teleological terms can as a political matter be counterproductive" (Barkin 2010: 170).

This observation is linked to the last point, that constructivism offers a way "to deal with the tension in realism between both a commitment to a political morality and an acceptance of moral relativism" (Barkin 2010: 172). Because realism is grounded in the logic of the social, it conceives political actions as being informed by the moral values of the societies from which it originates. But it faces a tension between the necessary relativism required in order to deal with other societies (which can have different values) and the promotion of a polity's own values, which is part of its cohesiveness. Constructivism can help in offering ways to distinguish between the social construction of values (which is an empirical data) from normative theory, thus allowing realists to understand values held by others without having to be relativist about their own normative preferences. A realist-constructivist research agenda thus needs to integrate a reflection about morality that avoids the joint traps of pure messianism and pure relativism.

These dimensions serve as analytical devices to explore and organize the themes addressed in Aron's own contribution to IR theories, in particular in his masterpiece *Paix et Guerre entre les Nations* (*Peace and War among Nations*).

Peace and War as a theory of foreign policy

At its core, *Peace and War* is a theory of foreign policy instead of a theory of international politics. Aron's main effort is trying to explain how the political units composing an international system behave the way they do, but without pretending to establish a systematic and predictive theory of their behaviour, which Aron thinks is a foolish and impossible task. This section first determines Aron's conception of a theory of international relations, before discussing his understanding of power and briefly mentioning his ontological agnosticism regarding the agent–structure problem.

Aron's conception of what a theory of international relations can accomplish is both traditional and ambitious: "define the specificity of a sub-system, furnish a list of principal variables, suggest hypothesis regarding the functioning of a system" (Aron 1967: 847). Aron then tries to establish what constitutes the specificities of international relations, which he argues are the "relations between politic units which all claim the right to do themselves justice and to be the only master of the decision to fight or not to fight" (Aron 1962: 20). In a very traditional way, Aron argues that the specificity of an international system is the possibility of war between the political units composing it, which we would today call the condition of anarchy: "states are not outside the state of nature when it comes to their mutual relations. There would be no theory of international relations if they were" (Aron 1962: 19). However, Aron is careful not to derive from the observation/hypothesis of anarchy more than it can deliver. First, he understands anarchy in a different way than neo-realist scholars do. Neo-realists have derived from the assumption of anarchy several conclusions regarding the difficulty for states to be safe in the international system, in particular regarding arms races or alliance formation. By doing so, they have overlooked the impact of hierarchical relations, which are now only beginning to be fully explored (Lake 2011; Bially Mattern and Zarakol 2016; Pouliot 2016). On the other hand, while Aron recognizes the importance of the "state of nature" and the political actor's willingness to ensure their security, he also observes the hierarchical nature of collective security management:

> political units are organized on a more or less official hierarchical scale, determined mostly by the strength that each of them is supposed to be able to mobilize: on the one hand great powers, on the other hand small powers; the former claiming the right to intervene in all matters, even those in which they have no direct stake, the latter having no ambition to act beyond their narrow sphere of interests and actions.
>
> (Aron 1962: 106–107)

While he does not systematically explore the consequences of this hierarchical dimension in his work, Aron is then careful not to be seduced by the logical implications of the theoretical assumption of anarchy, which would remove the study of international politics from a sound empirical grounding. Second, he acknowledges that he developed a theory of the international system, and not of international relations. He willingly excludes transnational relations and economic relations from his theory, arguing that these dimensions must be analytically distinguished for the purpose of the analysis. His understanding of the international system is that it is part of an *international society* comprising other elements (transnational flux, migrations, economic relations, etc.), but definitely the most important part because it is within an international system that the risk of war still exists, which causes the life or death of states and their citizens (an idea that the English school would attempt to challenge by reconceptualizing the relations between system and society). Hence, for analytical purposes, it makes sense to focus on a concept (international system) that can be theoretically and empirically circumscribed, and has such tremendous consequences for social units and the humans composing them. On the other hand, a theory of international relations trying to incorporate all elements of the international life would face overreach:

> I don't think that the formula *international society* or rather *world society* constitutes a real concept. It designates without describing it a totality that would include at the same time the inter-state system, the economic system, transnational movements, the various forms of exchanges between civil societies and supra-national institutions. Can we talk about an international system that would include all forms of international life? I doubt it.
> (Aron 1962: viii)

An international system is then composed of all political units recognizing that there is a possibility that they can be at war with each other. The concept of international system for Aron is then geographically and temporally limited (for example, there was an international system in Europe in the nineteenth century, another one in Asia, etc.), and to him one of the most important features of the twentieth century is the globalization of the international system: for the first time, all states can potentially be at war. The logical consequence of a focus on the possibility of war as a defining feature of an international system is Aron's emphasis on two "figures" of international relations, the diplomat and the soldier, who literally embody their state: "the ambassador[2] and the soldier *live* and *symbolize* international relations which, as interstate relations, can be narrowed down to diplomacy and war" (Aron 1962: 18). Here, Aron announces the type of research developed by Iver B. Neumann and others, for whom the conduct of international relations is embodied and governed by a logic of rituals that give meaning to interactions (Neumann 2012a, 2012b). But if international relations are interstate relations, and if the diplomat and the soldier are the living embodiment of such relations between political units, this means that *Peace and*

War is a theory of foreign policy, a theory of strategic-diplomatic conduct, and not a theory of international politics. Further proof is given by the title and subtitles of the chapters composing the first part ("Theory") of Aron's masterpiece:

- Chapter 1: Strategy and Diplomacy *or* on the unity of foreign policy
- Chapter 2: Power and Strength *or* on the means of foreign policy
- Chapter 3: Power, Glory and Idea *or* on the goals of foreign policy.

The three remaining chapters deal with the configuration of the international system and the way the organization of the international system itself influences the conduct of foreign policy. The second part of the book, entitled "Sociology", looks at the determinants of foreign policy based on a number of exogenous and endogenous characteristics of the states: space, population, resources, types of regimes, etc. As such, the entire theoretical apparatus built by Aron is organized in order to furnish the intellectual tools required to understand the behaviour of states in the international system: in *Peace and War*, he developed a theory of foreign policy, and not a theory of international politics.

Because *Peace and War* is a theory of foreign policy concerned with the conduct of diplomatic-strategic affairs in an international system characterized by the potential eruption of war, Aron devotes an important part of his analyses to the concept of power. Aron adopts a traditional conception of power: "I call power on the international stage a political unit's capability to impose its will to other units. In short, political power is not an absolute, but a human relation" (Aron 1962: 58), an unsurprising definition for the admirer of Max Weber that Aron was. Aron distinguishes between power and strength (*puissance* and *force*), the former being a relation and the latter being objectively measurable (size of armies, etc.). But by no means is strength the only (and best) predictor of power. Aron also establishes several conceptual distinctions, although he does not really elaborate on them in his book: a distinction between defensive power (capability for a political unit of not having another political unit imposing its will) and offensive power; and a distinction between a politics of strength and a politics of power. Most importantly, Aron warns that it is impossible to obtain a precise measure of power, for two reasons: first, power is relational and partly endogenous; second, the sources of power change over time because the normative context in which power is exercised changes over time. Aron warns that it is then critical to be sensitive to the historical context when studying and assessing power, but nevertheless attempts to come up with a generic list establishing the source of power:

> the power of a political unit depends on the scene of its action and on its capacity to use the resources, both human and materials, at its disposal: *environment, resources, collective action*, those are obviously, whatever the century and the modalities of competition between political units, the determinants of power.
>
> (Aron 1962: 65)

There is in Aron's conception an understanding that power is largely social, in the sense that it depends on how actors employ their resources to shape the environment depending on their internal cohesion and capacity for collective action. In short, Aron's conception of power is intertwined with strategy, thus preceding Lawrence Freedman's definition of strategy as "the art or creating power" (Freedman 2013: 9). Since power is based on strategy, it is both social and relational. Apparently, Aron can sometimes be oblivious to other forms of power: he overlooks reciprocal power (although he hints at it) and considers the potential pitfalls in the analysis of structural power a repudiation of this dimension of power itself (Baldwin 2016). Yet, his understanding is coherent with the delimitation of his field of inquiry as the international system, and his attempt to establish a theory of foreign policy. Within those parameters, Aron's understanding of power is sufficiently rich to serve useful analytical purposes, and some of his key distinctions could be explored in more detail in order to enrich the conceptual understanding of states' foreign policies.

Because of his definition of power, Aron does not give any ontological priority to either the agent or the structure in his theory. To be fair, he is obviously not phrasing the issue in terms of the agent–structure debate, and his observations on this issue are dispersed throughout the book, and can even appear contradictory at times. However, put together, they show that Aron does not favour the structure over the agent (or vice versa) but instead looks at their co-constitution, which invalidates the claim that Aron is a neo-classical realist, as in this case he would give ontological priority to the structure (Battistella 2012). On occasion, Aron seems to emphasize the role of the structure in determining the action of agents. For example, he writes that "power … depends on available means. The legitimate use of those means is, at each time period, defined by the international customs" (Aron 1962: 68), but also that "the main characteristic of an international system is the configuration of the balance of power" (Aron 1962: 104), which seems to indicate that he grants ontological priority to the structure, understood either as composed of norms (in a constructivist fashion) or as reflecting the distribution of power capabilities. Yet, Aron also writes that

> at each time period, the main actors determined the international system more than they were determined by it. Sometimes, a change of the regime of one of the main actors is enough to change the style, and perhaps the flow of international relations.
>
> (Aron 1962: 104)

In his *Clausewitz*, he argues that "actors create, to a certain extent, the reality to which they have the illusion to be submitted" (Aron 1976: 12). In fact, Aron summarizes his position regarding the agent–structure debate in a development that is worth quoting in full:

> The same persons do not arrive in power in all regimes, they do not act under the same conditions and under the same pressures. Assuming that the

same persons in different circumstances or different persons in the same circumstances would take equivalent decisions is a strange philosophy, and implies one of the two following theories: either diplomacy is rigorously determined by impersonal causes, with individual actors occupying the front stage but reciting a role learnt by heart; or the conduct of the political unit should be commanded by a "national interest" which could be rationally defined, the struggles of internal politics or regime change having no influence on this definition. These two philosophies are invalidated by the facts.
(Aron 1962: 283)

As such, Aron does not grant ontological priority to either the structure or the agent, but instead insists on their co-constitution and the equal importance of ideas and power for understanding the relations between the agents and the structure:

the calculation of forces and the dialectics of the regimes or the ideas are equally indispensable in order to interpret the conduct of diplomatic-strategic affairs in any time period; neither the goals nor the means, nor the licit and the illicit are adequately determined by the sole calculus of forces or the sole dialectics of ideas.
(Aron 1962: 155)

Because he insists on the co-constitution of agent and structure, Aron's theory is an attempt to determine the scope for agency in the international system.

Scope for agency in Aron's theory of the international system

Aron's effort to determine what the actors of the system can and cannot do (scope for agency) is separated into two steps. He first establishes a theory of the way power operates within the international system, before moving to a "sociology" of international relations.

The international system

For Aron, power and norms are both important in order to understand the shape of an international system. First, the distribution of power within the system serves as a first qualifier and distinguishes between bipolar and multipolar systems. Interestingly, Aron spends little time on this distinction in the book and does not really speculate on the consequences of this distinction for the conduct of foreign policy. Neither does he mention it again in his *Clausewitz*, nor in his *Memoirs*, in which he reflects on the validity of his analysis and its reception in Europe and in the United States. Part of the reasons explaining this lack of theoretical elaboration on what constitutes a cornerstone of structural realism might be that Aron considers the distinction as self-evident and banal (although he fails, like many, to consider the possibility of unipolarity). But the main reason is probably that he does not think that the distribution of power is the main, or even an important, explanatory factor to understand international dynamics. In particular, "alliances are not a mechanical effect of the distribution of power" (Aron 1962: 107). Aron notices three motivations for states to form an alliance: because they have an interest in it, for balancing purposes, or because of ideological affinities. In other terms, he identifies the traditional "balancing" motive, gives an extended definition of "bandwagoning" (which is not limited to security purposes) and includes an ideological component, thus making the analysis of alliance-formation mechanisms richer than the traditional realist understanding. Moreover, he introduces a distinction between "permanent allies" and "temporary allies". The former are allies who cannot conceivably become enemies in the foreseeable future. Therefore, a temporary increase of their power is not a concern for the other permanent allies. NATO members today can be considered "permanent allies". On the opposite, temporary allies are issue-specific, and can become enemies in the future. Therefore, in their case, the traditional alliance management concerns identified in the literature (preventing others to acquire more power) still apply (Snyder 1998; Weitsman 2003). But Aron introduces a conceptual distinction useful to understand what could otherwise be considered puzzles in the traditional alliance literature. For example, some authors have identified a "soft balancing" against the United States coming from European states (Pape 2005; Jones 2007), which would have been nonsensical to Aron: permanent allies do not perceive each other as potential threats, which explains why the eventual rise in European capabilities is not targeted at the United States in any way, and why the United States is not militarily concerned by it. A narrow focus on the distribution of power then leads to identifying useless and irrelevant puzzles.

This concern about ideas, and its correlative refusal to reduce international mechanisms to responses to the distribution of power, is not surprising, considering that Aron introduces an important category in order to analyse the international system: its nature. Aron explains:

> I call *homogeneous systems* those in which states belong to the same type, obey to the same conception of politics. On the opposite, I call *heterogeneous* those in which states are organized according to diverging principles and claim following contradictory values.
>
> (Aron 1962: 109)

With this dimension, Aron tries to capture the influence of norms, values and culture on international politics. He argues that homogeneous systems are more likely to be peaceful, because shared norms regulate the level of violence actors are willing to engage in against each other, prevent the demonization of the enemy (thus facilitating post-conflict negotiations) and guarantee the predictability of governments' behaviours, as they all play by the same rules. On the opposite, heterogeneous systems, in which norms are contested, favour the emergence of violent conflicts that are uneasily settled in the absence of a common normative framework. For example, the violence of the Napoleonic wars can be interpreted as a result of the heterogeneity introduced in the international system by the French Revolution, which contested the monarchic systems still in place in European countries. As such, Napoleon embodied the revolutionary ideal of overthrowing traditional authorities, and there could be no compromise found between the adversaries (Gueniffey 2014).

Aron's emphasis on the normative context precedes the liberal and constructivist concerns about the ways norms shape the international order. For example, Ikenberry's argument about a "liberal Leviathan" (Ikenberry 2011) established by the United States and stabilizing international relations easily feeds into Aron's analysis of what constitutes a homogeneous system. Similarly, constructivists have empirically documented the ways norms influenced the conduct of warfare, in particular showing how respect for international humanitarian law is linked to the degree of recognition belligerents have for each other (Farrell 2005), thus validating Aron's argument. Of course, homogeneity and heterogeneity are ideal-types, and real-world situations are more nuanced. Aron himself noticed the relative cultural homogeneity among European states before the First World War, which was nevertheless not sufficient to contain the heterogeneous dynamic introduced by the strong differences in regime types (and thus in political values) found in Europe at the time. During the Peloponnesian War, the cultural homogeneity of the Greek cities (and their common struggle against the Persians) did not prevent the conflict between Sparta and Athens from turning into an opposition between democratic and oligarchic systems. Therefore, all historical situations will involve aspects of homogeneity and parts of heterogeneity. It is then an empirical question to settle which tendency is dominating at a certain point in time, and Aron's conceptualization is a useful guide in that regard.

The first step in Aron's effort to determine a scope for agency is then to analyse the playing field on which actors will interact, which combines the distribution of power with the degree of homogeneity. Those two dimensions make some configurations and actions more likely, but they are not deterministic.

The actors

While the first step in Aron's analysis is to describe the stage of international interactions, the second step is to analyse the actors. What are their motives for action, and what are the means at their disposal? Aron's description of the motives for action is subtle, and its complexity does not lend itself to the easy reductions established by structural approaches. As mentioned, Aron begins with the idea that security is the first goal for a political group. But achieving security is obviously not the only foreign policy objective, and maximizing power can also be one. Aron has a broad definition of power, as he recognizes that it is not limited to physical sources, but also encompasses cultural attractiveness (what we would today call "soft power"): for him, political communities "do not want to be strong only to deter aggression and enjoy peace, but also to be feared, respected and admired" (Aron 1962: 83). In other terms, Aron settles the debate between defensive and offensive realism once and for all by highlighting its artificiality: both can be right depending on the circumstances and the historical context. Some states may seek security; others may seek power. But Aron adds an extra layer to his analysis of the motivations. To him, states may also look for *glory*, defined by the degree of recognition/admiration a political community gets from its counterparts. Aron carefully explains why the quest for glory is different from the "cultural attractiveness" dimension of power: because they trigger different behaviours. The best example can be given by looking at three different French statesmen: Clémenceau, Napoléon and Louis XIV. Clémenceau was looking for *security*. After the First World War, he wanted to make sure that France could not be attacked by Germany and was hoping to secure territorial guarantees in that regard. Napoleon wanted *power*. At some point, he wanted to rule Europe, and keep expanding France's power. Louis XIV was looking for *glory*. He took seriously Du Bellay's maxim "France: mother of arts, arms and laws", and was not looking for France to hold a large amount of territory in Europe, but certainly hoped that other European countries would look up to Paris as an inspiration and respect France's (and Louis') achievements. In other words, Aron was establishing *standing* as an important foreign policy motive, something that contemporary IR scholarship is only beginning to explore in detail (Lebow 2008; Paul et al. 2014). Instead of Thucydides' tired formula of "fear, honour and interest", Aron establishes a more useful trilogy of "security, power and glory" to understand foreign policy motives. Retrospectively, he exposes why the debates between structural realism and constructivism would ultimately be pointless: they each hold a kernel of the truth in their study of foreign policy motives and opposing them has little intellectual benefit.

Based on those motives, Aron establishes a typology of the different aspirations of states in the international system. First, in a traditional fashion, he opposes status quo and revisionist states, depending on whether those states are happy with an international situation or not. Interestingly, he notices that the status quo/revisionist distinction has little to do with determining the aggressor and the aggressed: a status quo state can still initiate a conflict if it feels that its victory would comfort its position, and revisionist states often masquerade their frustrations with peaceful declarations. It is then impossible to evaluate conflict initiations solely based on the status quo/revisionist categories (Rynning and Ringsmose 2008): a state can be both depending on the international context, and this does not predict its foreign policy. Aron also adds a dichotomy between traditional and revolutionary states, which stems from his distinction between homogeneous and heterogeneous systems. Traditional states can be revisionist or status quo states, but they operate within shared normative values. Revolutionary states may not be revisionist (they are content with the international boundaries, for example), but their very own values may be subversive to the international system. For example, during its first years, revolutionary France was not revisionist, but it was ontologically revolutionary for the European system, as the ideology France adopted was in total contradiction with the legitimacy principle adopted until then. This dual

Table 3.1 Categories of states according to Aron

	Status quo	Revisionist
Traditional	Austria-Hungary in 1815	Germany after 1918
Revolutionary	Early revolutionary France	Contemporary Russia?

analysis is an important conceptual addition as it offers a subtler distinction between categories of states than the usual status quo/revisionist dichotomy by taking into account the importance of ideological struggles.

In addition to this typology of states, Aron also tries to establish what he calls a "sociology" of international relations. In fact, it is a lengthy discussion of all the different factors that have an influence on states' behaviour: space (geography), number, resources, regime type or human nature. The discussion itself is quite classic, and goes through the traditional arguments regarding the sources of power: geography and size matter, numbers have ambiguous effects (can be a military advantage or an economic burden), democracies are more peaceful towards one another, etc. But here again, Aron refuses any deterministic argument, and highlights the contingency of human actions. Generally, he is trying to determine how those factors influence, but not determine, decisions.

Overall, Aron's discussion is subtle, and explores all the levels influencing action: the configuration of the international system, the ambitions of political leaders and the means at their disposal. Scattered through the book as they are, those discussions sometimes appear ad hoc, and with little connection with one another. But actually, they are connected by an impressive effort to determine, as precisely as possible, what the *scope* for agency in international relations is.

Historical context and reflexivity

Since his doctoral thesis on the philosophy of history, Raymond Aron was deeply perplexed by the relationship between the understanding of history and human action (Canguilhem 1992; Davis 2009). It is then not surprising that his understanding of international relations is deeply informed by a sensitivity for the importance of historical contexts. As previously discussed, for him, the meaning of power changes over time: "the sources of power are not the same from one century to another, and measuring power is, by nature, approximate" (Aron 1962: 64). It also means that it is pointless to try to predetermine states' interests and objectives in advance and deduce an analytical model from strong assumptions of so-called eternal desires such as "survival" or "security". For Aron,

> the concrete objectives political units establish for themselves evolve not only with the technological means of warfare and of production, but also with the historical ideas governing the organization and governance of societies ... One must also take into account what international lawyers call *custom*.
>
> (Aron 1962: 92)

Aron concludes this development with a very strong affirmation: "the diplomatico-strategic conduct is *customary*", and gives the example of the Franco-Russian agreements of 1917 as evidence of a "custom of bargaining" and "custom of protecting natural borders". In today's contemporary disciplinary language, Aron is describing a *diplomatic practice*, understood as a socially meaningful pattern of behaviour (Adler and Pouliot 2011; Bueger and Gadinger 2014). While this aspect is not prominent in the book (and is one of the many "gems" one can find through a close reading of *Paix et Guerre*), this is a clear sign of Aron's sensitivity to the importance of the historical contexts and the sedimentation of social dynamics, inherited from his training as a philosopher and a sociologist. But understanding the importance of the historical context also means not fetishizing past practices, themselves embedded within a specific time period. In a clear allusion to Kissinger, Aron is quite critical of those analysts who lament the loss of the "old ways" of diplomacy, a time when dispassionate diplomats were looking for a balance of power. Trying to reproduce this model in the ideological context of the Cold War was doomed to fail, as Kissinger's attempt eventually did (Hanhimäki 2004): the sensitivity to the historical context also means understanding how present times are different from the past.

This importance granted to the historical context is logically accompanied by a call for reflexivity. As a good Weberian, Aron argues that "what explains a decision is not so much the real situation than the idea the actor has about the situation" (Aron 1962: 308). Therefore, a good analytical strategy requires an attempt to reconstruct the multiple decision-making processes, cultural influences, personal preferences etc. that influence a specific decision. But it also means being reflexive about one's own processes, and admitting that what one can hold dear or true may not be shared by others.

Conclusion: Aron as a guide to foreign policy analysis

Using the framework of realist-constructivism as an analytical device helps in reconstructing Aron's understanding of international relations. Admittedly, Aron is a difficult read. *Paix et Guerre* is long, complex and definitely disconnected from the "puzzle-solving" type of writing that dominates the contemporary field of IR scholarship. In fact, many of Aron's "gems" are hidden in the text, and a close reading is necessary in order to appreciate the magnitude of the intellectual effort, and the depth of the insights that a familiarity with Aron's writings can provide.

Yet, the effort is particularly rewarding. Aron offers a subtle conceptualization of an international system taking into account both the importance of power and ideational contents. His attempt to clearly, and cautiously, delimit the scope for agency offers a warning against the false temptation to create parsimonious theories. No wonder that Waltz was identifying Aron as a prime target: the French author had demonstrated, 16 years before the publication of *Theory of International Politics*, that this effort was pointless and would only create artificial theoretical developments in IR, as it eventually did, culminating in the false "battle of paradigms". But Aron also explains that while a parsimonious general theory is pointless, a theory based on concept developments is possible, and necessary. Ironically, this is where theoretical development in the field seems to be going (Guzzini 2013; Berenskoetter 2016). In retrospect, Aron's prescience of contemporary theoretical developments (hierarchy, practice turn, etc.) is impressive, and he can be considered the intellectual forefather of such tendencies. But his understanding of alliance mechanisms or his integration of power distribution and global norms in order to understand the international system is miles ahead of his successors, and even sometimes of contemporary research. Had Aron been read more closely, and more widely, theoretical developments in the field of international relations would have been both quicker and more connected to the empirical world.

Ultimately, Aron offers a theory providing important insights on topics such as foreign policy, power transition, strategic balance, diplomacy and strategic affairs, and international stability. It is not everything in international relations, but it is an important part, which is in itself a sufficient justification for closely reading the French author.

Notes

1 Waltz himself establishes Aron as a clear target in his attempt to create a "scientific" theory of International Relations.
2 Understood as the diplomat, but also the head of state, the minister of foreign affairs, etc. It is the person who represents the political unit.

References

Adler, E. and Pouliot, V. (eds) (2011), *International Practices*. Cambridge: Cambridge University Press.
Aron, R. (1962), *Paix et Guerre entre les Nations*. Paris: Calmann-Lévy.
Aron, R. (1967), "Qu'est-ce qu'une Théorie des Relations Internationales?", *Revue Française de Science Politique*, 17:5, 837–861.
Aron, R. (1976), *Penser la Guerre: Clausewitz*. Paris: Gallimard.
Ashworth, L. (2002), "Did the Realist-Idealist Great Debate Ever Happen? A Revisionist History of International Relations", *International Relations*, 16:1, 33–51.
Baldwin, D.A. (2016), *Power and International Relations: A Conceptual Approach*. Princeton, NJ: Princeton University Press.
Barkin, S.J. (2010), *Realist Constructivism: Rethinking International Relations Theory*. Cambridge: Cambridge University Press.
Battistella, D. (2012), "Raymond Aron, Réaliste Néoclassique", *Études Internationales*, 43:3, 371–388.
Battistella, D. (2013), "La France", in Balzacq, T. and Ramel, F. (eds), *Traité de Relations Internationales*. Paris: Presses de Sciences Po, 157–180.
Bell, D. (2001), "International Relations: The Dawn of a Historiographical Turn?", *British Journal of Politics and International Relations*, 3:1, 115–126.
Bell, D. (2009), "Writing the World: Disciplinary History and Beyond", *International Affairs*, 85:1, 3–22.

Berenskoetter, F. (2016), "Approaches to Concept Analysis", *Millennium*, online early view.
Bially Mattern, J. and Zarakol, A. (2016), "Hierarchies in World Politics", *International Organization*, online early view.
Bueger, C. and Gadinger, F. (2014), *International Practice Theory: New Perspectives*. Basingstoke: Palgrave Macmillan.
Bull, H. (1977), *The Anarchical Society: A Study of World Order in World Politics*. Basingstoke: Palgrave.
Canguilhem, G. (1992), "Raymond Aron et la Philosophie Critique de l'Histoire", *Enquête*, 7, 1–8.
Davis, R.M. (2009), *A Politics of Understanding: The International Thought of Raymond Aron*. Baton Rouge, LA: Louisiana State University Press.
Farrell, T. (2005), *The Norms of War*. Boulder, CO: Lynne Rienner.
Freedman, L. (2013), *Strategy: A History*. Oxford: Oxford University Press.
Frost, B.-P. (1997), "Resurrecting a Neglected Theorist: The Philosophical Foundations of Raymond Aron's Theory of International Relations", *Review of International Studies*, 23:1, 143–166.
Goddard, S. (2008/2009), "When Right Makes Might: How Prussia Overturned the European Balance of Power", *International Security*, 33:3, 110–142.
Gueniffey, P. (2014), *Bonaparte*. Paris: Gallimard.
Guilhot, N. (2008), "The Realist Gambit: Postwar American Political Science and the Birth of IR Theory", *International Political Sociology*, 2:4, 281–304.
Guzzini, S. (2013), "The Ends of International Relations Theory: Stages of Reflexivity and Modes of Theorizing", *European Journal of International Relations*, 19:3, 521–541.
Hanhimäki, J. (2004), *The Flawed Architect: Henry Kissinger and American Foreign Policy*. Oxford: Oxford University Press.
Hoffmann, S. (2006), "Raymond Aron et la Théorie des Relations Internationales", *Politique Etrangère*, 58:4, 723–734.
Ikenberry, G.J. (2011), *Liberal Leviathan: The Origins, Crisis and Transformation of the American World Order*. Princeton, NJ: Princeton University Press.
Jackson, P.T. and Nexon, D. (2004), "Constructivist Realism or Realist-Constructivism?", *International Studies Review*, 6:2, 337–341.
Jones, S.G. (2007), *The Rise of European Security Cooperation*. Cambridge: Cambridge University Press.
Krebs, R. and Jackson, P.T. (2007), "Twisting Tongues and Twisting Arms: The Power of Political Rhetoric", *European Journal of International Relations*, 13:1, 35–66.
Lake, D.A. (2011), *Hierarchy in International Relations*. Ithaca, NY: Cornell University Press.
Lebow, R.N. (2008), *A Cultural Theory of International Relations*. Cambridge: Cambridge University Press.
Navon, E. (2001), "The 'Third Debate' Revisited", *Review of International Studies*, 27:4, 611–625.
Neumann, I.B. (2012a), *At Home with the Diplomats: Inside a European Foreign Ministry*. Ithaca, NY: Cornell University Press.
Neumann, I.B. (2012b), *Diplomatic Sites: A Critical Inquiry*. London: Hurst Publishers.
Pape, R.A. (2005), "Soft Balancing Against the United States", *Security Studies*, 30:1, 7–45.
Paul, T.V., Larson, D.W. and Wohlforth, W.C. (eds) (2014), *Status in World Politics*. Cambridge: Cambridge University Press.

Pouliot, V. (2016), *International Pecking Orders*. Cambridge: Cambridge University Press.
Rynning, S. and Ringsmose, J. (2008), "Why Are Revisionist States Revisionist? Reviving Classical Realism as an Approach to Understanding International Change", *International Politics*, 45:1, 19–39.
Schmidt, B.C. (ed.) (2012), *International Relations and the First Great Debate*. London: Routledge.
Snyder, G. (1998), *Alliance Politics*. Ithaca, NY: Cornell University Press.
Sterling-Folker, J. (2002), "Realism and the Constructivist Challenge: Rejecting, Reconstructing, or Rereading", *International Studies Review*, 4:1, 73–97.
Weitsman, P.A. (2003), *Dangerous Alliances: Proponents of Peace, Weapons of War*. Palo Alto, CA: Stanford University Press.
Wohlforth, W.C. (2008), "Realism", in Reus-Smit, C. and Snidal, D. (eds), *The Oxford Handbook of International Relations*. Oxford: Oxford University Press, 131–149.

4 Aron's oxymorus international ethics

Jean-Baptiste Jeangène Vilmer[1]

International relations (IR) theory is plagued by paradigmatism, the view that considers the various theories as mutually exclusive paradigms (Barkin 2010: 4). This is how it is taught in textbooks: realism, liberalism, Marxism, constructivism, English school, critical theory, feminism, post-structuralism, post-colonialism – the student must pick sides. This leads to several problems, including the caricature of these positions, and the labeling of academics in order to pit them against each other. Having to be *either* a realist *or* a liberal, for instance, leaves little room for nuance, and little hope for understanding Raymond Aron's conceptual framework. He is often presented like a mainstream classical realist, sometimes like a liberal, or a proto-constructivist; the truth is that Raymond Aron is unclassifiable. He can certainly be presented as a realist constructivist, as Olivier Schmitt does in his chapter. I will present him as a realist liberal. This will demonstrate the importance of non-paradigmatism.

In fact, Aron is the archetype – the best possible example of the fecundity of a non-paradigmatic approach. This corresponds with his own project to overcome the mutual-exclusivity mindset. As I will show, Aron was obsessed with finding the middle ground, the third way, between what he called the "antinomies" (a term he took from Kant) of political life: between realism and liberalism, cynicism and moralism, "morality of struggle" and "morality of law", ethic of responsibility and ethic of conviction, Machiavelli and Kant, conservatism and millenarism, despair and faith, etc.

However, as Hedley Bull pointed out, showing dilemmas and always recommending the middle ground does not constitute an ethical doctrine (Bull 1979: 179). Aron's ability to always simultaneously consider the merits of a proposal and its counter-proposal, to always balance the two and find the wisest position to be the middle ground, can even be frustrating for the reader looking for easy answers – but precious for the one looking for complexity of thought and not reducing it. Moreover, it was never his ambition to establish an ethical doctrine: he did not even believe in the possibility of IR theory ("there is no general theory of international relations"; Aron 2003: 93). There is no normative IR theory in Aron, only unavoidable normative implications of his sociological and theoretical approach to IR, because "normative implications are inherent in every [social sciences] theory" (Aron 2003: 575). The aim of this chapter is to structure these implications to reveal Aron's international ethics in three oxymorons, i.e., *appearances* of contradiction: a liberal realism, an inspired ethic of responsibility and a post-Kantian Machiavellianism.

A liberal realism

Aron claims to be a realist ("I belong, by temperament rather than conviction, to the realist school"; Aron 1958a: 13). Interestingly, when he also remembers having been a liberal in the 1920s, it is also "by temperament" ("then already, I was a liberal by temperament"; Aron 1983b), which tells us three things: (1) be it realism or liberalism, these classic IR theory schools seem to be nothing more than "temperaments" as far as he is concerned, which confirms his lack of interest for IR theory. (2) Like many progressive realists, he was first a liberal who became realist while observing at close quarters the rise of nationalism, fascism and even totalitarianism, and the corollary demise of the League of Nations and other inter-war dreams (Scheuerman 2011: 9). (3) If realism and liberalism are nothing but temperaments, and if Aron claims he had both, they are not incompatible – which opens the door to the possibility of a liberal realism or a realist liberalism.

With his own specificities, Aron indeed shares the realist axioms – that politics is determined by the struggle for power and international relations are determined by self-interested actors, mostly states, seeking to maximize their national interests in an anarchical context, where there is no global authority able to prevent the recourse to force. However, Aron also claims to be a liberal, and his ferocious fight against communism even made him known as a "passionate" one (Hoffmann 1985: 21). The often forgotten influence of the French philosopher Elie Halévy contributed greatly to Aron's conversion from theoretical to practical philosophy (the position of the "committed observer"), and from socialism to liberalism as early as the end of the 1930s. Halévy is the missing link between Tocqueville and Aron in the filiation of French liberal thought (Baverez 2006: 121).

Liberalism in its broadest sense is based on the ideal of individual freedom and believes in human progress, the possibility of improving the life of citizens. Although Aron does not believe in liberal progress in the Kantian sense – i.e., an ascendant linearity leading to the disappearance of the bellicose nature of man – he certainly believes that man is increasingly aware of the necessity to control this bellicose nature. He is liberal in the sense that such an effort presumes man's free will and autonomy. Aron also sees liberalism as a conception of the limitation of power which, while not equivalent to democracy, leads to it (through the principle of equality before the law) (Aron 1998: 138–139). Aron defends liberal democracy "on the basis of many criteria: effectiveness of institutions, individual liberty, equitable distribution, perhaps above all the kind of person created by the regime" (Aron 2010: 176), and insists that Western diplomacy should defend and even export liberal democratic values (Davis 2009: 173). Aron made a strong defense of liberal society but, contrary to philosophers like John Rawls, he did so in a historical, contextualized and concrete way. Rawls and others have an abstract and ahistorical approach that is very far from Aron's method. For this reason, some bring Aron closer to neoconservative liberals like Peter Berger or Irving Kristol, who are "mugged by reality", and do not hesitate to call him "the first neoconservative" (Anderson 1995). That is a mistake, as Aron does not satisfy any of the criteria of neoconservatism (supremacy, interventionism, militarism, regime change, unilateralism).

Aron denounces hard realism, which he calls "false realism": the one

> who asserts that man is a beast of prey and urges him to behave as such, ignores a whole side of human nature. Even in the relations between states, respect for ideas, aspiration to higher values and concern for obligations have been manifested.
>
> (Aron 2003: 609)

For him, realism "would be unrealistic if it considered the moral judgments men pass on the conduct of their rulers as negligible" (Aron 1967: 205).

> The sociologist does not appear to me to be doomed either to cynicism or to dogmatism. He does not necessarily become a cynic because the political or moral ideas which he calls upon in judging political regimes are part of reality itself. The great illusion of cynical thought, obsessed by the struggle for power, consists in neglecting another aspect of reality; the search for legitimate power, for recognized authority, for the *best* regime. Men have never thought of politics as exclusively defined by the struggle for power. Anyone who does not see that there is a "struggle for power" element is naïve; anyone who sees nothing but this aspect is a false realist.
>
> (Aron 1968: 24)

It would be unrealistic not to take morality into account, not so much because the actors *are* really ethical but rather because they must *look* so on the international stage, as Niebhur explained in 1954: "They cannot follow their interest without claiming to do so in obedience to some general scheme of values" (Guilhot 2011: 269). Like Niebuhr, Aron shows how states always justify their behavior with norms: diplomatic-strategic behavior "always attempts to justify itself, thereby admitting the authority of values or rules" (Aron 2003: 725). It does not mean that human action is governed by the search for values rather than interests, only that it is in the interests of IR actors to search for values. Therefore, contrary to a widespread prejudice, the two are not incompatible.

Moreover, these realist and liberal components are not at the same level of analysis. It is perfectly possible to recognize the realist constraints at the descriptive level (that states are never disinterested is an empirical fact, for instance) while aiming at ways to overcome them to make the world more just at the prescriptive level, i.e., defending some ideals (democratic values, for instance). This is exactly how Aron can be described as a liberal realist. He is not alone in that category, and nor was he at that time. Arnold Wolfers, who prefaced a book co-written by Aron (Aron 1957), is one of the most liberal of the classical realists, and therefore one of the closest to Aron. But the best representative of this trend is probably John Herz. His book *Political Realism and Political Idealism* (1951) addressed "the problem of how, starting from and not neglecting the power factor, one could yet arrive at 'liberal' objectives" (Herz 1981: 202). It is not certain whether Aron actually knew his work, and that makes their proximity even more spectacular. Herz's idea is to combine a realist base, "built, not on the sands of wishful thinking but on the rock of reality," and a liberal guiding star "that moves man to try to push developments in a different direction" (Herz 1951: 131).

An inspired ethic of responsibility

Aron's ethical reflection was structured by the early reading of Max Weber (Nelson and Colen 2015: 205), a common source for both IR classical realists and realist political philosophers (Scheuerman 2013: 802). To elucidate the relationship between politics and morality, Weber, in a 1919 lecture entitled *Politik als Beruf*, famously distinguished between the ethic of responsibility (*Verantwortungsethik*), which takes into account the consequences in moral evaluation and gives priority to results over intentions, as opposed to the ethic of conviction or inspiration (*Gesinnungsethik*) that defends a doctrinal belief regardless of consequences, and gives priority to the intentions over the results.

Aron presents the ethic of responsibility as a "means-ends interpretation of action ... an ethic defined by the search of effectiveness, and consequently by the selection of means suitable to the goal one wishes to attain" (1999: 252–253). It emphasizes the link between action and consequences, while the ethic of conviction emphasizes the link between action and intention. The choice between the two is the following:

> Either we swear to obey the law, whatever may happen, or we try our best to change the world in the direction we desire, to foresee the consequences of our acts in order to triumph over determinism and avoid bringing about, in the last resort, a situation contrary to that at which we aimed. Does the value of our acts derive from our intentions alone or from the consequences of these acts?
>
> (Aron 1964a: 84)

Against the ethics of conviction

First, Aron criticizes the ethics of conviction, and in particular its indifference to consequences: "No man is moral who acts exclusively according to the morality of conviction. No one has the right to disregard the consequences of his actions" (Aron 1963c: 53). Here, he follows closely Weber. The ethic of conviction is an ethic of ultimate ends, whatever the costs, a political idealism that Aron finds both unrealistic and dangerous. It is unrealistic in "the game of politics" because "no one, not the citizen, not the president of the student's union, not the journalist, says or writes exactly what he feels, indifferent to the consequences of his words or deeds, concerned solely with obeying his conscience" (Aron 1999: 255–256). A pure ethic of conviction would also be dangerous because it can foster support for the most extreme ideologies – "we repeatedly see the proponent of the 'ethics of conviction' suddenly turning into a chiliastic prophet" (Weber 1994: 361). This is actually what happened with Sartre, who "came to consent to extreme forms of violence in the service of the good cause" (Aron 2010: 951). "For moralism, if it leads to Max Weber's *Gesinnungsethik*, by failing to take account of the probable or possible consequences of the decisions taken, turns out to be immoral" (Aron 1967: 205).

For this reason, his rejection of the ethic of conviction, and more generally of idealism, is "not only pragmatic, it is also moral. Idealistic diplomacy slips too often into fanaticism; it divides states into good and evil, into peace-loving and bellicose" (Aron 2003: 584). He distrusts

> vague slogans such as 'to make the world safe for democracy' or 'to insure collective security' [because they] often tend to make wars bigger and worse. Selfishness is not obnoxious in the case of nations; it is reasonable; indeed only selfishness is moral. So-called idealistic policies always amount to an attempt to impose a certain conception of social or international organization. Political idealism ends by degenerating into imperialism.
> (Aron 1960: 80)

His opposition to the ethic of conviction has many manifestations. I will give only three examples. First, pacifism – the belief that war is a supreme evil that should be avoided at all costs – is widespread in the inter-war period (1918–1939). Aron will retrospectively think that such predominance "betrayed perhaps less confidence than anxiety" (Aron 1946: 85). Like most of his young comrades, under the influence of their philosophy teacher Alain, who wrote a persuasive pacifist pamphlet in 1921 (later translated with the title *Mars; Or the Truth about War*), Aron was initially a pacifist. His German years (1930–1931 in Cologne, 1931–1933 in Berlin), where he observed the rise of Nazism (his first mention of a concentration camp is in a September 1933 article in *Europe*), ended his pacifism once and for all (compare Aron 1931 and 1933a). It made him understand that the pacifist belief that war is necessarily worse than all other evils was not only false – "the results of the enemy's victory can be worse than the misfortune of war" (Aron 1983b: 58) – but also dangerous because the fear of war was precisely what totalitarianism needed in order to develop: "Let us have the courage to admit that the fear of war is often the tyrant's opportunity" (Aron 1958a: 73).

He henceforth rejected pacifism – which is "not a doctrine, but a faith" (Aron 1946: 88) – convinced that the policies of appeasement toward Germany had the pernicious effect of strengthening Hitler and making war more likely. When in

March 1936 German troops entered the Rhineland, Leon Blum, the head of the Popular Front, wrote a paper saying that force could have been used against Hitler but was not, and he was proud to have contributed to such a moral progress of humanity. He did not understand that, as Aron comments, "This 'moral progress' meant ... the near certainty of war" (Aron 1983b: 31). Four years earlier, Blum already distinguished himself after the defeat of the Nazis at the November 1932 elections by predicting that "Hitler lost all chance of gaining power" ... three months before he was appointed chancellor (Baverez 2006: 97–98). Hitler did not only count on his material power, he also counted on the reluctance of democracies to use force. This is how "pacifism, in refusing any risk of war, favored the politics which actually led to war" (Aron 1946: 95). This idea that pacifism is the enemy of peace (and, similarly, nationalism the enemy of the nation) has also been developed by Aron's friend Father Fessard, a Jesuit theologian, in *Pax Nostra* (1936).

For a second example, the ethic of conviction is also behind the categorical opposition to nuclear weapons during the Cold War, which Aron opposes because it is "made for motives of conscience and without calculating the risks and advantages" (Aron 2003: 634). Some pacifists, tempted to "save conventional wars to avoid atomic ones" (Aron 1963a: 226), can even, paradoxically, have a bellicose role. However, Aron is fully aware of the moral paradoxes of nuclear deterrence. He admits an "ethical antinomy which none can resolve" (Aron 1983a: 340): on the one hand, nuclear deterrence contributes to preventing major conventional wars; but, on the other hand, it involves threatening to kill large numbers of innocent people, and that is in itself "monstrous" (Aron 1983a: 339) – the main paradox being that, for the first time, forming the intention to do something wrong would be right (Kavka 1978).

A third example is the "peace versus justice" dilemma, which only became acute *after* Aron's death with the development of international criminal justice. After an armed conflict, those with whom we must negotiate a ceasefire and the return of peace are often the same people who have committed crimes (war crimes, crimes against humanity or genocide). Therefore, we must choose between prosecuting them in the name of justice and including them in the transition process in the name of peace. In this situation, there is usually a confrontation between two schools of thought: on the one hand, most politicians, diplomats, negotiators and realist observers prioritize peace over justice – they fear that such prosecutions against those suspected of committing crimes may create trouble and prevent a ceasefire and the return to peace. Therefore, they offer them official amnesties or secret arrangements to circumvent the sword of justice and persuade them to come to the negotiating table. On the other hand, most human rights activists, international institution representatives and lawyers prioritize justice over peace: they believe that peace obtained by impunity is illusory and temporary and that justice can have a pacifying effect, including discouraging future crimes. Hence the slogan "No peace without justice".

In this debate, a pure ethic of conviction position would prioritize justice over peace whatever the consequences, in conformity with the Holy Roman Emperor

Ferdinand I's motto *"Fiat justitia, et pereat mundus"* (Let justice be done, though the world perish). Against such an idealist stance, and even before the creation of the ad hoc tribunals and the international criminal court in the 1990s, Aron seems to favor an ethic of responsibility which prioritizes peace over justice:

> It is perhaps immoral, but it is most often wise, to spare the leaders of an enemy state, for otherwise these men will sacrifice the lives and wealth and possessions of their fellow citizens or their subjects in the vain hope of saving themselves.
>
> (Aron 2003: 115)

A consequentialist approach

In the language of contemporary normative ethics, the ethics of conviction/responsibility debate – a dated terminology – is instead called the deontologism/consequentalism debate. Aron, like most realists, seems mostly consequentialist: very early, in February 1933, he determined that "a good policy is defined by its effectiveness, not by its virtue" (Aron 1933b: 739–740). "The politician who obeys his heart without concerning himself with the consequences of his acts is failing the duties of his trust and is for this very reason immoral" (Aron 2003: 634).

He is definitely outcome- rather than intention-oriented when, for instance, he writes that "American policy in Vietnam, legitimate in its intention, became apparently immoral because of the destruction it entailed without attaining its objective" (Aron 1980: 8). When Aron expresses his skepticism about the intervention in Indochina, or when Morgenthau opposes the Vietnam War, their position is derived from the assessment of the chances of success, not from an objection to the will to intervene in itself. When the odds of success are too low or zero, even the most just causes should not be pursued. "Logic requires to compare cost and performance, to refuse excessive sacrifices if they are to yield only limited or mediocre profits" writes Aron (1993: 265) – echoing Morgenthau: "It is this impossibility to achieve – even with the best of intentions and the most extensive commitment of resources – what is presumed to be morally required that negates the moral obligation" (Morgenthau 1985: 110). If, in this case, it is impossible to save civilians without killing more of them, the responsibility to protect commands us to not intervene.

In other words, realists are not anti-interventionists, they are simply prudent. Most of the time, this prudence leads them to oppose the proposed intervention. But nothing precludes them, in a particularly favorable environment, to support it. When, the day after North Korea crossed the 38th Parallel on 25 June 1950, for example, the newspaper *Le Monde* thought it was "urgent to wait" before intervening, Aron replied that it was "urgent to act" (Aron 2010: 358).

While criticizing the ethic of conviction and favoring the ethic of responsibility, like Weber, Aron was fully aware that these two ethics are nothing but ideal-types (Breiner 2011: 108). The statesman *tends to* use the ethic of responsibility, because he needs to justify himself, and the citizen *tends to* use the ethic of conviction, on the basis of which he can criticize the statesman (Aron 1970a: 256). No one really follows the ethic of conviction: it is "an ideal type which no one can approximate too closely and still remain within the bounds of reasonable behavior" (Aron 1999: 256). A pure ethic of conviction would not be an ethic, but fanaticism. In politics, the two are intertwined because we must find "reasonable compromises" between the two demands (Aron 1985: 363–364). Here we find again his politics of compromise.

While criticizing Weber for the "extreme and somewhat radical form given to the antinomy between the two morals, responsibility and conviction" (Aron 1993: 252), Aron recognizes that Weber never meant that adopting the ethic of conviction implies a lack of responsibility for the consequences, and that adopting an ethic of responsibility implies having no conviction. He knew that applications of this abstract dichotomy would be mixed (Aron 1985: 362). Weber himself considered them as ideal-types, heuristic tools, but not irreconcilable realities. Quite the contrary: not only does the ethic of conviction not exclude responsibility and the ethic of responsibility does not exclude conviction (it is "based upon a through-going acceptance of a cultural or human value"; Aron 1964a: 91), but the objective should be to combine them: they "are not absolute opposites. They are complementary to one another, and only in combination do they produce the true human being who is *capable* of having a 'vocation for politics'" (Weber 1994: 368). For Aron as well, "the care for consequences completes, without contradicting them, the motives of action. One acts *by* conviction and *to* obtain certain results" (Aron 1963c: 53).

Does it mean that this is only an artificial opposition? No. Although the reasonable objective should be to combine them, and it is theoretically possible because they are not mutually exclusive per se, it is not feasible to do so in all situations. Aron warns that in extreme situations – and extreme situations are precisely where the "essence of politics" reveals itself – there are sometimes some "real antinomies of action" (Aron 1963c: 54).

> A politician must be both convinced and responsible. But when you have to lie or lose, kill or be defeated, what choice is moral? Truth, answers the moralist of conviction; success, answers the moralist of responsibility. The two choices are moral provided that the success desired by the latter is that of the City, not its own. The antinomy seems to me to be essential, even if, in the majority of cases, prudence suggests a reasonable compromise.
> (Aron 1963c: 54–55)

In short, Aron's approach to the conviction/responsibility dichotomy, like Weber's, is dialectical. First, he seems to favor one of the two: he is clearly preferring the ethic of responsibility as "the only [choice] compatible with politics and not condemned to perpetual contradictions" (Aron 1964a: 87). Second, he qualifies this first impression by *sublating* the opposition (this is the Hegelian phase of *Aufhebung*), adding that both are complementary and that a real ethic of responsibility needs to be inspired and guided by "convictions that transcend the order of utility" (Aron 2003: 634). Aron "believed in the ethics of consequences; but they were rooted in convictions" (Hoffmann 1983). Some calls this synthesis a "responsible ethic of conviction" (Bruun 2007: 272). In order to highlight the ethic of responsibility that both Weber and Aron favor, I would rather speak of an *inspired ethic of responsibility* – taking into account both the consequences of the person's actions (the political calculations) and their non-political values. Third, as is often forgotten, such a balance does not solve all problems. In extreme situations like war the antinomy is inevitable, and for Weber, like Aron, it is even "the mark of what authentically constitutes the human condition" (Aron 1963c: 56). Such an inevitability is another illustration of the tragic character of international relations.

Virtue ethics

Deontology and consequentialism are only two of the three main families of contemporary normative ethics. In his inclusive attitude, Aron did not forget the third one: virtue ethics. Both deontology and consequentialism assess the morality of the action. Virtue ethics assesses the morality of the agent. It emphasizes the virtues, or moral character (the Aristotelian *ethos*). Consequentialism relies on the rationalist assumption that human behavior can be explained by some kind of cost/benefit calculus. However, in international relations it is often difficult to measure gain: "what is the non-Sovietization of South Vietnam worth? ... Strategic analysis creates sometimes the illusion of a rigorous comparison between losses and gains ... but it is an illusion". Their incommensurability is mainly due to the fact that

> the stakes are never reduced to material realities (acquisition or loss of territory, destruction suffered or inflicted) but involve immaterial elements – prestige, diffusion of ideas or of a way of life, increased or reduced power, and power desired for its own sake.
>
> (Aron 1970b: 60)

Here, Aron the liberal realist is also proto-constructivist (see Olivier Schmitt's chapter).

> The determination of values is essential to the understanding of human conduct, because the latter is never strictly utilitarian. The rational calculations of speculators represent an activity, more or less widespread in different civilizations, which is always limited by a conception of the good life.
>
> (Aron 1962a: 137)

For both Aron and Mannheim, pluralism is a descriptive and a normative category, a fact of political life and a democratic value, which does not imply moral relativism (Mahoney 2001: 246).

Aron does not asses the morality of statesmen's actions *in abstracto*, and from an external viewpoint that would ignore the job's constraints. He limits his own "freedom of criticism" by asking himself "in his stead, what would I do?" (Aron 2010: 813). That is asking a virtue ethics question: not what to do, but what kind of person to be: if I had the statesman's knowledge and responsibilities, which actions would be open to me, regardless of the ethical justification for those actions? Hoffmann notes that this lack of distance can be problematic: it exposes him to the risk – opposite to the idealist "on Sirius" – of being deprived of hindsight (Hoffmann 1985: 21).

Another way to see a virtue ethics approach in Aron is, of course, through prudence, which he is not alone in defending. The fact that all the classical realists are heirs to the Aristotelian *phronesis*, a practical wisdom often translated as "prudence" that inspired an entire tradition of statecraft (Coll 1991; Lang 2007; Shapcott 2013) – including Edmund Burke who described prudence as "the god of this lower world" – definitely puts them in the virtue ethics camp. In 1954, Morgenthau wrote in his fourth "Principle of Political Realism" that realism "considers prudence – the weighing of the consequences of alternative political actions, to be the supreme virtue in politics" (Morgenthau 1985: 12). Later, Aron uses the exact same words: "prudence is the statesman's supreme virtue" (Aron 2003: 585). He confirms that he is indeed talking about the Aristotelian concept: "What tradition teaches is not cynicism but Aristotelian prudence – the supreme virtue in this world under the visited moon" (Aron 1974: 329). However, Aron's prudence has little to do with ancient wisdom: contrary to Aristotle, who linked *phronesis* to *sophia*, Aron's prudence is pragmatic and does not seem to be a heuristic quest, a pursuit of truth.

A post-Kantian Machiavellianism

Aron introduces the ethics of responsibility and conviction by stating that they "might be illustrated by referring to Machiavelli on the one hand and Kant on the other" (Aron 1999: 252). Indeed, in the final part of *Peace and War* devoted to "Praxeology", a normative IR theory, he identifies two main ethical problems: the Machiavellian problem and the Kantian problem (Châton 2012, 2017).

The Machiavellian problem

The Machiavellian problem is the problem of legitimate means. What means may the political leaders legitimately use? Can they use particularly immoral ones if it is in order to achieve great good? The Machiavellian problem is posed by the observation that effective means are often immoral. It is an insoluble contradiction because it is absurd to forbid politicians to use the means most likely to make them succeed, nor is it satisfactory to allow them the use of detestable means. One must then choose between "winning by losing the reasons for victory, or giving up victory in the hope of saving his soul" (Aron 1993: 272).

This dilemma is well known: for four centuries the "quarrel of Machiavellianism" reappears each time a political leader is accused of doing terrible things in the name of efficiency (Catherine de' Medici, Cardinal Mazarin, Frederick the Great, Napoleon Bonaparte, etc.). Similarly, Aron explains that Hitler, Stalin and Mussolini, of his contemporaries, led him to study Machiavelli (Aron 1993: 59). Therefore, the Italian Renaissance philosopher has first an instrumental value in Aron's work: he is used to understand and explain the conceptual framework of tyrannies, and is closely linked to Aron's work on totalitarianism.

Aron takes the aforementioned dilemma seriously: "There is no way out and the politician must accept the tragic of his condition" (Aron 1993: 272). The only thing to do is to avoid the extreme situations in which this dilemma appears. Unlike Machiavellianism in the vulgar and pejorative sense, which would be the choice of efficiency at any moral price, real Machiavellianism consists precisely in reducing the frequency of these situations in which the dilemma is inevitable. Real Machiavellianism is not a doctrine but "a certain way of thinking about politics", gathering the following elements: "a pessimistic conception of human nature ... a rationalist and experimental method ... and the exaltation of human will and action values" (Aron 1993: 197).

Aron dismisses two approaches. First, the idealist "morality of law": legalism, or some kind of legal deontological ethic, applied to international law. He rejects it as being not only naive (international law is often violated) but also immoral – because of the difference between legality and legitimacy which often conflict. Legal actions can be illegitimate and illegal ones can be legitimate. Hence a skepticism toward the Rule of Law, a legitimate ideal which could have a perverse effect if it is supposed to replace politics and prudence. Law itself does not suffice, and could be a cover for exactions (as we saw in 2014 in Ukraine: behind the legalist discourse of Putin lay a good example of *lawfare*, the use of law as a weapon of war). The Aronian is not a legalist, and that is why he can defend what were coined in 2000 as "illegal but legitimate" interventions, in reference to Kosovo.

The second approach he dismisses is the cynical "morality of struggle": a hard-core realism, or, as Aron puts it, an "absolute Machiavellism", saying that the statesman may use all available means. That refers to the "quarrel of Machiavellianism" with the Catholic philosopher Jacques Maritain, whom he never actually met but with whom he had an epistolary dialogue. In a 1941 international conference at the University of Chicago on "The Place of Ethics in Social Science", Maritain gave a talk he published the following year under the title "The End of Machiavellianism" in *The Review of Politics*, in which he distinguished two forms of Machiavellianism: a moderate one which preserves the common good as the end of politics and uses Machiavellianism only as a means of procuring such an end; and an absolute Machiavellianism, which is positivistic (politics is a not an art but a science of power) and amoral ("power and success have become supreme moral criteria") (Maritain 1942: 11–12). Maritain rejects both; he opposes Machiavellianism per se, believing that it "does not succeed" (Maritain 1942: 15). In a 1943 article, Aron finds Maritain's anti-Machiavellianism too naive, and based on faith more than history (Aron 1993: 384–395). Maritain answers that he tries to criticize Machiavellianism on a realist, not utopian basis (Maritain 1944: ch. 5). Aron appreciates the effort of finding the balance of a policy both moral and realistic between the abstract moralism that has the pernicious effect of leading men to cynicism by offering them an unrealistic ideal, and the nastiness of an absolute Machiavellianism. However, he thinks that Maritain underestimates "the imperfection, the inertia, the materiality of human and social nature" (Aron 1993: 394). In reality, they may not be talking about the same thing: Maritain is describing the Christian Man, while Aron is interested in the liberal one.

Aron distinguishes between domestic politics, where he agrees with Maritain to reject Machiavellianism and defends liberal and democratic values, human rights etc., and foreign policy, which is different because "states are in what Hobbes or Rousseau would have called a state of war" (Aron 1993: 434): international relations are anarchic in the sense that there is no global tribunal or police force capable of rendering justice and curbing violence so "each state remains responsible for its own security" (Aron 1970b: 55). Therefore, conflict is inevitable and the only possible ethic is an "ethics of restrained warfare": "as long as there are sovereign states, armed states, states in conflict with each other, there cannot be anything but a moderate Machiavellianism". Concretely, that means that terrible decisions should sometimes be taken in the name of "raison d'Etat" (Aron 1993: 434).

After Aron, Michael Walzer, the most famous twentieth-century Just War theorist, would defend a similar position on what he calls "the dirty hands problem" (Walzer 1973). Walzer uses it to justify the Allies' strategic bombing of German civilians during World War II, in the name of a "supreme emergency" (Walzer 2004: 46). Aron would have agreed.

For the same reason, Aron repeatedly insisted that foreign policy cannot be *based* on human rights. He is, of course, sympathetic to the defense of human rights, and praises non-governmental organizations (NGOs) for their "useful, respectable task, in which I participate to the extent possible", but states cannot behave like NGOs: even France, which gives in too often to the temptation of calling itself "the country of human rights" (what former Foreign Minister Hubert Védrine calls a "declaratory hypertrophy")

> cannot determine its friendships or make its decisions on the basis of the degree to which human rights are scorned or respected in the various countries. And I do not know of any country in history that founded its foreign policy solely on the virtues of its allies.
> (Aron 1983b: 247)

Human rights promotion can and even should be *a part of* foreign policy (Aron is a liberal), but they cannot be the base for it (he is not an idealist).

A morality of wisdom

Having dismissed both morality of law and morality of struggle, he then defends his *"morale de la sagesse"* (morality of wisdom). It is incorrectly translated as the "morality of prudence" in the English edition of *Paix et guerre*, even if Aronian wisdom is certainly prudential (Mahoney 2001: 244). Presented as a third way between idealism (morality of law) and absolute Machiavellianism (morality of struggle), it does not exclude force (unlike idealism) or ethical concern (unlike Machiavellianism). It neither divorces politics from morality, nor reduces it to morality. Politics is irreducible to morality because "the political problem is not a moral problem" (Aron 1933a: 99), but this does not mean that such realism cannot be balanced with ideals and values.

The morality of wisdom is not to be used in a principle or rule-based reasoning but in a case-based reasoning (casuistry). Aron is a contextualist, he stresses the specificities of each unique historical situation. "To be prudent is to act in accordance with the particular situation and the concrete data, and not in accordance with some system or out of passive obedience to a norm or pseudo-norm" (Aron 2003: 585). Therefore, Aron's international ethic is a situational or contextual ethic. Nuclear deterrence, for instance, should not be discussed in the abstract but it should be asked "who deters whom from what, by what threats, in what circumstances" (Aron 1963b: 40) – a formula Herman Kahn used in his book *On Escalation* (1965: 23). For interventionism, it means that the policy makers should decide on a case by case basis where to intervene, and where not. An Aronian can perfectly justify the selectivity of our actions, and easily answer to the "double standards" criticism (why Libya and not Syria? Because "the particular situation and the concrete data" are not the same, and the consequences of an intervention would not be the same).

This morality of wisdom is justified by the famous distinction between rational and reasonable: if the strategic-diplomatic conduct is not rational (Aron insists on the importance of "historical and psychological" dimensions), then IR actors are not calculating machines and they can be reasonable.

Aron's morality of wisdom is a morality of *moderation*, in line with Aristotle (being virtuous is being "skillful in aiming at the middle term"; Aristotle 2011: 35) and Montesquieu ("the spirit of republics is peace and moderation", "moderation governs men, not excesses"; Montesquieu 1989: 132), as explained by Bryan-Paul Frost in his chapter. It means that violence in general, and wars in particular, need to be limited. "Between the absurdity of total war and the impossibility of real peace, the hopes of humanity are confined to the possibility of limiting warfare" (Aron 1958b: 40). "Limited Warfare" is the title of the third part of *Les Guerres en chaîne* (1951), in which Aron explains that "The goal of the West is and must be to win limited war so as not to have to wage the total war" (Aron 1951: 497). Aron's recommendation is always "the control of escalation, the avoidance of an explosion of animosity into passionate and unrestricted brutality" (Aron 2003: 45); to avoid the "all or nothing" (go or not go) logic and defend the flexible response doctrine in the nuclear debate (Aron

1963a: 139; see also Malis' chapter), a doctrine which was elaborated in the 1960 Harvard/MIT seminar in which Aron participated during his sabbatical, the same year France conducted its first nuclear test (Baverez 2006: 399). In short, he sought to propose a "moderate strategy" (Aron 2003: 700).

Moderation is precisely the idea behind war ethics and international humanitarian law, to limit the consequences of war on people and goods. It opposes the direct approach of strategy famously embodied in Clausewitz's dictum: "To introduce the principle of moderation into the theory of war itself would always lead to logical absurdity" (Clausewitz 1976: 76). Direct strategy justifies total war, the hard-line approach of General MacArthur, requiring victory at all costs, the price being precisely that of ethics. The Russian bombings of Aleppo in 2016 are a more recent illustration of a direct approach that would have repulsed Aron. He is not alone: there is an entire tradition defending the "indirect approach" of strategy, aiming at precisely the opposite: the avoidance of frontal collision, and even of battle. The object of war is not to annihilate the adversary but to dominate them, that is, to impose one's will on them – "the effort of each state to impose its will on the other" is the first of the two elements in Clausewitz's definition of war that Aron adopts (Aron 1970b: 56). The best way to achieve this goal is to do so by spending the least energy and causing as little damage as possible. Like ethics, but for the sake of efficiency and economy of forces instead (Marshal Ferdinand Foch's first principle of war; Foch 1920: 48), the indirect strategy limits the effect of war on populations. This long tradition includes Sun Zu as much as the British strategist Liddell Hart, whom Aron considered "the most intelligent, and also the most typical, opponent of Clausewitz writing in the English language" (Aron 1983a: 234). Against Clausewitz, Liddell Hart argues that a perfect strategy would "produce a decision without any serious fighting" (Liddell Hart 1941: 190).

It is important to understand that Aron does not present his morality of wisdom as a solution and the Machiavelli problem remains unresolved: "the eternal problem of justifying the means by the end has no theoretical solution" (Aron 1994: 45). The morality of wisdom is not a solution, rather a guide for action: it "does not resolve the antinomies of strategic-diplomatic conduct, but it does attempt to find in each case the most acceptable compromise" (Aron 2003: 609). The notion of compromise is important because Aron used it before: in his 1938 dissertation, *Introduction to the Philosophy of History*, he prefers the "politics of compromise" over the "politics of reason". The politician of compromise (he refers to Max Weber as an example) tries to preserve certain values (peace, liberty) in a changing environment, without being handicapped by an unchanging conception of human nature. The politician of reason thinks he is a "confidant of Providence" (Aron 1961: 328).

The fact that the Machiavelli problem remains unresolved, and that all we can reach is a compromise, means that even in liberal democracies there will always be a certain amount of Machiavellianism – counterbalanced by other forces but still present. That is why Aron defends a "moderate Machiavellism" as opposed to an "absolute" one (Aurélio 2015: 240) – another instance of the centrality of moderation in his thought. A moderate Machiavelli is willing to dirty their hands if necessary. Convinced of the impossibility of a pacified world, they recognize that violence can be a legitimate means to defend liberal values – and, for example, fight against totalitarianism. However, contrary to absolute Machiavellianism which excludes nothing, moderate Machiavellianism excludes certain means like nuclear war or genocide. By defending the use of force when necessary and under certain conditions, Aron assumes there can be just wars, and even anticipatory action. Aron "was not against the notion of preemption or prevention, which could, in certain circumstances, be indispensable" (Hassner 2005: 1–2).

The Kantian problem

The Kantian problem is the cosmopolitan one, i.e., the problem of universal peace. The twentieth century of Raymond Aron in ambivalent in that respect: on one hand, there is more talk about human rights and more institutions than ever; on the other, it is the bloodiest century in the history of humanity, with two world wars and several genocides. As a matter of fact, the successive attempts to outlaw war and guarantee collective security failed. Therefore, Aron, like other realists, is skeptical about the efficiency of international law and institutions (Lefort 2007). He criticizes the League of Nations and the United Nations (UN), a "pseudo-parliament" which does not prevent "world society [from remaining] anarchic" (Aron 1983a: 411). "The United Nations does not have the capacity to ensure collective security, a concept for which we vainly seek a meaning in the present world situation" (Aron 1954: 22). He points out the contradiction between two missions of the UN: stating the law and limiting hostilities. When, for instance, North Korea, which was not recognized by the UN, invaded South Korea, the UN proclaimed the North to be an aggressor, but quickly opened negotiations with it and eventually recognized it. Aron understands and shares the consequentialist logic of it – "Standing by a formalistic position, refusing negotiations with the aggressor, would have meant the risk of prolonging and expanding the war" (in other words, the UN prioritized the ethic of responsibility over the ethic of conviction) – but the fact remains that there was a "contradiction between legal and expedient action" (Aron 1954: 24). He does not underestimate the importance of the UN either. As usual, he tries to be realist, meaning some kind of middle ground between the excesses of cynicism, on the one hand, and idealism, on the other: Aron believes it is a fact, not a value judgment, "that the establishment of the U.N. has not essentially changed international relations", i.e., "the essential characteristics of relations between states as we have known them for the past six thousand years" (Aron 1954: 26). It means that the essential factor is not the UN but

> the great powers' will to act. It would be a mistake through false realism not to recognize the necessity of this framework. It would be an equal mistake, through false idealism, to seek in the Charter the secret of salvation and a substitute for force.
>
> (Aron 1954: 25–26)

The cosmopolitan goal of building some kind of "world state" is utopian for a number of reasons: because hostility is natural to man, it cannot be eradicated, only moderated; because to bind a community you need an external enemy (Aron is influenced by Schmitt's friend–enemy distinction); because states will not give up their sovereignty and it would pose governance issues ("Which men would hold the supreme authority which would force the submission of states?" Aron 1951: 208); and because the world is too diverse, "There is no such thing as world opinion on the political level" (Aron 1962b: 722). Against the nineteenth-century idea of a "world conscience", Aron invites us to

> recognize the facts: in international relations, there is no world conscience – first, because the world is divided into two camps, each adhering to its own system of values; second, because even in those countries that subscribe to our system of values statesmen speak and act according to expediency. So much is this the case that if one of them, against his interest, were to proclaim a policy based upon pure morality, all observers would look for cynical motives behind such a noble and surprising conduct.
> (Aron 1954: 21)

That is why Aron does not speak of an "international community" – an expression widely used today despite the fact that no one knows exactly what it refers to: certainly a wish, but is it a reality? Aron prefers to talk of an international "society", a less homogeneous term (there are tensions between communities inside any given society), which is also favored by the English school. "The international society" is the title of the first chapter of his last book, *Les dernières années du siècle* (1984a), where he acknowledges that *Paix et Guerre* dealt only with "the interstate system" and took war in its traditional meaning of "the armed confrontation between states", while the interstate system is only "a particular aspect" of such a society (Aron 1984a: 19). It is the most important one, and should be given priority in the study of international relations – like all realists, Aron is state-centric – but it is not the only one. There are three types of phenomenon – transnational, international and supranational – that are not part of the interstate system but influence it and are influenced by it. The international society, or "world society", is the whole entity, "all these relations between states and private persons allowing us to dream of the unity of human species" (Aron 1984a: 25). However, Aron continues, it is not "a real concept", because it has "almost none of the characteristics of a society" (Aron 1984a: 26).

He prefers the Kantian expression of "asocial society" (Aron 1967: 204), which well reflects the permanent tension between conflict and cooperation – in both external and internal orders (in the latter, Aron defends the Machiavellian idea of a conflictual pluralism). "The society of states is by essence a-social, since it does not outlaw the recourse to force among the 'collective persons' that are its members" (Aron 1966: 480). "As long as international society preserves this mixed and, in a sense, contradictory character, the morality of international action will also be equivocal" (Aron 2003: 608). However, and because it is a tension, not a victory of conflict over cooperation, Aron does not totally exclude "the idea of a unifying, universal project for humanity" (Cozette 2008: 24). He insists that starting from a Hobbesian state of nature – a state of war in an anarchic world in the absence of a global tribunal and police – does not "deny the possibility of a more or less radical transformation of interstate relations" (Aron 1970b: 58). He leaves the door open to a better future.

Ideas of reason

Aron believes there are signs that humanity is heading in a cosmopolitan direction: compared to the Age of Metternich (the Concert of Europe), the interstate system is now spread over five continents and allows the exchange of everything (goods, ideas, currencies, etc.) (Aron 1984a: 151). Diplomacy is global too, even "total" because *"everything* is related and actors employ *all* means" (Aron 1959: 94), and "the unity of the diplomatic field is, firstly and above all, the expression of unity, on the road to fulfillment, of the human species" (Aron 1959: 88). However, such a common diplomacy, which gives the impression that a "world concert" has replaced the Concert of Europe, is nothing more than "the superficial uniformity of certain techniques": that diplomatic practices which were originally European have become widespread does not make the world uniform. Western technology is widespread too, but ways of life remain very diverse. Similarly, in IR there is an "infinite diversity of customs". Therefore, "The idea of world unity is the expression of a desire or of an illusion" (Aron 1954: 23). However, although there is no world unity *yet*, it does not mean that we are not heading in that direction.

Aron still believes in "The spread of the industrial society, the unification of mankind" and wonders whether there is some kind of "predestined fate, as foreseen by Auguste Comte: an industrial society that would set an example for all human communities and unite mankind for the first time ever" (Aron 2002: 477). In other words, he believed we have entered what Kant called "the cosmopolitan situation" (Hassner 2015b: 199), while being more prudent and skeptical than Kant (for whom universal peace was "the hidden plan of nature for mankind") as "we have no proof that ... from now on the rational process will reign in peace ... It is just a hope, supported by faith" (Aron 2002: 485). Therefore, he is not a Kantian, but a realist with Kantian aspirations. At first sight, that seems at odds with the conservatism of realism, but not with Scheuerman's interpretation of the classical realists being more open than we think to a global reform (Scheuerman 2011). Here it should recalled that Morgenthau eventually supported a Kantian cosmopolitan world state (Speer 1968; Craig 2007) that even the most liberal realists like Herz and Aron considered utopian.

Understanding the compatibility of realism and idealism, in the literal sense of having ideals rather than the vulgar one of being naive, depends on the Kantian notion of "idea of reason", "an idea that can never be entirely realized, but which animates action and indicates a goal" (Aron 2003: 735). World community and perpetual peace, the former being the means of the latter, are ideas of

Reason: impossible to accomplish, but still useful to guide action. Contrary to many other realists, Aron cares enough about the horizon of a perpetual peace to wonder about its conditions of possibility, and finds three of them. In a 1957 lecture at the London School of Economics, they were: the reduction of the gap between the rich (the Western minority) and the poor (the African and Asian masses); the end of the Cold War; and the constitution of a world community of nations accepting each other – each condition implying the previous one(s) (Aron 1958b: 41). Five years later in *Peace and War*, these conditions were different: the adoption by all important states of a democratic regime; the existence of a real international community; and the abandonment of external sovereignty, i.e., of the possibility to take the law into one's own hands. Aron is fully aware that this is only an optimistic mental experience, and that in reality these objectives are counterbalanced by "the desire for power and pride in surpassing other men" (Aron 1958b: 53) – the "revenge of passions" to which his disciple Hassner devoted his last book (Hassner 2015a). This ambivalence is rooted in the "double nature of man, both passionate and reasonable" (Aron 1959: 158). Therefore, perpetual peace and world community are a horizon, of which Aron sees "improbability in the short run, and yet, in spite of everything, the remote possibility of achieving it", and he urges the reader not to forget "the duty of hope" (Aron 1958b: 60). "The end of myths should not be the end of hope" (Aron 1946: 260). At the end of his *Memoirs*, he confirms: "I continue to think a happy end possible, far beyond the political horizon, an Idea of Reason" (Aron 2010: 986).

Such optimism can seem surprising from someone who is usually considered a pessimist. There are actually two kinds of pessimist: the resigned ones, like most of the "hard" realists, and those liberal realists like Aron: "The pessimists of my kind want incessantly improve society, fragment by fragment. The only thing is that they do not have a global solution (those believing in an impossible regime are usually considered optimists)" (Aron 2005: 1019). Aron described himself as an "active pessimist" who lost faith (in the 1930s), but kept hope (Aron 1971: 21). In line with his usual habit of sublating all antinomies, he could be better described as an "optimistic pessimist". Not all realists are entirely pessimistic: Machiavelli and Weber were, but Marx and Aron have an optimistic component because both are philosophies of progress, for very different reasons obviously (Marx believes in the end of capitalism, while Aron is a liberal). Weber is a major inspiration but Aron also criticizes his "Darwinian-Nietzschean vision of the world", excessively brutal and pessimistic, which is the conceptual framework of his *Machtpolitik* (Aron uses the German word for power politics on purpose, as it has a nationalist connotation and a pessimistic inspiration; see Aron 1964b: 45). Being a realist is certainly seeing the world as it is rather than as one would like it to be, but also rather than as one fears it to be – "The pessimistic deformation, inspired by the desire to demonstrate as inevitable and indispensable a policy of power, being no less dangerous than the idealistic deformation" (Aron 1993: 236).

To what extent is Aron Kantian?

When he arrived in Germany in 1930, the young Aron was definitely a neo-Kantian pacifist influenced by his Sorbonne master Leon Brunschwig, and destined to work like him on the philosophy of biology. At that time, he was "a pure product of ... neo-Kantian rationalism" (Aron 2010: 150). Referring to that period in his *Memoirs*, he writes: "I *was* a disciple of Kant" (Aron 1983b: 267) – I "was" and not I "am", because he changed. When he returned to Paris three years later, after having observed the rise of Nazism, read Marx and Weber and discovered phenomenology ("In studying phenomenology, I too experienced a kind of liberation from my neo-Kantian training"; Aron 2010: 103), he was no longer Kantian nor pacifist, and reoriented his work toward social sciences, convinced that the century's destiny was built up around two main ideologies, Nazism and communism (Baverez 2006: 94). "National Socialism had taught me the power of irrational forces; Max Weber had taught me the responsibility of each individual, not so much with respect to intentions as to the consequences of his choices" (Aron 2010: 118). World War II, which Baverez considers as "the most determining factor", prompted a reorientation of his works toward strategy and sociology (Baverez 2006: 184) and disabused him of his early "Kantian optimism" (Davis 2009: 36; Hoffmann 1985: 21). At exactly the same time he consolidated his realist attitude.

Indeed, Aron later equated Kantian ethics with the ethic of conviction, idealism and moralism and vigorously opposed them all: when he criticizes Sartre, who "was often lost in political affairs, precisely because he was essentially a moralist" (Aron 1983b: 146), he means that Sartre "never understood the duality of politics ... he was into *Gesinnungsethik*" (Aron 1981: 1054); he was "spontaneously Kantian, he was concerned with the intention of the other, much more than with the act itself" (Aron 2010: 268). Aron's ethics, mostly consequentialist with maybe some virtue ethics aspects, is definitely not Kantian: his morality of wisdom is not a principled or rule-based reasoning. His realism and criticism of idealism and liberalism, i.e., Kantian institutions (international law and organizations), are even anti-Kantian. Pierre Manent, who was close to him at the end of his life and pleads for an Aristotelian interpretation of Aron,[2] even writes that Aron "made perfectly attentive readers who were not much interested in politics believe he was a Kantian. But Aron was the least Kantian thinker there is; he sought no horizon beyond politics, no 'kingdom of ends,' no 'pure morality'" (Manent 2015: 27) – an interpretation that Mahoney finds "quite right" (Mahoney 2016: 232).

However, this is probably too strong: while Aron's ethics and political theory is not Kantian it does not mean there is no trace of Kant *at all* in his philosophy. When, at the end of his life, he reminds the reader that he *was* a disciple of Kant, it implies he is not anymore. However, he immediately adds:

> there is in Kant a concept to which I still subscribe: it is the idea of Reason, an image of a society that would be truly humanized. We can continue to

think, or dream or hope – in the light of the idea of Reason – for a humanized society.

(Aron 1983b: 267)

Aron still believes in a number of Kantian ideals, but only as ideas of Reason: as unreachable guides for action. From that perspective, he is certainly more Kantian, that is to say liberal, than many other realists. Raynaud concedes that Aron is not a pure Kantian but sees him as a "post-Hegelian Kantian" (Raynaud 2002: 130), to borrow an expression from Eric Weil, whom Aron met in Berlin in 1932. However, because the Hegelian dimension does not capture the realism counterbalancing his Kantian liberalism, and because Aron was at least as much a "liberal disciple of Machiavelli" (Aron 1984b: 96) as a realist disciple of Kant, it seems more adequate to capture his hybrid position by using these two references: a post-Kantian Machiavellianism.

Notes

1 I am grateful to Gwendal Châton, Bénédicte Renaud-Boulesteix and Olivier Schmitt for reading and commenting on a previous version of this chapter. This chapter also benefited from comments at the 2014 International Studies Association, a 2016 workshop at the Maison française des sciences de l'homme and a 2017 workshop at the American University of Paris.
2 There are two main interpretations of the Aronian practical philosophy, the Kantian and the Aristotelian – Raynaud thinks that "both are true" (Raynaud 2002: 124).

References

Anderson, B.C. (1995), "The Aronian Renewal", *First Things*, March, 61–64.
Aristotle (2011), *Aristotle's Nicomachean Ethics*. Chicago: University of Chicago Press.
Aron, R. (1931), "Simples propositions du pacifisme", *Libres Propos*, February, 81–83.
Aron, R. (1933a), "Réflexions sur le 'pacifisme intégral'", *Libres Propos*, February, 96–99.
Aron, R. (1933b), "Lettre ouverte d'un jeune Français à l'Allemagne", *Esprit*, 1, 735–743.
Aron, R. (1946), *L'Homme contre les tyrans*. Paris: Gallimard.
Aron, R. (1951), *Les Guerres en chaîne*. Paris: Gallimard.
Aron, R. (1954), "Limits to the Powers of the United Nations", *Annals of the American Academy of Political and Social Science*, 296, 20–26.
Aron, R. (1958a), *On War*. New York: W.W. Norton & Co.
Aron, R. (1958b), *War and Industrial Society*. London: Oxford University Press.
Aron, R. (1959), *La société industrielle et la guerre, suivi d'un Tableau de la diplomatie mondiale en 1958*. Paris: Plon.
Aron, R. (1960), "The Quest for a Philosophy of Foreign Affairs", in Hoffman, S. (ed.), *Contemporary Theory in International Relations*. Englewood Cliffs, NJ: Prentice-Hall.
Aron, R. (1961), *Introduction to the Philosophy of History*. Boston, MA: Beacon Press.
Aron, R. (1962a), *The Opium of the Intellectuals*. New York: Norton.
Aron, R. (1962b), "Reflections on American Diplomacy", *Daedalus*, 91:4, 717–732.
Aron, R. (1963a), *Le Grand débat*. Paris: Calmann-Lévy.

Aron, R. (1963b), Review (in French) of Strachey, J., *On the Prevention of War* (Macmillan, 1962), *Survival*, 5:1, 39–41.

Aron, R. (1963c), Preface to Weber, M., *Le Savant et le politique*. Paris: Plon 10/18, 7–69.

Aron, R. (1964a), *German Sociology*. New York: The Free Press of Glencoe.

Aron, R. (1964b), "*Macht, Power*, Puissance: prose démocratique ou poésie démoniaque?", *European Journal of Sociology*, 5:1, 26–51.

Aron, R. (1966), "The Anarchical Order of Power", *Daedalus*, 95:2, 479–502.

Aron, R. (1967), "What Is a Theory of International Relations?", *Journal of International Affairs*, 21:2, 185–206.

Aron, R. (1968), *Democracy and Totalitarianism*. London: Weidenfeld & Nicolson.

Aron, R. (1970a), *Main Currents in Sociological Thought II*. New York: Doubleday Anchor.

Aron, R. (1970b), "Theory and Theories in International Relations: A Conceptual Analysis", in Palmer, N.D. (ed.), *A Design for International Relations Research: Scope, Theory, Methods, and Relevance*. Philadelphia, PA: American Academy of Political and Social Science, 55–66.

Aron, R. (1971), *De la Condition historique du sociologue*. Paris: Gallimard.

Aron, R. (1974), *The Imperial Republic: The United States and the World 1945–1973*. Englewood Cliffs, NJ: Prentice-Hall.

Aron, R. (1978), "Pour le progrès: Après la chute des idoles", *Commentaire*, 1978:3, 233–243.

Aron, R. (1980), "On Dubious Battles", *Parameters*, 10:4, 2–9.

Aron, R. (1981), "Sur mon éducation philosophique et politique (I): Entretien avec Joachim Stark", *Commentaire*, 140:4, 1042–1056.

Aron, R. (1983a), *Clausewitz, Philosopher of War*. London: Routledge & Kegan Paul.

Aron, R. (1983b), *The Committed Observer*. Chicago, IL: Regnery Gateway.

Aron, R. (1984a), *Les dernières années du siècle*. Paris: Julliard.

Aron, R. (1984b), *Politics and History*. New Brunswick, NJ: Transaction Publishers.

Aron, R. (1985), *History, Truth, Liberty: Selected Writings of Raymond Aron*. Chicago, IL: University of Chicago Press.

Aron, R. (1993), *Machiavel et les tyrannies modernes*. Paris: Editions de Fallois.

Aron, R. (1994), *In Defence of Political Reason: Essays*. Lanham, MD: Rowman & Littlefield.

Aron, R. (1998), *Essai sur les libertés*. Paris: Hachette.

Aron, R. (1999), *Main Currents in Sociological Thought II*. New Brunswick, NJ: Transaction Publishers.

Aron, R. (2002), *The Dawn of Universal History: Selected Essays from a Witness of the Twentieth Century*. New York: Basic Books.

Aron, R. (2003), *Peace & War: A Theory of International Relations*. New Brunswick, NJ and London: Transaction Publishers.

Aron, R. (2005), *Penser la liberté, penser la démocratie*. Paris: Gallimard.

Aron, R. (2010), *Mémoires: Edition intégrale inédite*. Paris: Robert Laffont.

Aron, R., with Heckscher, A. (1957), *Diversity of Worlds: France and the United States Look at Their Common Problems*. New York: Reynal & Company.

Aurélio, D.P. (2015), "'Moderate Machiavellianism': Aron, Machiavelli, and the Modern Machiavellians", in Colen, J. and Dutartre-Michaut, E. (eds.), *The Companion to Raymond Aron*. New York: Palgrave Macmillan, 231–243.

Barkin, S. (2010), *Realist Constructivism: Rethinking International Relations Theory*. Cambridge: Cambridge University Press.

Baverez, N. (2006), *Raymond Aron: Un moraliste au temps des ideologies*. Paris: Perrin.
Brand, D.R. (1995), "Realists Make Strange Bedfellows: Kennan, Kissinger, and Aron", *Polity*, 28:2, 277–283.
Breiner, P. (2011), "Raymond Aron's Engagement with Weber: Recovery or Retreat?", *Journal of Classical Sociology*, 11:2, 99–122.
Bruun, H.H. (2007), *Science, Values and Politics in Max Weber's Methodology*, new expanded edition. Aldershot: Ashgate.
Bull, H. (1979), "Natural Law and International Relations", *British Journal of International Studies*, 5:2, 171–181.
Châton, G. (2012), "Pour un 'machiavélisme postkantien': Raymond Aron, théoricien réaliste hétérodoxe", *Etudes internationales*, 43:3, 389–403.
Châton, G. (2017), *Introduction à Raymond Aron*. Paris: La Découverte.
Clausewitz, C. von (1976), *On War*. Princeton, NJ: Princeton University Press.
Coll, A. (1991), "Normative Prudence as a Tradition of Statecraft", *Ethics & International Affairs*, 5:1, 33–51.
Cozette, M. (2008), "Raymond Aron and the Morality of Realism", Department of International Relations of the Australian National University, Working Paper 2008/5, online.
Craig, C. (2007), "Hans Morgenthau and the World State Revisited", in Williams, M.C. (ed.), *Realism Reconsidered: The Legacy of Hans J. Morgenthau in International Relations*. Oxford: Oxford University Press, 195–215.
Csizmadia, S. (2002), "L'interférence du libéralisme et du réalisme dans la pensée aronienne", in Fondation Joseph Károlyi et al. (eds.), *Raymond Aron et la liberté politique*. Paris: Editions de Fallois, 195–211.
Davis, R.M. (2009), *A Politics of Understanding: The International Thought of Raymond Aron*. Baton Rouge, LA: Louisiana State University.
Fessard, G. (1936), *Pax Nostra: examen de conscience international*. Paris: Grasset.
Foch, F. (1920), *The Principles of War*. New York: Henry Holt and Company.
Guilhot, N. (ed.) (2011), *The Invention of International Relations Theory*. New York: Columbia University Press.
Hassner, P. (2005), "Raymond Aron on the Use of Force and Legitimacy", U.S.–Europe Analysis Series, February, Brookings.
Hassner, P. (2015a), *La revanche des passions*. Paris: Fayard.
Hassner, P. (2015b), "Raymond Aron and Immanuel Kant: Politics between Morality and History", in Colen, J. and Dutartre-Michaut, E. (eds.), *The Companion to Raymond Aron*. New York: Palgrave Macmillan, 197–203.
Herz, J. (1951), *Political Realism and Political Idealism*. Chicago, IL: University of Chicago Press.
Herz, J. (1981), "Response" to Inis Claude, *International Studies Quarterly*, 25:2, 201–203.
Hoffmann, S. (1983), "Raymond Aron (1905–1983)", *New York Times*, December 8.
Hoffmann, S. (1985), "Raymond Aron and the Theory of International Relations", *International Studies Quarterly*, 29:1, 13–27.
Kahn, H. (1965), *On Escalation: Metaphors and Scenarios*. New York: Praeger.
Kavka, G.S. (1978), "Some Paradoxes of Deterrence", *The Journal of Philosophy*, 75:6, 285–302.
Lang, A.F., Jr. (2007), "Morgenthau, Agency and Aristotle", in Williams, M. (ed.), *Reconsidering Realism: The Legacy of Hans J. Morgenthau in International Relations*. Oxford: Oxford University Press, 18–41.

Lefort, C. (2007), "Raymond Aron, Critic of International Law: A Reading of *Peace and War*", in Frost, B.-P. and Mahoney, D. (eds.), *Political Reason in the Age of Ideology*. New Brunswick, NJ and London: Transaction Publishers, 211–226.

Liddell Hart, B.H. (1941), *The Strategy of Indirect Approach*. London: Faber & Faber.

Mahoney, D.J. (2001), "Raymond Aron and the Morality of Prudence", *Modern Age*, 43:3, 243–252.

Mahoney, D.J. (2016), "Liberal and a Classic: Pierre Manent's Neo-Aristotelian Reading of Raymond Aron", *Perspectives on Political Science*, 45:4, 230–236.

Manent, P. (2015), *Seeing Things Politically: Interviews with Bénédicte Delorme-Montini*. South Bend, IN: St. Augustine's Press.

Maritain, J. (1942), "The End of Machiavellianism", *The Review of Politics*, 4:1, 1–33.

Maritain, J. (1944), *Principes d'une politique humaniste*. New York: Editions de la Maison française.

Montesquieu (1989), *The Spirit of the Laws*. Cambridge: Cambridge University Press.

Morgenthau, H. (1985), *Politics among Nations*, 6th edn. New York: Knopf.

Nelson, S. and Colen, J. (2015), "Statesmanship and Ethics: Aron, Max Weber, and Politics as a Vocation", in Colen, J. and Dutartre-Michaut, E. (eds.), *The Companion to Raymond Aron*. New York: Palgrave Macmillan, 205–216.

Raynaud, P. (2002), "Raymond Aron et le jugement politique: Entre Aristote et Kant", in Fondation Joseph Károlyi et al. (eds.), *Raymond Aron et la liberté politique*. Paris: Editions de Fallois, 123–131.

Scheuerman, W.E. (2011), *The Realist Case for Global Reform*. Cambridge: Polity.

Scheuerman, W.E. (2013), "The Realist Revival in Political Philosophy, Or: Why New Is Not Always Improved", *International Politics*, 50:6, 798–814.

Shapcott, R. (2013), "Phronesis, Ethics, and Realism", *E-International Relations*, February 7, www.e-ir.info/2013/02/07/phronesis-ethics-and-realism.

Speer, J.P. (1968), "Hans Morgenthau and the World State", *World Politics*, 20:2, 207–227.

Walzer, M. (1973), "Political Action: The Problem of Dirty Hands", *Philosophy and Public Affairs*, 2:2, 160–180.

Walzer, M. (2004), *Arguing about War*. New Haven, CT: Yale University Press.

Weber, M. (1994), *Political Writings*. Cambridge: Cambridge University Press.

5 Raymond Aron, war and nuclear weapons

The primacy of politics paradox

Christian Malis†

The analysis of war played a central role in Raymond Aron's overall thought, as exemplified by the Herodotus quotation he chose to have engraved on the ceremonial sword he carried as an elected member of the *Académie des Sciences morales et politiques*: "No man should prefer war to peace, since in peace sons bury their fathers, but at war fathers bury their sons."

But is it not a bit of a paradox, since he had not directly participated in nor held any real military role during World War II? After 1945, he devoted a considerable amount of time and energy to strategy, more specifically to nuclear strategy, primarily insisting on the primacy of *politics* in the understanding of war. And this may be the supreme paradox of his life as a committed observer. I would like to show that he was probably *a personal victim of the primacy of politics*: through his unconscious desire to play a role in French politics, he "overplayed" his opposition to de Gaulle's *force de frappe*, becoming marginalized in the French political landscape. In 1976 he then authored his masterpiece *Penser la guerre, Clausewitz*. Like his "role models" Clausewitz but also Thucydides, Machiavelli and Tocqueville, he succeeded as a theoretician inasmuch as he failed as a practitioner.

Nuclear weapons played a triple role in the edification of Raymond Aron's intellectual work: obviously in the comments he made and positions he adopted inside the nuclear strategic debate from 1945 to 1983, but also in the genesis of his theory of international relations and of war (culminating in *Paix et guerre* and in *Penser la guerre, Clausewitz*), and lastly in his personal biography as a "committed observer" of the French and transatlantic strategic debates.

Theory, debate and personal involvement were dynamically interwoven in his original "modus operandi" as a thinker. The thought and work of Aron, at least with regard to the areas of international analysis and strategy, have been built by the continual cross-fertilizing of three levels of thinking:

- news comments in the press (mainly *Combat* (1945–1946), then *Le Figaro* (1947–1977), finally *L'Express* (1977–1983) (Aron 2005)) or topical (and often polemical) books dedicated to contemporary hot issues (*Le Grand Débat* (Aron 1963), *Plaidoyer pour l'Europe décadente* (Aron 1977));[1]

- framework books proposing to "step back" so as to understand broad trends and propose some kind of "immediate philosophy of history" (*Les Guerres en chaîne* (Aron 1951), *Espoir et peur du siècle* (Aron 1957), *Les Dernières années du siècle* (Aron 1984), etc.);
- conceptualization through theoretical works or treaties (*Paix et Guerre entre les nations* (Aron 1962), *Penser la guerre, Clausewitz* (Aron 1976)), usually leveraging traditional political philosophers from the "Tradition" (Clausewitz, Machiavelli, Montesquieu, Tocqueville).

This method combines the analysis of "issues remaining current because they are permanent" with "answers from the direct observation of reality" (Aron 1965b). The structure of *On War* (theory, sociology, history, praxeology) is an analytical development of it.

The political condition of mankind was demonstrated in the twentieth century by two pathologies, the study of which involves two major aspects of Aron's work as a sociologist: the totalitarian amplification of politics (a subject for other thinkers like Hannah Arendt, Karl Popper, Karl Jaspers), and the hyperbolic amplification of war. Historically, this condition originated at the end of the eighteenth century when war, with the French Revolution and the Napoleonic Wars, escaped the constraints that laws and customs had imposed on it since the Religious Wars and the Thirty Years' War. Hence the need for Aron to "think war". How does one re-constrain war? How does one put the genie back in the bottle when nuclear weapons cannot be "un-invented"?

In addition, the specific French context of the strategic debate is one of a "renaissance" or "golden age" of military strategic thought in 1945–1965, followed by a relative decline due to the top-down imposition of nuclear orthodoxy, the consequences of the repression of the Alger Coup on military free thinking and expression, and the centralization of the political decision-making process.[2] Among the galaxy of French thinkers, Aron belongs to the "Pleiade" with Pierre Gallois, Charles Ailleret, André Beaufre, Lucien Poirier and Camille Rougeron.

In this chapter, I intend to:

1. reconstruct the historical development of Aron's thought on nuclear weapons in relation to history and his own biography;[3]
2. assess the role of nuclear weapons in the framework of his theory of war, especially his assessment of the modification of classical patterns of international relations and strategy;
3. explain Aron's specific "radar signature" and influence inside the French/transatlantic strategic debate of the Cold War.

This will enable us to understand Aron's own primacy of politics paradox in nuclear matters.

The war matrix

Exiled in London from 1940 to 1944 after choosing to join de Gaulle's Free French movement in June 1940, Aron was physically hit by total war: in Mézières, in the Ardennes mountains, the mere sergeant had to retreat (with the 9th Army of General Corap) while not participating in any fighting. In London he was rejected from an armored unit and accepted the post of editor of *La France Libre*. Present-absent from the war (while his friend Romain Gary was a war pilot and another friend, André Malraux, had fought in Spain in 1937–1938), he would, for the rest of his life, commit himself to *thinking deeply, usefully and concretely* about the phenomenon of war, which, for him, had an existential and frustrating significance.

Chroniques de guerre (Aron 1990a) collects his articles on war and strategy. He was educated in the analysis of military issues by S. Szymonzyk, a Polish former communist and expert on Clausewitz, author of *La Guerre des Cinq Continents* (Szymonzyk 1943). At this time reading Delbrück more than Clausewitz initiated him into the sociological approach to war.

London was the matrix of Aron's strategic thinking which was to revolve around three main themes: the evil of total war; the need for a comprehensive understanding of military phenomena;[4] and the unprecedented French strategic equation (a new relation to Germany; the focus on power replaced by the focus on security; the future of the empire).

In the aftermath of World War II a new "intellectual military generation" asserted itself in the French strategic landscape. Aron is very much linked to it through personal links (dating back to London) with Pierre Gallois, Camille Rougeron and General André Beaufre. This generation rejected intellectual conservatism, and numerous vivid military reviews hosted a very dynamic strategic debate. Most of these thinkers were related by a common goal to put an end to the evil of total war that resulted from nationalist wars and was responsible for the overall French decline since Napoleon. However, Aron's thought surpassed all others with its globality and philosophical foundations.

In 1945, he also started a long-lasting interaction with American strategic thought. During the conflict the United States became (and has remained) the new nexus of worldwide military/strategic thought for four main reasons: the war alliance between academia and the Pentagon, which hired 8,000 scholars to help fight Hitlerism from 1942 (this was the origin of the future "defense intellectuals"); the US technical edge on nuclear weapons; specialized think tanks like RAND; and the US political decision-making process.

Les Guerres en chaîne (Aron 1951) was translated into English as *The Century of Total Wars*, a title chosen in reference to the rapid succession of two world wars. But the French title evokes the phenomenon of atomic reaction. It is used to designate the amplification of violence that was so characteristic of the early twentieth century. In fact, for Aron, and contrary to Bernard Brodie, it was not the atomic bomb as the ultimate weapon which first drew the attention of contemporary thinkers of war. The bomb is certainly at the technical end of the violence spectrum, but at the other end there is the partisan, for example, those in Greece, Burma and China, armed with ideology and a machine gun. Aron's "philosophy of history" at the end of the 1940s announces the one he will develop later in *Dimensions de la conscience historique* (Aron 1965a): total war does not create long-term trends (decolonization, the emergence of socialism as an alternative mode of industrialization, the decline of Europe) but gives them an apocalyptic shape.

In 1945–1946, unlike a few analysts and much of the military community in France, Aron understood the uniqueness of the device used on Hiroshima and Nagasaki. However, unlike Brodie (1946) and Admiral Raoul Castex (1945), he had no immediate intuition of two decisive changes: the substantial revaluation of the defensive power of a small state, however low down in the industrial hierarchy of powers; and the concept of *deterrence* formulated early on by Brodie. Was the bomb to foster the rise of the World State? With regard to post-war speculations about the advent of a world state, seen as an unavoidable consequence of the development of atomic weapons (illustrated in the philosophical novel *Heliopolis* by Ernst Jünger (1949)), Aron remained deeply skeptical. In the face of the US-proposed international control of atomic energy, he immediately guessed that the Soviet Union would never accept.

Finally, the United States' possession of a few bombs (actually a tiny stock in 1947) was not in his eyes the decisive barrier to an invasion of Europe by the Red Army. The imbalance of conventional forces (200 land divisions for Moscow) originated in the too rapid demobilization of the US military by Truman, which could be opposed to the "anticipated mobilization" of the Soviet totalitarian regime (and had been also a hallmark of the Third Reich). The military problem in 1947–1948 was, in Aron's eyes, simple: the Red Army had the means to invade Europe and thus take it hostage, but should be prevented from doing so by the prospect of a general war with the United States. What was dissuasive was the *global war potential* of America, atomic weapons being at the time only the most rapidly usable means to destroy a few vital Soviet centers. This early perception of a stalemate was the basis of Aron's famous diagnosis: "Impossible Peace, Unlikely War" (Aron 1948). A turning point occurred in 1949 with the explosion of the first Soviet A-bomb (much earlier than expected by the Western powers) and the hardening of East–West relations (the sovietization of East European regimes, the Berlin Blockade, the civil war in Greece, etc.).

Aron seriously, although briefly, envisaged in 1950, with the outbreak of the Korean War, the possibility of a Third World War. He consistently recommended to Western powers realistic war aims that would not entail fighting the hyperbolic war and attempting the destruction of the Soviet regime: open the Iron Curtain, restore communications between Russia and the rest of the world, impose international controls on atomic weapons, assure certain rights to individuals of all nations.

"Saving war": from primitive to complex nuclear thinking, 1949–1955

Contrary to what is sometimes written, Aron *was not* limited in his knowledge to common sense and open sources: he was actually quite close to Colonel Pierre Gallois, who was a member of the NATO New Approach Group which devised a new defense strategy in 1954–1955 based upon the extensive use of atomic tactical weapons (MC 48). As such, Gallois was one of the few real experts (with Colonel Ailleret, who conducted military exercises on a purely French side) on nuclear matters in France. The Soviet Union's development of nuclear weapons in 1949 persuaded Aron that a new era was opening in military history, perhaps even in the history of relations between states. Until then the bomb had, in his mind, played a more symbolic than real role in the Western military system.

To him, the conflict between the United States and the Soviet Union resulted from a natural and traditional rivalry between a great continental power and a great air and naval power, one oriented to the domination of Eurasia, the other concerned with a global balance. The Peloponnesian War had set an example of such a mechanism; the challenge now was to stop the development of war as a "destiny" (*"la guerre-destin"*). In 1951, the United States still retained a double superiority in the number of bombs and the number of vectors (strategic bombers of the Strategic Air Command). Therefore, for Aron, the aim should be to bridge the gap in conventional weapons while slowing, through the atomic threat, Soviet aggression.

Aron actually put his hope in a "mutual neutralization". This notion prefigured deterrence but differed in that it was a reciprocal moderation in escalating violence *in the framework of a conflict* (General de Lattre had also had this idea as early as 1945). Aron advocated a truly classic European rearmament. This would be subject to the creation of NATO and raised the painful issue of German rearmament, as explained by Mouric in Chapter 6. This conviction foreshadowed his future advocacy of a European nuclear force, a perspective which would be likely to neutralize a Western defense strategy based exclusively on the atom and as such was cousin to the much criticized "peripheral strategy".

Aron's distrust of the overconfidence in atomic weapons ("atomic Maginot Line") continued, as did his advocacy of rebalancing atomic forces and conventional forces in Western military strategy. This mistrust resulted in the vigorous denunciation of the doctrine of "massive retaliation" formulated by John Foster Dulles in 1954.

In this framework, Aron's "primitive" theory, featuring the trauma of hyperbolic war, was marked with two enduring principles: first, atomic doctrine should adopt the principle of flexible response/retaliation; second, the West had to "save" the purely tactical use of nuclear weapons.

The general structure of the international system – "Hobbesian" natural rivalry between "cold monsters" doomed to be always suspicious, often fighting, and sometimes destroying each other – and the special nature of the Soviet regime (with its congenital obsession with secrecy) always made Aron ultra-skeptical of the prospects for disarmament. New diplomatic initiatives were, however, taken by the Truman administration in 1949, and France made a great effort to this end in particular under the auspices of J. Moch. This public diplomacy concealed, however, its own national atomic effort conducted through the CEA (*Commissariat à l'Energie Atomique*). For Aron, atomic disarmament was a *myth*, as was the symmetric concept of "peace enforced only by mutual terror" that was to be found in Pierre Gallois' theory.

The belief that technological advances could compensate for national decline attained a kind of mystique among some French military thinkers and players like Gallois and Ailleret. However, while both campaigned in political circles for a national atomic force, Aron still believed that such an achievement was far beyond the reach of French power.

1955–1960: the pivot

The year 1955 was a turning point in multiple ways. There were the first new steps in the atomic military revolution, which is too often restricted to explosive power. In fact, the nuclear revolution came from the aggregation of multiple technological changes that were almost completed by 1955:

- thermonuclear explosive power;
- fissile affluence, enabling the unlimited multiplication of atomic devices;
- miniaturization of nuclear warheads, enabling their tactical use on board missiles, cannons, tactical aircraft: for NATO, Matador and Honest John, then Thor and Jupiter IRBM missiles in Turkey;
- the development of low-yield bombs (kilotonic/subkilotonic) which, inserted into the Western military arsenal in the late 1950s, enabled a continuity between conventional and nuclear means. This was one source of Gallois' conviction that deterrence would prevail;
- the development of intercontinental ballistic missiles (ICBM). This was again a revolutionary technology, whose mastery by the Soviets was proved to the world with the launch of Sputnik in October 1957. It enabled the possibility of reaching remote, undefended territories thousands of kilometers away;
- the development of nuclear submarines (actually in the late 1950s).

The year 1955 was also a biographical turning point as Aron chose to return to his academic career, a decisive choice prompted by his election at La Sorbonne. His notoriety as an insightful international affairs commentator had begun to be established from the beginning of the decade. This was when he really started in this new area of nuclear strategy. Coming to academia (although continuing to write for *Le Figaro*), he had more time for in-depth reflection and began to study Clausewitz deeply so as to understand the real impact of nuclear weapons on war and international relations. Very early, in parallel with the Anglo-Saxon analysts including the British, he developed the basic concepts of the theory. It was almost in the same motion that he became a militant supporter of a European atomic force, which, in his mind, had become a military necessity since US cities were now in the front line.

The Suez Crisis confirmed a new trend that Aron had foreseen: the unwritten alliance of superpowers against total war, which was potentially detrimental to their allies and to aspiring new atomic powers. Nuclear weapons in this context should be the basis of the necessary strategic autonomy of Europe with regard to the United States, while the classic Soviet power on the Old Continent was weakened by the manifestation of centrifugal forces in the "people's democracies" (the Hungarian revolution, October 1956). This reinforced Aron's old skepticism against atomic disarmament, which showed a renewed vigor in French opinion in the period 1955–1960, while the debate on a French atomic force took off. But a small stock of bombs *could not* be a deterrent capability: in this regard, the impasses of British military policy (with the reform of Duncan Sandys in 1957) seemed to Aron unambiguous, whereas at the same time Colonel Gallois advocated the adoption by France of a military policy oriented toward nuclear deterrence and a small professional army.

The "great debate": an intellectual civil war in France

The year 1960 was again a biographical turning point. Aron started his career as a semi-official opponent to Gaullism. He vehemently criticized de Gaulle's speech at the Ecole Militaire (November 3, 1959) announcing the *force de frappe*, and showed himself to be a harsh critic on his Algerian policy. This is a role he would overplay and in which he would trap himself. At the same he was very close to – but probably also manipulated by – the Kennedy administration.

There was a cross-over in this respect with Pierre Gallois. Aron became very well connected in Washington while Gallois lost the military network he had had during the Eisenhower administration through NATO. *Paix et guerre*, initiated by a series of articles in *Le Figaro*, contained an overly large "History" part (actually dedicated to the contemporary nuclear debate) and also manifested Aron's desire to influence the strategic debate of the time, as well as his aspiration to be more "committed" than "observer".

The 1960s also saw a crisis in nuclear strategy inseparable from the NATO crisis regarding the level of autonomy of European nations in the alliance and the degree of confidence that could guarantee US security. Genuine parity in the superpowers' ability to destroy each other was reached around 1959–1960 with the entry into service of ICBMs. Maxwell Taylor's book, *The Uncertain Trumpet* (1960), warned of the risks of a weakening of the US security guarantee and of a "delinkage" ("*découplage*") between the United States and Western Europe. In December 1960 the subject of arms control arose with clarity. The insistence on the subject was new in Aron's work and commentary; it was, for him, a solution to the structural instability of the balance of terror. Furthermore, Aron was very critical of de Gaulle's new military policy: in his mind, a small national nuclear strike force could be neither decisive – because second strike capability was out of reach for a small power – nor independent (due to the lack of homemade early warning capabilities). At the same time and symmetrically, he was shocked by the US policy of keeping nuclear secrets from its allies (except for the UK), even though the fear of Soviet spies may well have inspired such a stance.

Aron broke with Gallois after writing the preface to Gallois' *Stratégie de l'âge nucléaire* (Aron 1960); although laudatory, this preface includes decisive criticism about five points of Gallois' doctrine:

- the "proportionate deterrence" theory;
- the elimination of limited wars due to the risk of escalation;
- the defensive potential of s small national strike force;
- the generalization of atomic weapons as an instrument of peace;
- the significance of conventional forces in Europe.

In 1960–1961 Aron participated in a decisive seminar at Harvard. There he was initiated into the methods and refinements of flexible response. He met with McGeorge Bundy, W. Rostow, Robert Bowie, Marshall Shulman, Max Millican, Jerome Wiener, Fred Iklé and other future members of the Kennedy administration. He therefore finished framing his own theoretical conceptions, writing the two last parts of *Peace and War*, even in advance of the public statement of Kennedy's new military conceptions. Aron was the only French strategist to benefit from such contacts: Gallois was isolated; Beaufre very centered on France; and Lucien Poirier (the future author of the French nuclear doctrine at the *Centre de Prospective et d'Evaluation*) had not yet produced much work on nuclear strategy. Aron would try to build a bridge between Europe and the United States, as he did in a more general way between American social sciences and the European sociological tradition. The Harvard seminar was a small intellectual revolution for Aron, providing a firm basis for conceptions which had been floating until then: the models approach convinced him that automatic nuclear stability in the Gallois mode was a myth; that the multiplication of nuclear powers was dangerous; that a gradual response was an answer to the Atomic Maginot line. These were also points of convergence with Beaufre which would bring the two men closer in the late 1960s.

Although Gallois is the invisible counterpart to and target of Aron in *Peace and War* (Aron 1962), Aron was opposed both to the simplifications of the optimistic nuclear school of thought and to the depoliticized models of US analysts. The primacy of political analysis was summarized in his favorite formula to summarize deterrence issues: "Who discourages whom? From what? In which circumstances? With which means?" In the absence of *experience*, the antinomy of nuclear strategy – stability at a high level necessarily results in less stability at lower levels of conflict – could not be resolved in a theoretical way. In fact, the atmosphere of the debate deteriorated in France in the early 1960s. The stakes were high, the memory of 1940 and the atmosphere of suspicion created by the Algerian War exacerbated the debate. This explains the incredible vehemence of

Aron toward Gallois in *The Great Debate* (Aron 1963). Gallois was presented as a "theoretician for a poor country". This atmosphere artificially amplified real disagreements between Aron and the government's line. As a matter of fact, General de Gaulle himself sought, although informally, ways to Europeanize the strike force, provided that French predominance would be preserved. And Gallois advocated a European force as well and even proposed to de Gaulle an agreement with Washington based upon the "double key" principle. With the publication of Gallois' *Paradoxes de la paix* (Gallois 1967) and Ailleret's "Tous azimuts" article (Ailleret 1967), the temptation of some kind of armed neutralism seemed to emerge in French strategic policy. This was strongly condemned by Aron. Ultimately, he appeared in the early years of the 1970s to be the leader of what might be called the "Euro-Atlantic" school of thought, which included supporters of a European nuclear defense, and of an agreement with the United States on the principle of flexible response. In this school we find Valluy, Stehlin, Beaufre (the latter much less European, but very much concerned about the instability of deterrence). Amid the triumph of the Gaullist military policy, their voices gradually faded. The stage was actually occupied by those who, following Gallois, believed in an end to war because of nuclear weapons, like Alexandre Sanguinetti, Léo Hamon, Charles Ailleret.

From the beginning to the end of this period the German issue was always present, immediately or in the background, to explain the most critical directions of the French military policy from the EDC (European Defence Community) to the national atomic program. With the strike force and the French withdrawal from NATO, this aspect of the problem became less acute, since France had now acquired a real margin of military superiority over its historical adversary, as well as a new symbolic stature. Aron did not support a "German Bomb" but in 1962–1963 envisaged a European formula, under dual control, allowing Germany to obtain atomic weapons. He personally advocated this solution when meeting with McGeorge Bundy and Kennedy in Washington. Basically unconvinced by Washington's obsession with possible reactions from Moscow, he would have liked France to be the spokesperson of German atomic aspirations. In the end, Kennedy tried to rebuild Atlantic unity through the Multi-Lateral Force (MLF) proposal, and later by linking European nations in the nuclear decision-making process through the Nuclear Planning Group. Since the beginning, Aron's perception of the German strategic problem had differed from that of General de Gaulle. In 1945 the *Combat* columnist had precociously proclaimed the end of the German hegemon ("1945 is the 1815 of Germany"), advocating a Franco-German reconciliation. Early in favor of the rearmament of Germany, he had been indignantly opposed to a "Plan Pléven", which was, to his mind, inspired by mistrust and the desire for control of the German neighbor. He also denounced this concern for French predominance in the *Rassemblement du Peuple Français*, the party created by de Gaulle in 1947, in the last campaign phase of the EDC. *Gaullo regnante*, he criticized both phases of the president's general German policy: the phase of Franco-German understanding, not in itself, but for its anti-American dimension, and because it was attached to an insufficiently inclusive conception of European unity; and the suspicion phase, from 1964, because he regretted what looked like the sacrifice of the consolidation of Franco-German reconciliation in favor of illusory prospects of a peace settlement in Europe by an agreement with the Soviets ("*Détente, Entente, Coopération*"). In fact, in his eyes Germany had always been the key European issue because it was central to the balance of power. Although, in this regard, in the 1960s he denounced the frantic search for a strategic agreement with Moscow, overall he shared with officials in Washington the general idea that the specific role of France vis-à-vis the Federal Republic should be to contain Germany by integrating with it, and by associating Bonn with high ambitions susceptible to averting the hope of a quick reunification: building Europe and containing the Soviet threat.

1968–1976: Aron's rise to the extreme of theory

In this period, Aron resembled more and more his role-model thinkers Thucydides, Machiavelli, Tocqueville, Clausewitz, and, in a different way, Delbrück, who had major intellectual achievements after failing in the realm of action. Furthermore, the general strategic context had evolved. Internal NATO relations had been pacified after de Gaulle's withdrawal from NATO's integrated command structures. The Nuclear Planning Group had been set up inside NATO, and the Ailleret–Lemnitzer Agreements regulated the French involvement in a European battle (using the French "*corps de bataille*" as an operational reserve for a counter-strike in Germany, August 1967).

In France passions had declined since the "*force de frappe*" was declared operational in October 1964. The two main stakes of the French strategic problem were, first, the appropriate type of alliance to maximize national security while not being too subservient (the 1940 syndrome). Answers had been found through the refusal of the British model (or a Nassau-type agreement with Washington), the withdrawal of 1966 and the creation of an independent strike force. The second stake was the type of military influence that France would be able to exert outside its frontiers. Gallois advocated armed neutralism (disagreeing with de Gaulle), and this trend was not absent from Ailleret's "Tous azimuts" article (Ailleret 1967). In this respect, President Valery Giscard d'Estaing (1974–1981) was to modernize the French military posture by increasing conventional budgets and creating an expeditionary force (which intervened in Kolwezi), but Aron did not participate much in this debate. Lastly, the main concepts of nuclear strategy had been identified (Aron 1968) and Aron was less excited by "pseudo-strategy" in the Hermann Kahn style. In his articles, he alternated between the Vietnam War and, to some extent, non-proliferation (NPT, Space Treaty) and arms control talks and agreements (SALT I 1972, SALT II 1979).

In 1976, French official strategic thinking had regressed, the orthodoxy being set out in a *Livre Blanc* (1972). Aron had missed the strategic duo that might have been possible with General Beaufre in the *Institut Français d'Etudes*

Stratégiques, which never really took off. Aron veered toward very speculative thinking, starting with the *Collège de France* lessons on a theory of military action and a theory of political action, based upon Clausewitz and Sun Zu, which announced *Penser la guerre* (Aron 1976). Aron read Clausewitz as an epistemologist anxious to discover the secrets of the theoretical elaboration of a policy area. This undertaking completed the intellectual project initiated by the *Introduction à la philosophie de l'histoire* (Aron 1938). "Existentially", he turned 65 in 1970 and had definitively renounced the temptation to be a truly active protagonist of history-in-the-making and politics, and as an intellectual he instead considered it useful to spend the rest of his life completing his work "for posterity". His only concrete incursion into the French strategic arena was a famous lunch in July 1974 with Giscard d'Estaing, Gallois and Beaufre about nuclear strategy, which did not achieve much of a result (Malis 2009: 562–564).

According to Raymond Aron, Clausewitz had been about to reach a perfect and comprehensive theory of war, making full use of the cardinal principle of the subordination of the military to politics, a theory which would therefore have intellectually integrated Sun Zu's "alternative" approach. The German writer simply had not had enough time to achieve this "great unification", which Aron considers himself to have probably reached. Indeed, Clausewitz insisted disproportionately on the "decisive battle" that was actually relevant to *one* type of diplomatic constellation (that of classical Greece or Europe of the nineteenth century, for example, where states respected the principle of their existence), while Sun Zu emphasizes non-military maneuvers or low-intensity military action because the destiny of the state could be decided with one lost battle. Comparatively with "neo-Clausewitzian" nuclear analysts (more or less all of those for whom nuclear weapons do not transform the asocial/Hobbesian structure of international relations), Aron derives from the author of *On War* a more profound idea, which is the "heterogeneity of the work and of its material" (Aron 1976: 1982–1983). This heterogeneity reaches its climax with nuclear weapons, a "limit case" which, by the same token, highlights the intrinsic political nature of an act of war. For Aron, two master ideas structure Clausewitz's theory: the principle of annihilation; and the supremacy of political rationality over the military instrument. These principles are linkable to the "grammar" and the "logic" of war. The second principle is also expressed by what Aron calls the "Formula": "War is the continuation of politics through other means", or better, "through the introduction of other means". Nuclear weapons confirm the latter principle and modify the meaning of the former. The ascent to extremes being inconceivable, the descent to mere armed observation becomes mandatory; nuclear weapons are weapons for *deterrence* (negative goal: defend, prevent the enemy from taking) and not for *action* (positive goal). Contrary to what was (erroneously) done by Roosevelt–Churchill in World War II, the West should therefore renounce absolute goals and the final destruction of the enemy in its rivalry with the Soviet Union, especially in Europe.

What has changed in the grammar of war?

If the nature of war remains unchanged, its grammar is altered in multiple ways. Nuclear war has its specific grammar – the basic concepts of first/second strike, counter-city or counter-force strategy, tactical/strategic use of weapons, etc. – the efficiency of which is linked in the last analysis to physics. But *concrete experience* is lacking, except the first and still unique case of Hiroshima–Nagasaki. That is why nuclear "models" by American analysts, despite their Byzantine refinement, remained for Aron pseudo-strategy, because they cannot be prescriptive, nor even provide forecast capability (the Cuban Missile Crisis scenario had not been contemplated). Regarding the principle of annihilation, which was now forbidden between nuclear states because of "Mutually Assured Destruction" (MAD), it actually remained terribly real and effective through *revolutionary war* (guerrilla techniques of popular war used for revolutionary goals), a type of war which is perhaps more dangerous for humanity than the "unfindable" nuclear war ("*guerre introuvable*") since it has the potential to "upset the world order" (Aron 1957: 296).

Lastly, Aron tried to analyze to what extent nuclear weapons transform the nature and morphology of war by answering three questions. First, is diplomacy transformed as a draft payment, compared to which war is a cash payment ("*les traites de la dissuasion*")? Aron rejected the concept of "compellence" by Schelling or the "pseudo-strategic scenarios/models literature in the H. Kahn style", since both blur the still valid conceptual distinction between peace and war. However, the "crisis" is not – contrary to what had been suggested in *Peace and War* – the nuclear-era equivalent of war in previous history. Could we then say that, for Aron, the handling of nuclear weapons is first and foremost "diplomacy", and that there would be a new "nuclear diplomacy"? I don't think so. As early as 1954, Aron had criticized the "brinkmanship diplomacy", of which Dulles was supposed to be a practitioner, then he rejected de Gaulle's conception of nuclear weapons as unusable for positive diplomatic goals. In fact, for him traditional rules of diplomacy had not changed – his deep analysis of the Cuban Crisis in *Penser la guerre* and then *Les Dernières années du siècle* (1984) do not evoke a "nuclear crisis" but a classical diplomatic crisis "under the nuclear shadow". Diplomacy keeps classical rules but takes into account weapons which forbid military escalation and the rise to the extreme of violence.

The quest for *stability*, the equivalent of "balance of power" in the nuclear age, requires arms control. Aron had been skeptical in *Peace and War* about the feasibility of setting quantitative ceilings for nuclear weapons, and of "freezing" nuclear competition between superpowers in the absence of *political* solutions to their conflict (specifically regarding the status of Berlin and more generally a peace settlement in Europe). He then looks uncertain in 1976, four years after SALT I. We will see that this uncertainty will transform into hostility to a process conducive to the strategic military superiority of the Soviet Union, with the risk of Europe's "Finlandization". Aron's praxeology relies on two main prescriptive principles: proportionality and communication. The proportionality rule requires making ante and stake proportionate ("*proportionner la mise à l'enjeu*"); the communication rule requires maintaining communication between enemies "so as to avoid mistakes by excess or by default". That is what Roosevelt (and Churchill) had failed to practice during World War II, demanding unconditional surrender from Nazi Germany and bombing its cities, thus leaving no recourse for the German people other than to remain bound to Hitler's undertaking, and offering Stalin the opportunity to dominate Eastern Europe. Truman began to understand the proportionality rule with the Korean War (refusing to use nuclear weapons and to increase conventional commitment in a theater which was secondary compared with Europe), and Kennedy implemented it in the aftermath of the Cuban Crisis (Red Telephone, withdrawal of Jupiter IRBMs from Europe). Ultimately, for Aron, nuclear weapons *do not* fundamentally transform the "ordinary course of international relations". In this perspective Aron proposes, even 15 years later, an interpretation of the Cuban Crisis as a "crisis involving the threat of nuclear weapons", and not as a "nuclear crisis".

In this respect, Aron can be distinguished from the school of European philosophers like Karl Jaspers, Jean Guitton or, more recently, René Girard, for whom a new era in the history of humanity has begun, requesting "a jump" and a "metastrategy" (Guitton), or the replacement of "understanding" (applied to the practical organization of the world) with "reason" applied to ultimate meanings and to freedom (Jaspers 1963).

1977–1983: final testament and last fight

Aron's participation in the strategic debate after *Penser la guerre* (Aron 1976) can be found in his weekly commentary in *L'Express* (1977–1983), but also in *Les Dernières années du siècle*, a testament book, comparable in ambition to Spengler's *Decisive Years*, in which he attempts a retrospective intellectual assessment 20 years after the "Treaty". The two main issues of interest are Aron's severe assessment of the arms control policy as conducted by Washington, and his final commitment to the "Euromissile" debate in the context of an unprecedented unanimity between the main protagonists of the French strategic debate with "restarts" in the late 1970s.

In the field of arms control, Aron's judgment in the 1970s evolved toward harsh criticism: arms control only served to conceal a sort of American military retreat. In *Plaidoyer pour l'Europe décadente* (Aron 1977), *Le Spectateur engagé* (Aron 1983) and *Les Dernières années du siècle*, he shows an identical anxiety: "A specter is haunting Europe: the Red army":

> Only the red phone serves the purposes of arms control, namely reducing the risk of misunderstandings, wars by accident. Other agreements tend to raise obstacles in the way of candidates for the nuclear club, rather than slow the qualitative arms race.

Here he is line with Gallois in *L'Europe change de maître* (1972).

On nuclear proliferation, his approach is more nuanced but still in continuity with the positions taken in the 1950s while A. Wohlstetter sparked debate on the "N+1 country": unlike Kenneth Waltz, Aron considers proliferation as globally dangerous. Aron, even though less hostile than Gallois, accuses arms control, in conjunction with the philosophy of "détente", to have led the United States and Europe to this very dangerous situation at the end of the 1970s:

> The cult of Détente for its own sake explains the official support granted to the Carter Administration by NATO's heads of State. In the same spirit they hesitate to displease Brejnev by criticizing SALT II. The deterioration of the balance of power generates visible symptoms of self-finlandisation.
> (Aron 2005: 188)

With the SS-20, Moscow seemed in a position to land the final blow on an Atlantic alliance whose leader seemed to have renounced leadership after the Vietnam disaster, and whose coherence seemed plagued by the German *Ostpolitik*. Again the real pivot was Western Germany: if Bonn renounced the Pershing and capitulated to the hundreds of thousands of people in the pacifist movement encouraged by Moscow's propaganda, the cohesion of Europe and of the West may well be lost forever. The "*découplage*" would open the door to Soviet domination in Europe without firing a shot, a goal tirelessly pursued by the Kremlin since the end of World War II. Less vehemently committed than in the 1960s, Aron was now in line with diplomats like F. de Rose, strategists like Pierre Gallois or journalists like Michel Tatu (1983), who endorsed the Euromissile option as a way to efficiently renew the flexible response doctrine of which he had always been a supporter (Aron 1984). This new alignment of French strategists, after the controversies of the 1960s, also took shape in the face of the "No first use" proposal made in 1982 in *Foreign Affairs* by the "Gang of Four" – McGeorge Bundy, Robert McNamara, Gerard Smith and George Kennan, pleading for no first use of nuclear weapons by the United States, a policy which would be compensated by an increase in Europe's conventional military effort.

Conclusion: moderation, wisdom, prudence

Concluding this journey in Aron's life and work, we find six key synthetic elements.

Aron's reading of Clausewitz and Girard's interpretation

Aron was confident he had achieved the Clausewitzian synthesis: war is the continuation of politics by other means, not only in the narrow sense but also in a broader sense: the nature of the inter-state context determines the types of wars for which the operational requirements must necessarily vary. In general, he always protested what might be called the strategic technicism. It is the sin of the theorists who disregard the policy context and overestimate the military factors (theories of revolutionary war in Algeria by French colonels; American analysts of the Kennedy team). His "finalization" of Clausewitz is opposed to Girard's (2007) own "finalization" which leaves no space between "apocalypse" and "reconciliation".

Wisdom and understanding of the State personified

Contrary to dangerous behaviors it is the "understanding of the State personified" which is the most conducive to the wisdom required in the nuclear age. In this respect, Aron is opposed to Graham Allison's analysis (*Essence of Decision*, 1971) from a descriptive as well as prescriptive point of view. The political understanding must not confuse war and politics – Lenin did of course, but still kept a clear conscience of the singularity of the means of organized military violence (and so did the Soviets). The head of state must keep himself above the compromises of bureaucratic policy highlighted by Allison; unfortunately, this was not the case with the negotiations of arms controls.

In a sense, popular war is more dangerous than the "unfindable" nuclear war

Despite Clausewitz warning about the "Wondrous Trinity" – "The problem is to maintain the theory in the middle of these three trends, such as suspended between three centers of attraction", in Aron's view the Americans overestimate the military term, the Soviets the political term and the Chinese the popular term.

However, the popular element, which can be found in revolutionary warfare, is maybe more dangerous than nuclear weapons to the international order since with popular/revolutionary war the pursuit of the enemy's annihilation remains primary. In this respect, the ultimate paradox of atomic weapons is perhaps to finally foster restraint in the use of the destructive power of technology, while guerrilla warfare, born in the eighteenth century as a popular answer to national regular armies (the Spanish War), reopens the possibilities of hyperbolic war. Passions, not weapons, make wars.

In retrospect, let us admit Aron was right. With the extinction of the Cold War's ideological conflict, another model of nuclear deterrence began to be established, based upon limited stocks and a general concept closer to "existential deterrence". But conversely, revolutionary war dramatically reignited with jihadism. Its specific danger is that, by igniting popular passions, jihadism spread the virus of civil war not only inside Islam (Sunnis vs Shia, Salafist vs Nationalist, Sunnis vs Sunnis), but also in Western Europe, Africa and even Eastern Asia.

Peace, prudence, faith

Balance of terror is not true peace. Here Aron is close to the position expressed by Pope John Paul II about deterrence in 1982. From the early 1960s Aron had anticipated the dangers of a world unified by technology and communication but spiritually disunited by what people "consider as sacred" ("*L'aube de l'histoire universelle*" in *Dimensions de la conscience historique* (Aron 1965a)). At the end of his life Aron came back to Rousseau's reflections on war, especially the "*fragments sur la guerre*" (Rousseau 1964). For Rousseau, peace is not only the photographic negative of war, but a "divine plenitude". For Aron, it is necessary to accept that we will always live in the shadow of war because of the *political condition* of humanity which translates into a legitimate and never-ending plurality (as long as history goes on). In this respect, he presents himself as quite close to the antique wisdom of Judaism and Christianity: war is avoidable, but real peace is not obtainable on earth; it will always come from a dynamic conquest (Mahoney 2002).

Aron's position toward the "French strategic school"

French strategic culture is singular and built upon one main directional line: how to preserve the mastery of France's destiny (B. Colson). However, there were two "hemispheres" in French nuclear thinking, Aron being the representative and even the *chef de file* of the Euro-Atlantic school with people like Beaufre or, later, François de Rose: historically this school has politically lost the game against the "sovereign school" embodied by Gallois or Poirier. More broadly, it sees, despite Aron's contempt, the French strategic school as a "provincial" subsidiary of the American school. It was more a kind of French branch of the "Atomic Brotherhood" born with Hiroshima, of which Brodie was an archetypal representative. Kaplan (1983) has underlined their common and mystical conviction to constitute some kind of small elite community, responsible for influencing world leaders (a mindset close to the Jesuits). US and most French strategists were united by a quasi-religious conviction that a new age had begun for humanity. In this respect, Aron is much more on the agnostic side.

The ultimate paradox: was Aron himself a victim of the primacy of politics?

Aron may well have been an unconscious victim of his desire to play a role in French politics. He then "overplayed" his opposition to the *force de frappe*, though he honestly recognized in 1966 that "probably no other course was possible". He had denied the deterrence value of a small strike force that threatens from one's own destruction, while also recognizing that "uncertainty" and "ambiguity" were psychopolitical elements inseparable from nuclear diplomacy. This is why, even with Aron, it is difficult to fully separate thought from existence.

Notes

1 A comprehensive view of Aron's positions on nuclear matters requires going extensively through the *Figaro* articles edited by G.H. Soutou (Aron 1990b, 1994, 1997).

2 The Fifth Republic is very much centralized at the executive level, while the Fourth Republic looked much more the US system with a strong involvement of the parliament enabling a very dynamic strategic debate, which culminated at the beginning of the 1960s with the nuclear "*Grand Débat*".
3 It is possible to adopt a conceptual approach and reconstruct Aron's conceptions on nuclear weapons and strategy starting from Clausewitz's definitions of war and Aron's final Clausewitzian synthesis in *Penser la guerre*, as Barry Cooper did in his very interesting "Raymond Aron and Nuclear War" (Cooper 2011). My own perspective will be primarily that of a historian and built around dates that we can consider as pivotal for either biographical or historic reasons, and usually for both.
4 For example: the sociological understanding of Germany's war capability through the concepts of enlarged strategy, anticipated mobilization, totalitarian revolution, then applied to the Soviet Union.

References

Ailleret, C. (1967, December), "Défense dirigée ou défense tous azimuts", in *Revue de Défense Nationale*. Paris: Revue de Défense Nationale.
Allison, G. (1971), *Essence of Decision: Explaining the Cuban Missile Crisis*. Boston, MA: Little, Brown.
Aron, R. (1938), *Introduction à la philosophie de l'histoire*. Paris: Gallimard.
Aron, R. (1948), *Le Grand Schisme*. Paris: Gallimard.
Aron, R. (1951), *Les Guerres en chaîne*. Paris: Gallimard.
Aron, R. (1957), *Espoir et peur du siècle*. Paris: Calmann-Lévy.
Aron, R. (1960), "Préface", in Gallois, P., *Stratégie de l'âge nucléaire*. Paris: Calmann-Lévy.
Aron, R. (1962), *Paix et Guerre entre les Nations*. Paris: Calmann-Lévy.
Aron, R. (1963), *Le Grand Débat, initiation à la stratégie atomique*. Paris: Calmann-Lévy.
Aron, R. (1965a), "L'aube de l'histoire universelle", in *Dimensions de la conscience historique*. Paris: 10/18.
Aron, R. (1965b), *Essai sur les libertés*. Paris: Calmann-Levy.
Aron, R. (1968), "Remarques sur l'évolution de la pensée stratégique (1945–1968): Ascension et déclin de l'analyse stratégique", *Archives européennes de sociologie*, 9:1968.
Aron, R. (1976), *Penser la Guerre: Clausewitz*. Paris: Gallimard (2 vols.).
Aron, R. (1977), *Plaidoyer pour l'Europe décadente*. Paris: Robert Laffont.
Aron, R. (1984), *Les Dernières années du siècle*. Paris: Commentaire Julliard.
Aron, R. (1990a), *Chroniques de guerre: La France libre (1940–1945)*. Ed. Bachelier, C. Paris: Gallimard.
Aron, R. (1990b), *Les Articles du Figaro*: vol. 1, "La guerre froide (1947–1955)", ed. G.H. Soutou; (1994), vol. 2, "La Coexistence (1955–1965)"; (1997), vol. 3, "Les crises (1965–1977)". Paris: de Fallois.
Aron, R. (2005), *De Giscard à Mitterrand (1977–1983)*. Paris: de Fallois.
Brodie, B. (1946), *The Absolute Weapon: Atomic Power and World Order*. New York: Harcourt, Brace and Company.
Castex, R. (1945, October), "Aperçus sur la bombe atomique", *Revue Défense Nationale*. Paris.
Cooper, B. (2011), "Raymond Aron and Nuclear War", *Journal of Classical Sociology*, 11:2, 203–224.

Gallois, P. (1960), *Stratégie de l'âge nucléaire*. Paris: Calmann-Lévy.
Gallois, P. (1967), *Paradoxes de la paix*. Paris: Presses du Temps Présent.
Gallois, P. (1972), *L'Europe change de maître*. Paris: L'Herne.
Girard, R. (2007), *Achever Clausewitz*. Paris: Carnets Nord.
Jaspers, K. (1963), *La Bombe atomique et l'avenir de l'homme*. Paris: Buchet-Chastel.
Kaplan, F. (1983), *The Wizards of Armageddon*. New York: Simon & Schuster.
Mahoney, D. (2002), "Dépasser le nihilisme: Raymond Aron et la morale de la prudence", in *Raymond Aron et la liberté politique*. Paris: De Fallois, 133–148.
Malis, C. (2009), *Pierre-Marie Gallois: Géopolitique, histoire, stratégie*. Paris: L'Age d'homme.
Rousseau, J.-J. (1964), "Fragments sur la guerre", in *Œuvres Complètes, III*. Paris: NRF/Bibliothèque de la Pléïade.
Soutou, G.-H. (2001), *La Guerre de Cinquante Ans*. Paris: Fayard.
Szymonzyk, S. (1943), *La Guerre des cinq continents*. London: Hamish Hamilton.
Tatu, M. (1983), *La Bataille des Euromissiles*. Paris: Le Seuil.
Taylor, M. (1960), *The Uncertain Trumpet*. New York: Harper & Brothers.
Université de Franche-Comté–Institut Charles-de-Gaulle (1984), *L'Aventure de la bombe: De Gaulle et la dissuasion nucléaire 1958–1969*, actes de colloque. Paris: Plon.

6 Raymond Aron and the idea of Europe

Joël Mouric

The European idea, or the idea of a politically united Europe, has been ever present in Raymond Aron's thought on international relations. Yet, his statements in the interviews collected in *The Committed Observer* at the end of his life betray some ambiguity (Aron 1981). While desiring that Jean Monnet's vision would materialize, he also claimed his faith in nationhood. Obviously, as he said in the opening of his 1975 lectures on Europe in Brussels, Aron had been "a veteran" of the European movement (Aron 1976a), to the extent that some authors could consider him a peculiar, yet fervent, supporter of European integration. Aron's memoirs and his articles on foreign policy in *Le Figaro* may lead to the latter conclusion. A more global view of his works, however, makes it clear that he considered the existence of nations to constitute the distinctive character of the European polity (Launey 1995). In that perspective, one should not forget that Aron, while investing much of his time in daily commentary on world affairs and politics, was and remained a philosopher who intended to think the world within the framework of a system. While his views on Europe might have been influenced by the conjecture of the time, his conception of Europe, once established, proved to be a very stable one (Bonfreschi 2014), which was based on the political reality of nations. In this chapter, we shall see how Aron's idea of Europe was shaped by his experience as a young French philosopher confronted by the threat of Nazi tyranny, then how he started to theorize the situation of Europe during the early years of the Cold War. In the last part, we shall see which "praxeology" – or conduct of policies and strategy – Aron recommended for Europe.

A European education: the European idea as a political myth

As a young *normalien*, Raymond Aron shared the pacifist ideals of his generation, shocked by the slaughter of the First World War. In his very first article, "What the university youth of Europe wants", he claimed that "to become aware of the interdependence of nations, of the common life, economic and intellectual, which unites European countries, this is not the pursuit of a utopia, but bringing thought and reality together" (Aron 1926). The young Aron was influenced by the spirit of Locarno and supported the efforts of Aristide Briand to build a collective security system within the framework of the League of Nations. In 1925, he attended a session of the League in Geneva, where he met Bertrand de Jouvenel. And from 1928 onwards, he took part in the *Decades de Pontigny*, annual meetings of the French intellectual elite organized by Paul Desjardins. Those meetings strongly supported Briand's collective security policies. And Aron was still vaguely socialist and passionately pacifist when he arrived in Germany in March 1930 as a lecturer, first in Cologne, then in Berlin (Baverez 1993). His "Letters from Germany", published in *Libres Propos*, Alain's journal, reflect his commitment to the *Verständingung*, the reconciliation between France and Germany (Stark 1993). Within a few months, however, he would witness the rise of national-socialism, with the NSDAP rising from 12 to 107 seats in the September 1930 *Reichstag* election.

The awareness of the Nazi totalitarian threat triggered a conversion from idealism to realism, whose first victim was Aron's ingenuous European leanings. In May 1931, he wrote: "The European idea is only the idea of economists and a few scribblers. It does not live in the soul of the crowds. It is a mere word, barely a concept, nothing like a myth" (Aron 1931: 222–223). This is the first occurrence of the concept of "political myth" in his writings. Borrowed from Georges Sorel, the notion of political myth refers to an inspiring idea, likely to mobilize people for action (Bottici 2007). The European idea was the first victim of Aron's conversion to political realism. The priority was now to resist, by force if need be, the rise of Nazi Germany, which he considered a catastrophe for Europe. In Aron's mind, the European idea, the idea of a politically united Europe, was no longer relevant. This is exemplified in his thesis, *Introduction to the Philosophy of History*, in which the possibility of a united Europe is discussed, but with blatant irony, against the Hegelian views represented by authors like Julien Benda (1933): "Let us admit", wrote Aron, "that history necessarily leads to a united Europe: comforted by that knowledge, the historian would contemplate without fear the last European wars, remnants of a finishing era" (Aron 1938: 179). Scepticism would now be the weapon of free citizens against the looming "era of tyrannies" (Halévy 1938). Between his return from Germany in April 1933 and the defence of his thesis five years later, Aron had become closer to Élie Halévy, the historian of England. Thus, he embraced the ideals of political liberalism and insisted that political freedom had to be defended at the national level, by the citizens themselves.

The defeat of France made Aron an exile in London for most of the war, from where, in the columns of the Free French journal, *La France Libre*, he would comment on the war and its aftermath. In those years, building the "New Europe" became the main motto of Goebbels' propaganda (Bruneteau 2003). And many French writers succumbed to the temptation of intellectual collaboration. Aron wrote against them and their treason. Among his targets was Alfred Fabre-Luce (1942) who, in the first two volumes of his *Journal de France*, had enthusiastically embraced the new Europe. In a series of articles, whose title was inspired by Maurice Barrès, "Au service de l'ennemi", Aron chastised Fabre-Luce and his fellow collaborators. Aron also contributed to publications funded by the British government in defence of the Free Europe against Hitler's Europe. Yet, through his contribution to the "battle of propagandas" and beyond it, he outlined his vision of the Old World. First of all, he did not believe in the inevitability of great spaces run by managers within the framework of a totalitarian state. Thus, Aron blamed James Burnham (1941), whose *Managerial Revolution* prophesied the victory of the dictatorships, and Carl Schmitt (1941), who, as the leading jurist of the Third Reich, had presented the Nazi great space as the German version of the Monroe doctrine.

The lesson from the war, if any, was the endurance of European nations. A totalitarian ideology, not nationalism in itself, had triggered the Second World War. In September 1942, while the Battle of Stalingrad was raging, he wrote, after a remark by the German historian Hans Delbrück about the wars of liberation against Napoleon: "people, autonomous nationalities, have now a vital strength that no violence can overcome" (Aron 1942). And shortly afterwards, he concluded that, after the war, "Europe [would] still be made of nationalities" (Aron 1943). As for German history, Aron first saw it as a continuum from Bismarck to Wilhelm II and Hitler. In 1945, however, once victory was achieved, he would differentiate between Bismarck and Hitler: the German Reich of the former was legitimate as a nation state; the Reich of the latter had been tantamount to endless war and unprecedented tyranny. What was now to be avoided was a power vacuum in the heart of Europe. The nagging questions of the postwar years were all about the fate of Europe, whose situation was critical. Can Europe unite? Can Europe feed itself? Defend itself? Those were Aron's questions after the end of the Second World War.

A vision of Europe based on the primacy and autonomy of the political

After the end of the war, Aron did not return to university, because he felt the temptation or the duty to get involved in politics. The tasks were huge, at the national as well as at the European level. They implied restoring democracy, dealing with economic recovery and defence. Aron's commitment was both national and European. At the national level, he joined de Gaulle's Rassemblement du Peuple Français (RPF) in 1947, with the intention to bring about a new intellectual and moral reform of France in the tradition of Ernest Renan (1871). First of all, the RPF was an answer to the Soviet threat, in a country where the French communist party, boosted by the prestige gained from his role in the Resistance, had become the strongest political party, sweeping almost one-third of the votes in the 1947 local elections, but also switching to insurrectional strikes and sabotage once excluded from the government. This is the political situation described in Aron's essay, *Le Grand schisme* (1948). But Aron was simultaneously resolved to do his part in the reconciliation between France and Germany. "The dream of my youth – French–German reconciliation – the ruse of reason gave us a second opportunity to achieve it: this one should not be missed" (Aron 1983: 251). More than ever, the relationship with Germany was at the core of his European commitment, because it was strategically essential. Against those of his countrymen who warned about an upcoming revival of German power, Aron claimed that 1945 was the 1815 of Germany. And, as he taught his students at the newly established cradle of the French political elite, the École Nationale d'Administration, "if one wants a Europe made of nations, inevitably, there must be a Germany". In his courses, Aron made it clear that Stalin would take advantage of the power vacuum in the heart of Europe. What he feared was the "balkanization" of the Old Continent, each nation torn by ideological strife and soon exposed to the terrors of civil war, like the Corcyreans in Thucydides' narrative. And in 1951, in *The Century of Total War*, Aron asked

> What is there that is essential in the European idea, as it was propagated in recent years? To my mind, it is a simple and obvious proposition, which Mr. Churchill grasped immediately and which propagandists and intellectuals have since obscured, namely, that Western Europe must build up its military strength, and that strength can only emerge from a reconciliation between France and Germany. *The European idea is useless, sterile, if it does not foster that dialog.*
>
> (Aron 1951: 413)

Therefore, Aron took part in the European movement. Approached by the liberal jurist and former Free French economist René Courtin (Bonfreschi 2014: 188), he joined the "Comité français pour l'Europe unie", associated with Churchill's United Europe Movement. The idea was to promote European integration from the top, starting from the political elite. And in May 1949, following the creation of the Council of Europe, Aron signed the "Appeal for the creation of a European political authority". Other prominent members of the Gaullist RPF, like Michel Debré and Michelet, signed the document (Bonfreschi 2014). The Appeal emphasized the Soviet threat and the urgency of political integration beyond the technical decisions then being implemented. It was based on practical defence more than idealism. Even though Aron became a member of the Executive Committee of the European movement, whose honorary presidents were Blum, Churchill, De Gasperi and Spaak, he nevertheless made his scepticism clear after attending the Congress of Europe in the Hague, presided over by Churchill in 1948: the Congress was mostly a meeting of former leaders and lacked political legitimacy (Mouric 2013: 14).

Practically, Aron embarked on a series of lectures and speeches, mostly in Austria and occupied Germany. The speeches were intended to bring about reconciliation, and to unify the Europeans, by praising the benefits of Western integration compared to the Soviet rule. He spoke in Vienna in 1946, then in several German cities. Those writings can be understood in two ways, which sometimes causes confusion about Aron's conception of Europe. On the one hand, they were part of the propaganda in support of Western integration. The political myth of Europe was the only available option to counter the spread of the communist ideology. Of course, the Germans wanted something else, they wanted the reunification of their country. Aron's forthright answer was that it was not possible, and would not be in the foreseeable future. This argumentation represents the bulk of his speech to German students in Frankfurt on 30 June 1952. Stalin had just issued his notes proposing reunification in exchange for neutrality. Against those deceitful proposals, Aron made a plea for European integration and freedom. And his conclusion is arguably the most striking piece of pro-European oratory he ever produced:

> The European community or the Atlantic community is not a motto for the enthusiasm of one single day. It is the final aim of the effort that gives sense to a whole life or assigns a goal to a generation.
>
> (Aron: 1952a)

Aron, however, had bluntly outlined the limits of the European myth just two years before in *The Century of Total War*, claiming that

> The European idea is empty, it has neither the transcendence of Messianic ideologies nor the immanence of concrete patriotism. It was created by intellectuals, and that fact accounts at once for its genuine appeal to the mind and its feeble echo in the heart.
>
> (Aron 1954: 316)

Yet, Europe should not only be considered in terms of statistics. Aron did not forget the families deprived of a father, killed, missing in action, or POW, presumably for many years. He alluded to the German cities laid in ruins by the Allied zone bombings. In Burkean tones, he announced that

> The recovery of Europe, that shall be discussed, is thus neither purely material, not entirely moral. It would be nonsense to wonder about the spiritual inspiration of tomorrow's Europe while forgetting the families without a man, the homes without a fire and the misery of the crowds. It would be nonsense to calculate the number of working hours required to rebuild some neighbourhood of Berlin or Frankfurt, thus forgetting that the past that lived in those old stones is gone for ever, neglecting the risk that in the new buildings a new society may appear, without any organic link to its tradition.
>
> (Aron 1954: 64–65)

The destruction of cultural and political traditions might create a vacuum that could benefit new tyrannies. Europe had to live in "a kind of dialectic tension" between the nostalgic remembrance of the imperial tradition and the pride of national peculiarities: "Europeans miss their vocation if they follow only one of those concepts, since the truth of each always depend on the other one" (Aron 1954: 67). Though it was no easy task to define the European identity, Aron tried to do it by emphasizing the principles of political liberalism: "As Max Weber said: without a minimum of human rights, we can't live any longer. I believe that totalitarianism denies that minimum" (Aron 1954: 77).

At the global level, what Europeans had in common in 1945 was their decline. In an article for the *Bulletin of the Atomic Scientists*, Aron stated that the bomb, then the monopoly of the two superpowers, epitomized the decline of Europe. And against Leo Szilard (1949), one of the inventors of the bomb, who recommended the neutralization of Europe as the best means to preserve peace, Aron made the case for the reinforcement of the Atlantic alliance. This, he went on, would be the decisive test of the willingness of Western Europeans to defend their freedom (Aron 1950). While many intellectuals believed in European neutrality, Aron always strived against that illusion. Some observers mistook him for a warmonger. Yet Aron's formula to define the situation of the Cold War, "peace impossible, war unlikely", was based on the assumption that European unity – despite the claims of the neutralists, who were asking for a common withdrawal of the great powers – was impossible and would remain beyond reach for a long time:

> I hear the objection: which other method do you see to restore European unity? Let's say it bluntly: for the time being, there is none. The restoration of European unity may be the aim of the second phase. The aim of the first is to stop the expansion of sovietism and to rebuild the economy of the countries westwards from the Iron Curtain. Let's not endanger the fulfilment of that task by dreaming of a momentarily inaccessible peace.
> (Aron 1948: 49–50)

The main obstacle to European unity was indeed the Soviet domination of Central and Eastern Europe, which had begun in 1946 with the sovietization of East Germany. One of his most decisive battles was when Aron defended the Atlantic pact against Etienne Gilson, who believed it to be dangerous for the Europeans, since there was no guarantee that the United States would fight for Europe. Gilson proposed a heavily armed neutrality as an alternative. And at the beginning, de Gaulle, who still believed in US isolationism, agreed with him. Aron (1952c) fought back in *Liberté de l'esprit*, the Gaullist journal directed by Claude Mauriac. He first emphasized that a neutral Europe would be militarily weak. Only the US commitment in Europe – already existing, but strengthened by the alliance – could re-establish the balance of power at the regional level. Then, he blamed Gilson for mistaking two things: on the one hand, the preference for a democratic socialism, equally distant from the Soviet model and the American economic liberalism; on the other hand, the place that Europe should have within the system of international relations. If the former position was legitimate, the choice of neutrality was a mistake, for Stalinist communism only knew friends or enemies. Aron's plea against European neutrality paved the way towards his criticism of ideologies that would lead, in 1955, to *The Opium of the Intellectuals*. Yet, it also had immediate and far-reaching consequences. Claude Mauriac (1970) wrote that de Gaulle, after reading Aron's article, changed his mind and granted him his full support. Starting from the top, Aron had decisively influenced the whole Gaullist movement towards accepting the Atlantic alliance, at a time when France was the most reluctant nation among the Allies.

While Aron's thought was obviously based on the primacy of the political and of foreign policy, he did not neglect the economy, which was part of the balance or imbalance of power. In *France and Europe*, arguably his very first essay aimed at the American political elite, he described the common destiny of Western European nations in the aftermath of the Second World War, starting from a quotation by Marshall Smuts, the South African leader, who had claimed that "France has disappeared, for a generation at least, as a great power":

> Isolated, the countries of Europe are weak and powerless. None has any longer the resources necessary for a great army; none offers any longer a market for mass production; none can any longer afford the luxury of an independent diplomacy. Faced with the Soviet threat, they will stand or fall together. Supposing a Sovietized France, Germany would soon succumb in turn. If the Soviet zone extended to the Rhine, it would reach the Atlantic a few months or a few years later. The global constellation consolidates even those who regarded themselves as hereditary enemies. The 250 million Europeans of the West, insofar as they remain divided into national states, prisoners of parochial quarrels, will remain a curiosity of history. United, they would raise themselves to the level of the strongest.
> (Aron 1949b: 8–9)

Though a determined supporter of European integration, Aron did not underestimate the difficulties. Back in 1949, they were political: "Germany cannot be integrated in a federal Europe by dictating conditions inspired by the tradition of power politics" (Aron 1949b: 11). The difficulties were also at the economic level, since the methods implemented by the European countries were often at odds: "the European economic organization has retained the idea of planning rather than unification" (Aron 1949b: 14).

For Aron, the apogee of European free trade had taken place prior to the First World War. Therefore, Aron was sceptical of the idea of the Schuman Plan. While he wholeheartedly supported the reconciliation between France and Germany, he was not convinced that the European Coal and Steel Community could work. Even though he had, two years before, claimed that Europe needed a project for the steel industry, not national plans, Aron believed that only a political decision could bring about political unity, so he was always reluctant to endorse Jean Monnet's method of functional integration. "Oddly enough", wrote Aron,

> when it comes to European unity, one would relentlessly ask for the most while the least cannot be achieved. We dream of customs union or economic

> unities while we can neither restore the convertibility of currencies nor abolish quantitative restrictions or lower customs duties. All too often, the gossip on European unity is used as an alibi for inaction ... We shall only advance towards integration if each country puts its affairs in order beforehand.
>
> (Aron 1952b: 21–22)

As ever, Aron would come back to the geopolitical situation and the primacy of foreign policy:

> The unity of the Six would be a mere caricature of European unity, for Europe cannot stop in the midst of Germany. I fear that all too often one talks about European unity, Europe of the OEEC or Europe of the Schuman Plan to forget the division of Germany and Europe. As long as the Iron Curtain does exist, there will be nothing but expedients. The cooperation of the Six, with or without a federation, is one of those expedients – expedients whose urgency may be emphasized, yet not mistaken for the genuine aim.
>
> (Aron 1952b: 21–22)

Aron would repeat the same objection when the EEC came under discussion. Could a political entity be derived from a common market? As a matter of fact, Aron was very consistent in his criticism of the Monnet method. The critical moment had been, from his point of view, the failure of the European Defence Community (EDC), rejected by the French parliament on 30 August 1954. When the project arose in 1950, Aron wanted a rearmament of Western Europe and his reaction was moderate. Nevertheless, he pointed out that the project did not take into account the diverging interests of the EDC members: France was still an imperial and Mediterranean power, while the Federal Republic of Germany was mostly concerned about the Soviet threat and a hypothetical reunification. Above all, the idea of a European constitution, embedded in the EDC project, worried him, because there was no European people, so that the consent of the governed was not guaranteed at all. Therefore, he eventually developed an all-out attack against Jean Monnet's approach. On 30 August 1954, to Aron's relief, the EDC was rejected by the French National Assembly. The alternative, the creation of the West German *Bundeswehr* integrated into NATO, was, in Aron's eyes, much more convincing for the defence of Europe. Henceforth, he thought that Monnet's project was dead (Aron and Lerner 1956). The European climax was over. As the situation was much less tense after the death of Stalin and the conclusion of the EDC debate, Aron returned to the university. There, he would work as a sociologist, but also as an international relations theorist and expert in strategy.

A praxeology for Europe

In "Nations and Empires", a 1957 article, Aron questioned the very idea of European integration, going so far as to evoke a European fanaticism:

> A federal state requires more than passive consent. Yet, it looks like national feelings were stronger than the European feeling. The fanatics of the European ideal hold nationalisms for negative because they hinder the realization of their ideal. Those feelings are also negative in regard to communism, whose spread is seemingly equal to the expansion of the Soviet empire. Obstacles to a democratic federation of the Western European states, national feelings are also an obstacle to communism, whose purported universalism hides the leading role of the Russian state. They are, for now, conservative, thus irritating for those who are looking towards the future.
>
> (Aron 1961: 173)

So, Aron not only doubted the possibility of a European federal state, because he did not see any European patriotism appear, he also remembered that nationalisms remained the main force that could stir up peoples against Soviet imperialism. This analysis directly followed from his wartime reflections in *La France Libre*. The nations had thwarted Hitler's Europe. Likewise, they were able to impede the sovietization of Central and Eastern Europe. Aron admired the Hungarian revolution of 1956: "What had been deemed impossible, a people overthrowing a totalitarian state all by himself, suddenly became reality. The mottos of 1848, liberty, nation, justice, were recovering, against the bureaucratic tyranny and the Russian domination, their eternal freshness" (Aron 1957a). Therefore, Aron was reluctant to condemn nationalism as such. While the abuses of chauvinism should be avoided, a moderate nationalism based on the historical existence of nations as political communities was legitimate.

Conversely, the French philosopher was more hostile than ever to any philosophy of history or ideology that would claim knowledge of the sense of history. Since the 1930s, he had consistently criticized the "confidants of Providence". It is no coincidence that, in the same year that the Treaty of Rome was signed, he wrote this provocative passage in *Espoir et peur du siècle*:

> Was the conquest of Europe by the Third Reich as much or less justified than that of the Classical world by Rome? Nothing forbids us to imagine that our great-nephews, living in a Europe unified by Hitler's perverse genius, would have blessed, within a few centuries, the one who, at the price of tens of million corpses would have enabled Europe, now free of internecine wars, to maintain her rank.
>
> (Aron 1957b: 209)

Accordingly, Alfred Fabre-Luce could write to Aron about his lukewarm stance on the Common Market: "You are denying your enthusiasm".[1] In the following years, Aron would acknowledge the economic success of the EEC, though underlining that the establishment of the Fifth Republic in France had been the political condition of that success. Besides, Aron developed his views on Europe within his theoretical *magnum opus*, published in 1962: *Peace and War: A Theory of International Relations*.

There, Aron claims that "war belongs to all eras and all civilizations" (Aron 1962: 157). If war is always part of the reality of international relations, the discrimination between friends and foes cannot be ignored. And Aron's views on Europe in *Peace and War* reflect that pessimistic realism:

> It is against the threat of the USSR that the Atlantic bloc has forged a common will. It is to recover some independence towards the Great powers that European states try to unite. Should the conflict between the Giants vanish by the stroke of a magic wand: what would remain of European integration or of the Atlantic bloc?
>
> (Aron 1962: 740–741)

The fundamental objection of Aron towards Jean Monnet's project was always the same: European unity must be sought for itself, it is indispensable neither to economic prosperity, for which a free trade zone could suffice, nor to defence, for which the Europeans had decided to rely on the Atlantic alliance. As a matter of fact, neither of the "fathers of Europe", Jean Monnet and Robert Schuman, was even mentioned in *Peace and War*, where, on the contrary, one can find the names of Charles de Gaulle, Konrad Adenauer and Winston Churchill, each statesman having presided over the destiny of his own nation in critical circumstances. Notwithstanding the pessimistic or negative tone of his remarks, Aron believed in the possibility of Europe preserving its freedom while avoiding destruction. He summed it up in the formula "to survive is to win". Based on his interpretation of Clausewitz, derived from Delbrück's, it was intended to confront the problems of European defence while avoiding the dangers of escalation and total war, which were, as theorized in Clausewitz's treatise, inherent to war in itself. Aron argued that war is, above all, a political fact. Hence the possibility of waging a limited war. In 1955, Aron had thoroughly read Clausewitz's treatise and in *Peace and War* he proposed a strategy for Europe, within the context of the Cold War and nuclear deterrence. Later, in the 1980s, shortly after Aron's death, the American neoconservatives would reject those views (Pipes 1984).

While Aron did not believe in the birth of a European federal state, he was nevertheless determined to defend the peaceful relations that Europe owed to its integration. That is why, in 1966, he reacted against de Gaulle's sovereign moves: France's empty chair in the EEC, the withdrawal from NATO and the "great design" towards the Soviet Union. Monnet then asked Aron to join him in a common action. But that proposal, the only one ever, was a dead end. In a letter to Pierre Chatenet, then chairman of Euratom, Aron stated that his main idea was not that Europe coincided with the community of the Six, nor that the common institutions were necessary to prosperity and peace. "My main conviction", he wrote,

> is that international relations of a rather new kind had gradually developed within the Western world, particularly among the Six. I fear that, for

multiple reasons (the policy of the French government is only one among others), we are coming back to relations of a more traditional kind, which I cannot be delighted at.[2]

For the same reason, Aron criticized the events of May 1968, for he believed that the youth, in a state of denial, was rejecting historical awareness. His criticism peaked in 1977 in his essay *In Defence of Decadent Europe*, which drew a comparison between prosperous Western Europe, in which traditional authorities – the army, the church – were being increasingly challenged, and Eastern Europe, under the Soviet yoke, in which economic achievements were far behind, but discipline more firmly established in favour of the leaders. Western Europe was experiencing an ominous crisis of civilization. Therefore, in 1976–1977, Aron backed Alexander Solzhenitsyn in his polemic against Jean-Paul Sartre and Simone de Beauvoir. The Russian dissident blamed the French intellectuals for their support of the Soviet Union and their ignorance of the political consequences of their ideological stance. Solzhenitsyn was not a liberal, but he bluntly reminded the Europeans of the political realities. Aron's article was published in the 100th issue of *Survey* (Aron 1977b). Sir Nicholas Henderson, the British ambassador in Paris, sent him, along with his own congratulations, a review by Bernard Levin in *The Times*, who praised: "A fierce, yet telling study on Sartre by Aron who has been, for so long, the honour of Europe".[3] Thus, Aron was doing his part in the moral rearmament of the West. The creation of *Commentaire* in 1978 – a journal committed to the advancement of European integration – had the same aim.

At the strategic level, Aron was a staunch opponent of the Conference of Helsinki in 1975. As early as 1962, in *Peace and War*, he had warned against the illusion of collective security policies, whose limits were epitomized by the League of Nations. With hindsight, one could argue that Aron underestimated the effectiveness of the human rights requirements embedded in the Helsinki Final Act, which would provide the dissidents with a powerful international leverage against the communist regimes. What Aron doubted was the determination of the Westerners not to recognize the status quo in Europe. And, as it was based on the pledge to respect the existing borders, it looked like Helsinki was tantamount to the recognition which Aron believed should not be conceded.

A second test of the willingness of the Europeans to defend themselves was the Euromissile crisis. By 1976, the Soviet Union had deployed new SS-20 medium-range ballistic missiles. Mobile and powerful, the SS-20 could target NATO headquarters but could not reach American territory, so that it threatened to unlink the United States from its European allies. In 1979, NATO took a "double decision": unless the SS-20s could be removed by negotiation, in 1983 NATO would deploy 572 "Euromissiles" in Europe. The peace movements organized huge demonstrations, especially in the Federal Republic of Germany where the motto "better red than dead" was becoming popular. Aron, who had just sided with West Germany when the Bonn Republic was suffering the attacks of the Baader-Meinhof group, once again committed himself and called for the implementation of the double decision. More than ever, the Cold War was a test of will. Aron died on 17 October 1983. His last article was in support of deploying the Pershing missiles. When he died, Aron did not foresee the coming collapse of the Soviet Union. In 1983, its new leader was Yuri Andropov, whose determination to reform and strengthen the system Aron did not doubt. Even though he was aware of the historical significance of the election of a Polish pope in 1978, with whom he discussed the situation of Europe, Aron did not believe that Solidarnosc, the Polish movement led by Lech Walesa, would end differently from what had happened before in the people's democracies. When General Jaruzelski came to power, he thought that, once again, "normalization" had prevailed.

Aron, certainly, was not a prophet of European unity. Nor was he a Eurosceptic, a word that has flourished since the 1992 Maastricht Treaty. Yet, his thought, opposed to any philosophy of history, belongs to the category of scepticism. As early as 1956, he had denounced, as we have seen, what he called European fanaticism. In 1975 in Paris, he warned European statesmen that the passive consent of the peoples of Europe to the process of integration was not guaranteed forever:

> As a matter of fact, the Community no longer works, it can only progress through the will of the leaders. Should that will falter, and obstacles would become impossible to overcome. Should it disappear, only an international bureaucracy would remain.
>
> (Aron 2005)

Foremost as ever was defence and the acceptance of his duties by the citizen. One had to make the difference between the individual as economic or political subject. In 1974 in New York, Aron had reminded his audience of the political tradition of Europe, in which the citizen must participate in national defence. This implied a condemnation of conscientious objectors as well as the claim that a multinational citizenship was hardly possible. Based on the political philosophy of Edmund Burke, Aron would claim that even human rights could not be defended, unless some states decided to fight for them and their citizens risked their own lives for that cause. As an example, he recalled the fate of the European Jews during the Second World War, many of whom had died while others, like himself, were forced into exile after having lost their civil rights. As a political philosopher, Aron believed in education. But the events of May 1968 had shown that the university itself could be impeded from accomplishing its mission if ideologies replaced the transmission and creation of scientific knowledge. *In Defence of Decadent Europe* was intended as a vindication of Western Europe's superiority compared to the "other Europe" in the East and against her self-deprecating tendencies. Successful though the book might be, Aron did not place much importance on it. His main pride was *Clausewitz, Philosopher of War*, which, in turn, we may consider his great book on Europe.

Against the possible loss of political awareness in Europe, Aron chose to rely on Clausewitz, whom he considered a European citizen, even a liberal conservative. Clausewitz, indeed, wrote Aron, had undergone a similar experience to his when his country was defeated by Napoleon in Jena, and later on, when Prussia became Napoleon's ally and some Prussians, among them Clausewitz, joined the army of the tsar to go on fighting against Napoleon. And Clausewitz, who had perfectly described the dangers of military escalation, was also the theorist who stated that the *Bürger* or citizen was ultimately responsible for the defence of his homeland. *Clausewitz, Philosopher of War* ends with a reminder to Europeans who might be tempted to forget their duties:

> French, Jewish by birth, how could I forget that France owes its liberation to the strength of its allies, Israel its existence to its arms, a chance of survival to its resolution and to the American determination to fight if necessary.
> (Aron 1976b: 286)

Conclusion

In his 1976 speech for the bicentennial of the United States, just after praising the great American democracy, Aron advised that Europeans should not seek a model in the American polity: while the latter was based on its constitution, Europeans belong, in the first place, to their nations. Obviously, the idea of a constitutional patriotism does not belong to Aron's political thought. Neither a nationalist like de Gaulle, nor a federalist like Monnet, Aron was not Habermasian either.

Raymond Aron's position on Europe is quite original. It may disappoint those who are looking for a great vision of power, the promise of a federal state or the idea of a post-national citizenship. What makes his idea of Europe consistent is his resolve not to indulge in wishful thinking, to learn the lessons of past experiences, yet without neglecting the new circumstances that may arise. This precluded him from accepting any philosophy of history or any illusion of knowing the sense of history beforehand. And this applies to the Marxist–Leninist ideology as well as to Europeanism. The consistence and stability of Aron's thought on Europe was based on his determination to foster the cohesion of the Western alliance, to which European integration, and primarily the reconciliation between France and Germany, was essential. His pledge to political realism and the harshness of polemics in the time of ideologies explain why he mostly commented on the circumstances of the Cold War, to the extent that many readers may think that he lacked the ability to see beyond the historical context of his time, and that his works may be out of date. While Aron, in *Peace and War*'s third part, "History", focused on the situation of the early 1960s, he nevertheless developed a strategy to overcome that situation, a strategy that was vindicated by history at the end of the 1980s. On Europe, Aron was right in observing the decline of the political myth, demonstrated by the loss of interest by the public and the increasingly technocratic complexity of European institutions. While never precluding the emergence of a European federal state, Aron just warned that it might not happen and that Europeans, tempted to see themselves beyond the horrors of a tragic history, nevertheless continue to live in the dangerous world of history, characterized by the ever-present possibility of war.

Notes

1. NAF 28060, Box 206. Fabre-Luce, letter to Raymond Aron on 14 May 1957.
2. NAF 28060, box 142, letter from Raymond Aron to Pierre Chatenet, 20 December 1966.
3. NAF 28060, box 127.

References

Aron, R. (1926), "Ce que pense la jeunesse universitaire d'Europe", *Bibliothèque universelle et Revue de Genève*, December, 789–794.
Aron, R. (1931), "Révision des traités: Lettre d'Allemagne", *Libres Propos*, May, 222–223.
Aron, R. (1938), *Introduction à la philosophie de l'histoire*. Paris: Gallimard.
Aron, R. (1942), "Bataille des propagandes", *La France libre*, 4:23, 372–379.
Aron, R. (1943), "Destin des nationalités", *La France libre*, 5:29, 16 March, 339–347.
Aron, R. (1946), *Perspectives sur l'avenir de l'Europe*. Lecture given on 26 November 1946, pp. 2–3. Bibliothèque Nationale, NAF 28060, Box 1.
Aron, R. (1948), *Le Grand Schisme*. Paris: Gallimard.
Aron, R. (1949a), "Le Pacte atlantique", *Liberté de l'esprit*, no. 3, April.
Aron, R. (1949b), *France and Europe*. The Human Affairs pamphlets. Hinsdale, IL: Henry Regnery.
Aron, R. (1950), "The Atomic Bomb and Europe", *Bulletin of the Atomic Scientists*, 6:4, 110–114.
Aron, R. (1951), *Les Guerres en chaîne*. Paris: Gallimard.
Aron, R. (1952a), "Discours aux étudiants allemands", *Preuves*, 18–19, August–September.
Aron, R. (1952b), "L'Unité économique de l'Europe", *La Revue Libre*, no. 2, 3–22.
Aron, R. (1952c), "En quête d'une sratégie", *Liberté de l'Esprit*, 29/30, 65–70, 111–116.
Aron, R. (1954), *The Century of Total War*. London: Derek Vershoyle.
Aron, R. (1957a), "Une Révolution antitotalitaire", in Lasky, M. and François, B. (eds), *La Révolution hongroise: histoire du soulèvement d'octobre*. Paris: Plon.
Aron, R. (1957b), *Espoir et peur du siècle*. Paris: Calmann-Lévy.
Aron, R. (1961), *Dimensions de la conscience historique*. Paris: Plon.
Aron, R. (1962), *Paix et guerre entre les nations*. Paris: Calmann-Lévy.
Aron, R. (1976a), *L'Europe des crises*. Brussels: Bruylant.
Aron, R. (1976b), *Penser la guerre, Clausewitz*. Paris: Gallimard.
Aron, R. (1977a), *Plaidoyer pour l'Europe décadente*. Paris: Robert Laffont.
Aron, R. (1977b), "Alexander Solzhenitsyn and European 'Leftism'", *Survey, a Journal of East–West Studies*, 100, 233–241.
Aron, R. (1981), *Le Spectateur engagé*. Paris: Julliard.
Aron, R. (1983), *Mémoires*. Paris: Julliard.
Aron, R. (2005), "L'Europe, avenir d'un mythe", lecture given on 13 May 1975. *Cités*, no. 24.
Aron, R. and Lerner, D. (1956), *La Querelle de la CED: Essais d'analyse sociologique*, Cahiers de la Fondation nationale des sciences politiques. Paris: Armand Colin.
Baverez, N. (1993), *Raymond Aron: Un moraliste au temps des idéologies*. Paris: Flammarion.
Benda, J. (1933), *Discours à la nation européenne*. Paris: Gallimard.
Bonfreschi, L. (2014), *Raymond Aron e il gollismo 1940–1969*. Soveria Mannelli: Rubbettino.

Bottici, C. (2007), *A Philosophy of Political Myth*. Cambridge: Cambridge University Press.
Bruneteau, B. (2003), *L'Europe nouvelle de Hitler: Une illusion des intellectuels de la France de Vichy*. Paris: Éditions du Rocher.
Burnham, J. (1941), *The Managerial Revolution: What Is Happening in the World*. New York: John Day.
Fabre-Luce, A. (1942), *Journal de la France*, March 1939–July 1940. Brussels: Editions de La Toison d'Or.
Halévy, E. (1938), *L'ère des tyrannies: Études sur le socialisme et la guerre*. Paris: Gallimard.
Launay, S. (1995), *La pensée politique de Raymond Aron*. Paris: PUF.
Lipgens, W. and Loth, W. (1988), *Documents on the History of European Integration: Vol. 3: The Struggle for European Union by Political Parties and Pressure Groups in Western European Countries 1945–1950*. Berlin: De Gruyter.
Mauriac, C. (1970), *Un autre de Gaulle, journal 1944–1954*. Paris: Hachette.
Mouric, J. (2013), *Raymond Aron et l'Europe*. Rennes: PUR.
Pipes, R. (1984), *Survival Is Not Enough*. New York: Simon & Schuster.
Renan, E. (1871), *La réforme intellectuelle et morale de la France*. Paris: Michel Lévy.
Schmitt, C. (1941), *Völkerrechtliche Großraumordnung. Mit Interventionsverbot für raumfremde Mächte. Ein Beitrag zum Reichsbegriff im Völkerrecht*. Leipzig: Deutscher Rechtsverlag.
Stark, J. (1993), *Raymond Aron: Über Deutschland und den Nationalsozialismus, Frühe politische Schriften 1930–1939*. Opladen: Leske und Budrich.
Szilard, L. (1949), "Shall We Face the Facts?" *Bulletin of the Atomic Scientists*, 5:10, 269–273.

7 Beyond Soviet and American models of industrialization
Aron's third way approach to global development

Daniel Steinmetz-Jenkins

Introduction

The Congress for Culture Freedom's (CCF) 1955 conference in Milan may be considered one of the epochal intellectual moments of the second half of the twentieth century. In mid-September 1955, more than 140 scholars from all over the world took part in the four-day conference, the largest in the history of the organization. The key idea that guided the conference was the notion of the "end of ideology." Although the concept had different formulations at the time, it was Raymond Aron's version of the doctrine that set the agenda for not just the conference but the future of the CCF. In this regard, the afterword to Aron's highly successful book, *L'Opium des intellectuels*, published just months before the conference, titled "The End of the Ideological Age," is of crucial importance (Aron 1955a). Aron's concluding thoughts in the book provided the conceptual tools to do away with traditional political divisions so as to allow for reconciliation among, or at least clarification of, real differences of value.

As the guiding inspiration for the 1955 Milan conference, Aron was given the task of writing the pilot paper that would establish the terms by which the Congress hoped to reconstruct the idea of freedom. The title of this pre-circulated paper was "De quoi disputent les Nations," which first appeared in the French journal *Nouvelle Revue Française* in 1954 (Aron 1954a) and a year later in *Encounter* with the title "Nation and Ideologies" (Aron 1955b). This small article was later reformulated and placed in the afterword of *The Opium of the Intellectuals*. "We are becoming," Aron declares,

> ever more aware that the political categories of the last century – Left and Right, liberal and socialist, traditionalist and revolutionary – have lost their relevance. They imply the existence of conflicts, which experience has since reconciled, and they lump together ideas and men whom the course of history has drawn into opposing camps.
>
> (Aron 1955a: 24)

In Aron's judgment, Western Europe was moving into a "non-millennial socialism and a non-reactionary conservatism" (Aron 1955a: 24) that offered both peaceful governance and peaceful opposition. He viewed ideological controversies in Western societies as fading since the welfare state had proven it could reconcile divergent demands and, in turn, deflect revolutionary passions. The best way to maintain the system, argued Aron, required political elites to engage in various "degrees and methods of compromise" (Aron 1955a: 33).

A few months after the Milan conference, a report of the proceedings written by the sociologist Edward Shils appeared in the CCF journal *Encounter*. Shils noted that the general agreement of the participants over the waning of ideology, together with the belief that the Soviet Union was losing the cultural Cold War, gave the conference the feeling of a "post victory ball" (Shils 1955: 54). Yet a tidal wave of pushback challenged such optimism: on the third and fourth days of the conference, representatives from "underdeveloped nations" naturally wondered how the end of ideology applied to their respective countries. If "freedom's defenders" had any chance of staving off the communist temptation facing recently decolonized countries, they argued, it would require the United States and Western Europe to invest significantly in the economic development of new states. Moreover, the same participants also stressed the positive role that nationalism and long-held traditions were playing in the political formation of post-colonial Africa and Asia.

As Shils recognized, however, Western representatives at the conference were deeply troubled by these statements. They were skeptical about a purely economic approach to development and thus "put off by the economism of the Africans and Asians" (Shils 1955: 55). Moreover, the end of ideology thesis had regulated nationalism to a nasty doctrine made obsolete by World War II. If anything, Shils concludes, the Asian and African representatives "underscored the danger of western complacency at having weathered the storm of ideologies" (Shils 1955: 56).

The real significance of the Milan meeting, then, is not that it led to the end of ideology debate fiasco – as most notably associated with the work of Daniel Bell – in the United States. Rather, it was the second half of the conference that forced the CCF to take up a new problematic: the relationship between the end of ideology and the "underdeveloped world." As General Secretary Nicolas Nabokov noted, perhaps "the most urgent question discussed at the Milan conference concerned the economic development of technologically ill equipped countries" (Nabokov 1956). As the CCF switched its gaze from Europe to Africa, Asia, and Latin America, a new theoretical challenge thus presented itself: how to construct an alternative theory of modernization that looked beyond the laissez-faire and Marxist ideologies that the Milan conference had deemed passé. This theory of modernization would duly recognize the cultural and political particularity of emerging nation states. It would also have to account for the so-called convergence between the West and the Soviet Union, which the optimism at the Milan event assumed.

Aron rose to meet the challenge facing the CCF by crafting a conception of modernization that tried to get around the horns of the theoretical dilemmas that emerged in Milan. The initial testing ground for this was a series of lectures

Aron gave at the Sorbonne between November 1955 (just two months after Milan) and May 1958, later billed as the "Sorbonne Trilogy." The first of these lectures, titled "Le développement de la société industrielle," was published in 1962 with the title, *Dix-huit leçons sur la société industrielle*, and became wildly popular among the French governing elite. Aron's lectures in 1957 and 1958 were also published with the titles *La Lutte des classes* (1964) and *Démocratie et totalitarisme* (1965).

The aim of these lectures was to articulate a theory of industrial society – the dawn of universal history, as Aron called it – that nevertheless highlighted what he began to describe as the "autonomy" or "primacy" of the political. In the words of Ralf Dahrendorf, this led Aron to embrace an unusual view of convergence theory:

> Aron treated political and socioeconomic developments as if they were almost totally separate. This enabled him to combine his unreserved defence of democracy and the rule of law with the expectation that all industrial societies would develop similar if not identical structures of economy and society ... Aron did not succumb to the belief that a convergence of systems would be a good thing and therefore desirable.
> (Dahrendorf 2011: 102)

To collapse the distinction between the political and the industrial constitutes the essence of what Aron deemed to be ideology. Aron's distinction between the political and the social-economic, however, makes most sense when put into a wider international context in which cultural, religious, and political diversity stood threatened by *both* Soviet and American ideological systems. Aron's critique of the American ideological system, however, often took place within the confines of the CCF.

This chapter argues that Aron's emphasis on the "autonomy of the political" cannot be limited to his critique of the French Marxist scene of the 1950s and 1960s. The concept must also be connected to the emerging debates over systems convergence and global development theory put forward by Cold War liberals in the United States. The CCF played a key role in facilitating these debates. Aron was in disagreement with the optimism of his American colleagues, who, he believed, naively supposed that the Western model could be transferred to the underdeveloped world. His theory of industrial society, it will be argued, must be seen as an alternative to various schools of American modernization theory. In this sense Aron could be viewed as siding with Asian representatives of the CCF who were worried about the disastrous impact of industrialization on their respective political cultures and traditions.

I illustrate these claims by providing the first scholarly engagement with Aron's decades-long critical interaction with the thought of W.W. Rostow. Aron criticized Rostow's stages of economic growth for assuming Western values and patterns of development that ignored the geographical, physical, and historical particularities of developing nation states. By the mid-1960s, Aron gave critical attention, in articles appearing in *Le Figaro*, to the misguided foreign policy of the Kennedy and Johnson administrations, which he believed to be heavily indebted to Rostow's thought. Most interestingly, Indian intellectuals associated with the CCF, such as V.K.R.V. Rao and A.B. Shah, appropriated Aron's views of industrialization when criticizing Rostow's thought. Ultimately, it will be demonstrated that Aron's involvement in CCF conferences and seminars, in addition to his own published articles, shows him to be often at odds with his American colleagues' optimism concerning the transfer of Western political values abroad and their misguided faith in technical knowledge.

Industrialization, global development, and the primacy of the political

By the late 1950s, convergence theories abounded on all sides of the political spectrum in France, signifying the Cold War's decline in political intensity. Debates over systems convergence in France and the United States were driven by different political motives. De Gaulle believed, for instance, that the decay of communist ideology would lead to a political convergence within Western Europe and the return to traditional national interest between Russia and France. In his view this would make possible a restructuring of the European system that would overcome the Cold War (Loth and Soutou 2010: 125).

De Gaulle's position also entailed, observes the historian Georges-Henri Soutou, "negative convergence": "this was the view that both superpowers in fact were accomplices in the international system, implicitly agreeing to divide the world into two spheres of influence" (Loth and Soutou 2010: 26). De Gaulle envisioned France playing the historical role of resisting this "double hegemony" by taking the lead in European political affairs and forming alliances with the Third World. This position allowed Gaullists to form bridges with segments of the French Left that were disillusioned with the Soviet Union and repelled by American imperialism.

Such optimistic takes on convergence in France were often driven by economic assumptions that entailed qualitative political transformations of the Soviet Union. In 1958, for example, the economist François Perroux published his seminal two-volume book, *La Coexistence pacifique*, in which he argued that "Trade would encourage the Soviet Union to switch from a general, ideologically based opposition to the West to a willingness to cooperate" (Loth and Soutou 2010: 28). Views such as Perroux's, claims Soutou, became the standard take at the Quai-d'Orsay after 1964.

Roughly around the same time, the convergence debate took off in the United States. Khrushchev's reforms pushed American social scientists away from seeing the Soviet Union as totalitarian and instead through the lenses of economic growth and social transformation. A great example of this can be found in the early writings of Zbigniew Brzezinski. A participant in CCF gatherings, in 1956 Brzezinski interpreted the Soviet Union to be a totalitarian regime, only to prefer the concept of convergence a decade later in a book co-written with

Samuel Huntington, *Political Power: USA/USSR*, which Aron quoted on a few occasions (Malia 1999: 379).

The CCF became a major stage for facilitating this discussion, and Aron played a key intellectual role. In 1957, alongside Daniel Bell, Richard Pipes, and others, Aron presented a paper titled "Soviet Society and the Future of Freedom" at the CCF's "Changes and Soviet Society" conference in Oxford (Aron 1957a). Under the auspices of the CCF, the next year he participated in a discussion of George Kennan's Reith lectures titled "Russia, the Atom, the West" (Lasky 1958). This was followed in 1959 by the CCF-sponsored "Colloques de Rheinfelden," where Aron and George F. Kennan debated to what extent the Soviet Union would progress along the lines of the liberal West (Aron *et al.* 1960). It is thus no wonder that Aron is still regularly portrayed in France and the United States as one of the godfathers of convergence theory (Malia 1999: 380).

What is most remarkable about Aron's reputation as a convergence theorist is that it coincided at the very moment he was promoting "the political." Thus, at a moment of détente – when convergence theories abounded alongside a cottage industry of optimistic takes on global development – Aron began to caution his readers about what he described as the autonomy or the primacy of the political (Aron 1967a). As far as I can tell, the first time Aron explicitly makes recourse to the phrase "the primacy of the political" was in his 1957–1958 Sorbonne lectures, "esquisse d'une théorie des regimes politique," later published in 1965 under the title *Démocratie et totalitarisme* (Aron 1965). However, the same notion is implicitly on display in the preceding two lectures (Aron 1963a, 1964). Viewed in this context, it makes little sense to limit Aron's appeals to "the political" to a critique of Marxist universalism. The backdrop here is not simply French Marxism but the CCF's post-Milan attempt to reconcile the end of ideology thesis with a theory of global development. In this regard, Aron also appealed to the concept of the political when arguing against ideologies of liberal universalism, as represented by the triumphalism of mid-century American modernization theory.

Commissioned by both *Le Figaro* and the CCF to report on the political situation in Asia, Aron spent around six weeks in 1953 visiting India, Japan, China, and South Korea. During this time he interviewed Shigeru Yoshida and Jawaharlal Nehru, gave a talk before the Japanese branch of the CCF, met with numerous Asian intellectuals and journalists, and wrote roughly a dozen articles for *Le Figaro* on the political and economic state of Asia (Aron 1990a: 1091–1105). Based on his *Mémoires* and newspaper articles, Aron's trip proved pivotal in two major ways for his thinking on emerging states and global development that is incipiently on display in *The Opium of the Intellectuals*, which he began to formulate after Milan.

Before Aron departed for Asia, Jean Fourastié published his *Machinisme et bien-être*. A colleague of Aron's at Sciences Po, Fourastié was very much under the influence of Colin Clark's *The Conditions of Economic Progress*, and suggested in his book, in Aron's words, that the essential phenomena of the modern economy is the increase in value produced per head of the working population (Aron 1967b: 113). By arguing that growth was the major category of economic theory, Clark and Fourastié made it both legitimate and necessary to analyze the economic features common at the global level. Aron came away from his travels to Asia in many ways convinced by Fourastié's argument. There he witnessed the burgeoning of industrial societies that had more in common with the industrial ills of nineteenth-century Britain than post-war Europe or the United States. In *Opium of the Intellectuals* he reported:

> My visit to Asia helped to convince me that the major concept of our time is that of industrial society. Europe, as seen from Asia, does not consist of two fundamentally different worlds, the Soviet world, and the Western world. It is one single reality: industrial society.
>
> (Aron 1962: 42)

When Aron sensed a global industrial convergence, he grew concerned about the political and cultural effects that the demand to industrialize had inflicted on developing countries (Aron 1990a: 1111). "Chinese, Hindus, Moslems," declared Aron, "have been subjugated, humiliated, and exploited by the makers of the machine" (quoted in Stankiewicz 1964: 7). From this time on Aron would continually underscore to his overly optimistic CCF colleagues the horrific cultural and social consequences of industrialization.

In an article sharply critical of US foreign policy that appeared in *Confluence* in 1953, Aron observed that out of 100 articles appearing in the American press to address Truman's Point Four Program, "not one can be found which analyses its political conditions" (Aron 1953: 6–7). He then rhetorically raised the question whether it is not obvious that the rationalizing of an economy presupposes a certain judicial and political environment. Aron's criticism of the Point Four Program shares much in common with his critique of Marxism. In fact, the *Confluence* article specifically described Point Four as the "American ideology":

> Does not the error lie in forgetting that freedoms (personal, electoral, etc.), desirable as they may be, do not create the state and cannot flourish in simply any environment ... American influence, incapable of supporting the leaders in accord with the true American Ideology is reduced to supporting any available de facto potentate.
>
> (Aron 1953: 8)

Interestingly, when Henry Kissinger edited the draft of Aron's *Confluence* article, he found it so critical of the United States that he asked Aron if he could add to it some of Aron's previous material critical of Marxism (Kissinger 1952).

Aron continued this line of thought in a critical article of the West and the social-economic situation of India that appeared in *Preuves* in May 1954. In "L'Asie entre Marx et Malthus," he declared that

> Whatever one may think of the foreign policy of the present Prime Minister, it is neither generous nor intelligent to reply to his neutralist declarations by

> the suppression or reduction of economic aid. The free world has a major interest in the success of India's economic efforts.
>
> (Aron 1954b: 49)

Aron concluded the argument, however, by pointing out that India's future success would not be the result of simply "spreading institutions from one society to another" or by "transferring experts or technical experts" from the West (Aron 1954: 49). What would be necessary is for Indian leaders to find the proper balance between implementing necessary reforms and being mindful of local traditions and cultural practices.

After Aron returned from Asia to write *Opium of the Intellectuals*, it is no wonder that he rebuked Western intellectuals for wanting to hastily issue Western forms of political governance into India and China:

> No European country ever went through the phase of economic development which India and China are now experiencing, under a regime that was representative and democratic. Nowhere, during the long years when industrial populations were growing rapidly, factory chimneys looming up over the suburbs and railways and bridges being constructed, were personal liberties, universal suffrage and the parliamentary system combined.
>
> (Aron 2009: 259)

These same concerns make their appearance in the Sorbonne trilogy. In *Dix-huit leçons sur la société industrielle*, Aron affirmed that traditional societies are thrown into confusion by the phenomenon of economic growth. He immediately turns to Japan to make the point. The reformers of the Meiji Era, observes Aron, had to appropriate the whole equipment of Western society. Thus, "in a non-Western country the cause of growth is this complete transformation" (Aron 1967b). This passage must be linked to Aron's *Figaro* articles of 1953 in which he observes that such a transformation is "brutal" and costly to the Japanese way of life and culture.

Aron then alludes to his comments about India made in *The Opium of the Intellectuals*, observing that "when a European society was at the level of development of present-day India, there was neither aviation nor electronics" (Aron 1967b: 134). All comparisons between societies at non-contemporary stages of development, Aron asserted, are risky: "There is a qualitative difference between the imitation of the development of European society by non-European societies, and the creation of this industrial society by Europe itself" (Aron 1967b: 134). Nevertheless, since industrialization constituted the new universal norm, Aron believed it inevitable and indispensable that industrial production be instituted in India. However, these changes, Aron asserted, would "require such far reaching social and psychological transformations that one hesitates over the decisive question as to what type of government will make this historical change possible" (Aron 1967b: 134–135).

Consistent with this line of reasoning, Aron remained silent on how exactly emerging states should go about achieving modernization. Clearly the poverty divide between advanced and developing countries had to be reduced. When speaking at the Colloque Rheinfelden in 1959, Aron commented that it is intolerable for two-thirds of the world to continue living in growing poverty while one-third live relatively affluent lives. Societies such as India and China, reasoned Aron, would potentially narrow the divide between the Soviet Union and the United States, as the technological equipment gaps between the countries are narrowed. Aron even predicted that by 2007 China would have a larger industrial output than the Soviet Union (Aron 1957b: 221, 228).

The narrowing of the development gap did not mean that India or China would coincide with or resemble either Soviet or American industrial societies. Aron did, in fact, think that industrial society could be transferred, but that the universal values often accompanying it assumed a "secularization of thought and a certain attitude towards this world" unique to the West. As such, Aron sought to challenge not industrial society, which he ambiguously viewed as the new norm, but secular Western values that threatened to destroy the political, ideological, and cultural heterogeneity of the international system.

In this regard, *La Tragédie algérienne*, published in the spring of 1957, is pivotal for understanding Aron's thinking on global development. As Aron exhorted his fellow French citizens to recognize the right of Algerian statehood, he also acknowledged the possibility that the leaders of the Front de libération nationale would set up a theocratic or totalitarian regime: a major argument being made in France against Algerian independence. Aron conceded this by prioritizing the right of the nation over the "Western demand for individual rights." The history of Western societies, Aron argued, showed their development to be no different, and Europeans, charged Aron, would be hypocritical to deny this.

> In Europe, the right to self-determination may be seen as an application of the idea of liberalism. The unity of Germany and Italy called for by the liberal bourgeoisie could or might have facilitated the progress of liberal institutions. But even in Europe, the nation and liberal ideas did not chime together for long.
>
> (Aron 2002: 425)

For most of their modern histories Europeans governments were themselves ravaged by absolutist forms of nationalism that had far more influence in the nineteenth and early twentieth centuries than the liberal tradition of individual rights. As he states,

> whether independent Indians or Egyptians enjoy more or less liberal institutions is up to them. People of color, whom the westerns have humiliated, use a Western vocabulary to voice their claims, but if they were given the choice between liberal institutions under Western tutelage or tyrannical ones in an independent state, the fact is that most of them would chose the second alternative.
>
> (Aron 2002: 426)

This passage embodies Aron's thinking on decolonization and development. Aron appeared entirely disinterested in putting forward any plan or model of action concerning how development should be pursued from one nation state to the next (Aron 1963a). By the late 1950s, the grounds were thus set for Aron's criticisms of various American schools of modernization theory.

W.W. Rostow

In 1958 W.W. Rostow was awarded a Reflection Year Grant from the Carnegie Corporation and moved to Cambridge University, which offered to host him for the academic year. Rostow used the time off from MIT to conduct research for the work that came to define the field of modernization theory: *The Stages of Economic Growth: A Non-Communist Manifesto* (Rostow 1960). The book famously identified five stages of growth that all nations pass through in their historical development: traditional society, preconditions for takeoff, takeoff, the drive to maturity, and the age of mass consumption. As the historian David Milne remarks, "Rostow believed that it was incumbent upon the United States to push those nations languishing in the first two stages toward greater material progress – blunting the appeal of Marxist Leninism along the way" (Milne 2008: 62). Rostow proclaimed his development scheme to be universally applicable. As such, it differed very little from the historical materialism of Marxism except an alternative twist: the end of history is liberal capitalism. Not surprisingly, as Milne is quick to observe, Rostow's stance was overwhelmingly optimistic in anticipating that, if backed by US financial assistance, underdeveloped nations could successfully move through the stages of development until they entered the stratosphere of liberal democracy.

During Rostow's research year at Cambridge, he was invited by the CCF to participate in a seminar, Les Colloques des Rheinfelden, centered on the paper Aron gave on development: "Industrial Society and the Political Dialogues of the West" (Aron 1963b). In all likelihood it was the first time the two met. What Rostow encountered was a theory of development whose pessimism stood in vivid contrast to his own. It was not just Rostow who was taken aback by Aron's ambiguous stance on industrial society; nearly every scholar invited to the seminar had a similar reaction (Aron 1963b: 122–139).

Aron commented that a major problem with the CCF meetings since Milan, particularly the 1957 Tokyo conference devoted to economic reform in the Third World, was their myopic focus on the Westernization of non-Western societies. The fact that the seminars were devoted to the problems of transferring Western institutions to the non-Western world compelled Aron to ask: "Shouldn't the West take a long hard look at itself?" (Aron 1963b: 56). The post-Milan seminars assumed, he argued, that the West was sufficiently sure of itself that it could examine its possible universalization without at the same time examining itself. The problem, Aron continued, is that even as developing nation states sought to appropriate American technology and economic models, it did not automatically follow that they wanted to accept American-style political institutions.

Aron, then, declared that Rostow's position assumed the universalization of American values "without really knowing what its own political philosophy is ... beyond mere economic growth" (Aron 1963b: 57–58). This is problematic, stressed Aron, since there is no necessary incompatibility between industrial society and a variety of political and moral organizations. Rostow's response revealed the undying optimism of his philosophical outlook: "Are we so badly off?" he asked. Relying on Montesquieu, he then went on to declare that some cultural and governmental forms are indeed better than others and that "the natural law of progress" ultimately results in republicanism:

> Considered in relation to Montesquieu's analysis, Mr. Aron's questions become that of determining whether the countries of the East and of the West, those of Asia, Europe, Africa, and North and South America, despite their diversity, share a core of values which in fact determines the lines of the development ... One can speculate as to whether the values men seek in social organization do not have a common content throughout the world.
> (Aron 1963b: 197)

Aron, who knew more than a little about Montesquieu, was hardly impressed. One month later he took to the pages of *Le Figaro* to pen a critical article on Rostow's thought, which was almost unknown in France at the time, titled "Marxisme et contre marxisme" (Aron 1990b: 553–556). In this article, Aron argued that Rostow's various stages were so general as to be useless: Rostow did not take into consideration the geographical differences between France, England, Japan, Germany, and the United States that helped facilitate their industrial rise; nor was Rostow mindful of their differing technological capacities. The *Figaro* article, however, touched on only a few of Aron's concerns.

A year later, he took to the newly founded *Archives Européennes de Sociologie* to offer a damning critique of the recently published *Stages of Economic Growth*. Aron complained that Rostow's various stages of development were too confining and too vague. The concept of traditional society struck Aron as being of little use since it claimed to monolithically apply to all underdeveloped communities. It made little sense to him that the communities of New Guinea and various tribes in Africa must be grouped together with the long histories of China or India. "The only features these have in common," Aron observed, "is that they are neither modern nor industrialized" (Aron 1960: 299). As such, the notion of traditional society was so broad as to be hardly useful. He then argued that Rostow's preconditions of takeoff were hazy since the beginnings of modernization are different depending on whether it is something that develops internally or as a result of contact with the West.

Moreover, the third stage – the transitional "takeoff" period – begged the question as to what degree problems and stages are the same in countries that gave birth to industrial society versus those that imported industrialization or imitated it. The takeoff of Brazil in 1960, for instance, assumed modern techniques and a rapid population increase. However, the takeoff period of France in

1830 was devoid of antibiotics, refrigerators, and automobiles. Accordingly, Aron concludes that "the growth of each nation has its own history. *A fortiori*, the modernization of human society considered as a unity also has its history, which is both unique (*einmalig*) and peculiar (*einzigartig*)" (Aron 1960: 299). Thus, for Aron it is rigid and potentially dangerous to attempt to define a universal scheme of growth, as Rostow proposed, requiring every nation to go through the same phases and follow the same path.

Aron countered Rostow by claiming that a more interesting approach to development would chart a specific country's path to modernization, which may or may not resemble that of another. It is exactly here that Aron appeals to the primacy of the political and the constitutive role it plays in shaping a given country's developmental trajectory. Aron turns to the Meiji Restoration, which saw an authoritarian regime establish compulsory education, the rationalization of the legal system and civil service, and the creation of a semi-private entrepreneurial system. Tradition was not lost with change since the traditional ruling class brought about the changes and maintained power. "There are no grounds for believing," concluded Aron, "that all advanced societies must be of the same type" (Aron 1960: 302).

There are good reasons for thinking that Aron's criticisms of Rostow decisively influenced the Asian contingent of the CCF. In 1960, V.K.R.V. Rao, a leading Indian economist, gave a lecture in Paris at the Institut de science économique appliquée, titled "Some Reflections on the Economic Utopia." His talk is primarily devoted to challenging the basic theses of *Stages of Economic Growth*. Rao's wording is incredibly similar to Aron's argument about India and development that appeared in his *Opium of the Intellectuals*:

> [Rostow's] economic history is rather naïve in its main thesis. Economic development in the very countries he has been talking about took place under conditions that cannot by any modern standard be described as those of a free or democratic society. But there can be no doubt that democratic freedom in the Western World succeeded rather than preceded the precondition and early take-off stages in the major areas of the Western World ... Rostow fails to perceive in Western economic development this basic element of exploitation [made] possible only under nondemocratic conditions.
>
> (Rao 1964: 313, 314)

A year later, he presented a paper at a UNESCO seminar on social development. Explicitly referencing Aron, he complained that Rostow's first stage had reduced *all* traditional societies to being inherently backward. He then approvingly embraced Aron's argument that science, industry, and rationality constitute means, rather than political ends, which are driven by "the ethical and spiritual development of human personality" (Rao and Shah 1965: 70).

Rao's paper at UNESCO became a focal point of discussion for the CCF's 1961 seminar held in New Delhi, called "Tradition and Modernity in India."

Two dozen Indian academics and writers, including Rao and A.B. Shao, participated in this event. An edited volume of the proceedings appeared four years later. The text does not mention Aron's name, but the introduction makes it clear that Rao's Aronian-inspired views on the origins of Western modernization constitutes the consensus perspective of the book.

Aron remained steadfast in his critique of Rostow throughout the 1960s. In 1961 the newly elected President Kennedy hired Rostow to serve as deputy to the national security advisor, McGeorge Bundy. Kennedy came to office eager to outdo Khrushchev's bold January 6 proclamation that the end of history led to socialism and that the Soviet Union would wholeheartedly assist the Third World to achieve liberation from colonization. To safeguard the developing world from the communist temptation, especially in light of Castro's rise in Cuba, Rostow directly encouraged the president to institute a "Marshall Plan" for Latin America. As Milne comments, "Latin America had to be nudged toward Rostowian 'take-off,' for communists claimed that their creed alone could solve the obdurate socioeconomic problems afflicting the former Spanish colonies" (Milne 2008: 78). The door was now open for Rostow to see the practical application of his rather fine-tuned theory of development.

Inspired by Rostow's vision, in 1961 Kennedy launched the Alliance for Progress program that lavished billions on aid programs to assist the development of Latin American states. The Alliance program eventually snowballed into the president establishing the Agency for International Development, which witnessed a 65 percent increase in government funding for the Third World. Aron was quick to point out in the pages of *Le Figaro* the practical limitations of Kennedy's Rostovian-inspired policies. In a column titled "Du plan Marshall au plan Kennedy," he remarked that Kennedy's policies were inspired "par les conceptions de W. Rostow," whose thinking about development is curiously defined by what is in the best interests of the United States.

He then explicitly criticized Rostow's ten-year plan, which affirmed that more than half of the underdeveloped population could access, with the aid of industrialized countries, "à la a phase of economic growth" (Aron 1960: 817). This, Aron, implied, would almost necessitate the 20 republics of Latin America to undergo an economic revolution. But surely, Aron reasoned, "the transitions from traditional society to modern society is long and difficult; it demands intellectual social, and economic reforms sometimes taking decades" (Aron 1960: 815). Is the great but underdeveloped civilization of India, inquired Aron, really on the brink of "taking off towards modernity," as understood by Rostow?

A little more than a decade later, Aron wrote in *The Imperial Republic* that the universally decried bankruptcy of the Rostovian-inspired Alliance for Progress was due to the impracticality of a policy that claimed it could enable other nations to share in its own prosperity and civilization, and in a brief amount of time. The problem, Aron noted, is that the United States did not reach its age or prosperity in a mere decade or two. The "error," remarked Aron, "lies in failing to see that the growth rate of [developing nations] is not very different from that of the now developed countries at a comparable stage in the growth" (Aron

1974: 251). Aron's explanation for the failures of the Alliance for Progress are really no different than his criticisms of Truman's Point Four Program: both myopically prioritize an American ideology over the particularity of geographical, political, cultural, and religious conditions that entail brutal changes, and unforeseen consequences for developing nations.

As Rostow's influence in government grew, so did Aron's desire to distance his position from *Stages of Economic Growth*. From 1961 to 1964, Aron furthered his criticism against Rostow in three scholarly articles, published collectively in 1966 in a book titled *Trois essais sur l'âge industriel*. A year later the English translation of *Dix-huit leçons sur la société industrielle* appeared, the entire preface of which highlights Aron's differences with Rostow.

> These lectures do not have the same aims as *The Stages of Economic Growth* ... they are in no sense a *non-communist manifesto* ... It certainly does not support the thesis embraced by Western thinkers of the convergence of all industrial societies.
>
> (Aron 1967b: 5)

Against the tendencies of Rostow, Aron asserted that the notion of industrial society is just as concerned about the differences between nations as much as their similarities. One could not lump Europe, the Soviet Union, or the United States together in a common trajectory of development since the techniques, institutions, and mentality of the people were different in each case. As Aron put it:

> We have learned to mistrust these vast interpretations, at once seductive and misleading, in terms of the economic system. Neither the stage of maturity, nor that of high mass consumption has manifested the same political and social characteristics at all times and places.
>
> (Aron 1967b: 6)

Aron concludes the preface by stating that, unlike with the claims of Rostow or Marxism, his notion of industrial society neither offers a grand synthesis, nor does it culminate in a prophecy. Rather, it offers a mere sketch of some of the main trends of the time, and a deleterious trend, Aron discerned, was Rostow's influence on American foreign policy.

Conclusion: global development, Rostow, and the Vietnam War

Well before the end of ideology debate took off in 1960, the triumphalist and parochial overtones of the various CCF gatherings clearly bothered Aron. If Milan signaled the CCF's turn toward development in the Third World, the follow-up conferences had, to Aron's consternation, reduced modernization to Westernization. A case in point is the 1958 CCF conference in Rhodes, Greece, titled "Representative Government and Public Liberty in the New States." The stated aim of the conference, which included representatives from Asia and Africa, concerned problems of democracy in the new states and a discussion of the means by which free institutions can be sustained and strengthened.

At Rhodes, Aron clearly recognized that the Western Euro-American wing of the CCF had reduced global development to the imposition of Euro-American values abroad. But what works in Britain, stressed Aron, might not necessarily work elsewhere. As he put it, "if democrats are to try to make democracy work elsewhere, especially in Africa and Asia, can we afford to keep our attention focused exclusively on our attractive western features?" (Aron 1958). Aron went on to suggest that the establishment of parliamentary democracy in the developing states, as things currently stood, was a utopian dream; a pluralistic party system assumed a level of national unity and general agreement that did not exist in the new states. Or, "some of the so-called 'new states' have emerged without the minimum of national unity which is necessary for democratic political controversy" (Aron 1958). The contradiction, as he noted, is that liberal values presuppose liberal institutions to maintain them; in developing nations such institutions are typically ineffectual.

Upon hearing Aron's pronouncements at Rhodes, his colleagues wondered if he thought Western-style democracy even possible for the new states. The Swiss journalist Francois Bondy responded that emerging states in Asia and Africa start at political democracy, which supposedly would lead them down the path to becoming full capitalist economies. "I wonder," Bondy asked, "is the process of starting with the latest model of democracy and then retrieving the early steps of capitalism possible?" Aron's rejoinder to Bondy explicitly illuminates his skepticism regarding transferring political democracy to the new states:

> What I would like to say is that the present experience is without parallel in world history. We take institutions which have grown up slowly in the West and we transplant them in countries where often neither the state nor the nation exist and where the tasks to be achieved are enormous, and were, in fact, never achieved in the West with constitutional procedures and party systems.
>
> (Aron 1958)

This was eventually followed by Aron's mysterious concluding remarks: "the most impressive fact, but perhaps depressive too, is that we intellectuals, coming from all parts of the world, all speak the same language. We use the same words, the same vocabulary; we work with the same concepts" (Aron 1958). Aron thus sought to remind his colleagues of the linguistic particularities of what they took to be the universal political norm.

It is no wonder that a decade later, as the Vietnam War spun out of control, Aron, in the words of the sociologist John A. Hall, "became a harsh critic of the mechanical, and thus false, conception of theory that guided American" foreign policy (Hall 1981: 173). Although Rostow appears intermittently in Aron's explicit criticism of the Vietnam War, one passage from *The Imperial Republic* reveals what Aron thought about Rostow's potential influence:

> Walter Rostow developed an interpretation of contemporary history to which [he] pinned [his] faith ... The North Vietnamese, he claimed, were the last prophets of revolutionary romanticism, and Vietnam was a decisive test of counterinsurgency, because if South Vietnam held out and won, the United States would have deterred the doctrinaires of the revolt of the countryside against the cities, the last proponents of Communist expansion by force, once and for all. Whether Kennedy or Johnson believed in these reasons or justifications, the war created its logic.
>
> (Aron 1974: 104)

Rostow, argued Aron, viewed North Vietnamese communist ideology as a temporary phase of societal immaturity that a counterinsurgency of increased bombing could ultimately defeat. This policy ultimately failed, Aron pointed out, since political and nationalistic reasons – not economic – were the major factors motivating North Vietnamese war efforts to unify the state.

Again, this is exactly where Aron directed the idea of the primacy of the political against the ideology of American foreign policy. As Aron put it: "I will ask myself" whether a single such specialist who is "able to speak the language of the country, knowing little of the Vietnamese people, their customs, or history, can claim the title of expert" (Aron 1983: 195). Is this not exactly the same judgment Aron had arrived at when criticizing his CCF colleagues at Rhodes?

References

Aron, R. (1953), "The Diffusion of Ideologies," *Confluence*, 2:1, 3–12.
Aron, R. (1954a), "De quoi disputent les nations?" *Nouvelle Revue Française*, 22, 612–637.
Aron, R. (1954b), "Between Malthus and Marx," *Encounter* 3:11, August, 44–49.
Aron, R. (1955a), *L'Opium des intellectuels*. Paris: Calmann-Lévy.
Aron, R. (1955b), "Nations and Ideology," *Encounter*, 16, 24–33.
Aron, R. (1957a), "Soviet Society and the Future of Freedom," *International Association for Cultural Freedom Records*, Box 405, Folder 2.
Aron, R. (1957b), *Espoir et peur du siècle: Essais non partisan*. Paris: Calmann-Lévy.
Aron, R. (1958), "A Round Table Discussion of the Differences between East and West," *International Association for Cultural Freedom Records*, Box 409, Folder 4.
Aron, R. (1960), "Notes Critiques: Les étapes de la croissance économique," *Archives Européennes de Sociologie*, 1:2, 299.
Aron, R. (1962), *The Opium of the Intellectuals*, 2nd edn. New York: Norton.
Aron, R. (ed.) (1963a), *World Technology and Human Destiny*. Ann Arbor, MI: University of Michigan Press.
Aron, R. (1963b), "Industrial Society and the Political Dialogues of the West," in Aron, R. (ed.), *World Technology and Human Destiny*. Ann Arbor, MI: University of Michigan Press, 3–26.

Aron, R. (1964), *La Lutte des classes*. Paris: Éditions Gallimard.
Aron, R. (1965), *Démocratie et totalitarisme*. Paris: Éditions Gallimard.
Aron, R. (1967a), *Les étapes de la pensée sociologique*. Paris: Gallimard.
Aron, R. (1967b), *Eighteen Lectures on Industrial Society*. London: Weidenfeld & Nicolson.
Aron, R. (1974), *The Imperial Republic: The United States and the World, 1945–1973*. Englewood Cliffs, NJ: Prentice-Hall.
Aron, R. (1983), *Politics and History*. New Brunswick, NJ: Transaction Publishers.
Aron, R. (1990a), *Le Guerre Froide: Les articles de politique internationale dans Le Figaro de Juin 1947 à Mai 1955*, 1. Paris: Fallois.
Aron, R. (1990b), *La Coexistence: Les articles de politique internationale dans Le Figaro – Mai 1955 à Février 1965*, 2. Paris: Fallois.
Aron, R. (2002), *The Dawn of Universal History*. New York: Basic Books.
Aron, R. (2009), *The Opium of the Intellectuals*, 4th edn. New Brunswick, NJ: Transaction Publishers.
Aron, R., Kennan, G.F., and Oppenheimer, R. (eds.) (1960), *Colloques de Rheinfelden*. Paris: Calmann-Lévy.
Dahrendorf, R. (2011), *The Modern Social Conflict: The Politics of Liberty*. London: Transaction Publishers.
Hall, J. (1981), *Diagnoses of Our Time: Six Views of Our Social Condition*. London: Heinemann Educational Books.
Kissinger, H. (1952), *Archives Privées Raymond Aron*, Boîte 152 (August 20, 1952).
Lasky, M. (ed.) (1958), *The West, the Atom and Russia: A Roundtable Discussion of the Views of George Kennan*. Paris: A Publication of the Congress for Cultural Freedom.
Loth, W., and Soutou, G.H. (2010), *The Making of Détente: Eastern and Western Europe in the Cold War, 1965–1975*. Abingdon: Routledge.
Malia, M. (1999), *Russia under Western Eyes: From the Bronze Horseman to the Lenin Mausoleum*. Cambridge, MA: Harvard University Press.
Milne, D. (2008), *America's Rasputin: Walt Rostow and the Vietnam War*. New York: Hill and Wang.
Nabokov, N. (1956), *International Association for Cultural Freedom Records*. Box 402, Folder 11.
Rao, V.K.R.V. (1964), *Essays in Economic Development*. Bombay: Asia Publishing House.
Rao, V.K.R.V., and Shah, A.B. (eds.) (1965), *Tradition and Modernity in India*. Bombay: Manaktalas.
Shils, E. (1955), "Letter from Milan: The End of Ideology," *Encounter*, 20 (November), 54: www.unz.org/Pub/Encounter-1955nov-00052.
Stankiewicz, W.J. (ed.) (1964), *Political Thought Since World War II*. London: The Free Press of Glencoe Collier-Macmillan Limited.

8 Raymond Aron's heritage for the International Relations discipline
The French school of sociological liberalism

Thomas Meszaros and Antony Dabila

Was Raymond Aron a realist, neorealist, liberal or something else? This question is still debated today, as illustrated in Schmitt's original understanding of Aron's approach as a theory of foreign policy (see Chapter 3). Aron did not take part in the quarrel between the positivist, systemic approach of Morton Kaplan and the liberal, juridical and historical conception of Hedley Bull. Even if he is intellectually drawn toward the traditional approach he associated with sociology, history, philosophy and economics rather than the "modern" approach inspired by the behaviorist revolution, he nevertheless recognizes its value. His liberal conception was also different from that of English school. More sociological than strictly juridical and historical, his thought follows the works of Tocqueville, Weber and Clausewitz. He had "chosen affinities" with these authors. He shared their hurt and sadness in the face of violence, which he would also study in an objective way. Since his first intellectual steps, he understood the importance of producing thoughts on the question of the relationship between societies and politics without sacrificing his objectivity toward a philosophical ideal, with *realism* as an epistemological principle.

> I have discovered different people from myself in modern society, of the likes of Hitler and those who followed him. From this time on, I have, so to speak, been purified once and for all, of that I would call academic idealism. I have had the feeling at one and the same time, that politics is tragic and that one could only have reasonable opinions if one respected, as far as is possible, others and accepted differences of opinion.
>
> (Aron 2006: 904–905)

Aron was resolutely realistic in his approach to science, that is to say, with his attitude toward politics and in his own intellectual thought process (see Frost 1997; Hassner 2007; Roche 2011a, 2011b; Battistella 2012a, 2012b). But he was not a realist in the classic sense of International Relations (IR) theory. Steadfastly anti-totalitarian, he considered that a "sincerely humanistic society", such as inspired by Kant, was possible and he shared with Rickert, Dilthey and Weber a "liberal conception of the philosophy of history" (Aron 1981: 315; Canguilhem 1985). His attachment to the freedom of human action was totally incompatible with a teleological and deterministic view of history (Bourricaud 1985; Holeindre 2012). As an adept of reasonable and moderate thought, inspired by Aristotle's Middle Way (*in medio stat virtus*), he believed in virtue and prudence in politics and in the importance of conduct which was "reasonable", especially in this nuclear age. This *via media* between a *realistic* imperative and a liberal conception illustrates Aron's desire to overcome the limitations of these two traditional approaches (Châton 2012; Holeindre 2012: 331). More skeptical than realist, more relativistic than rational, he discussed all the hypotheses in order to develop his thoughts, rejecting all rigid ideas. His both realistic and rationalistic perspectives, his "liberal realism" (Jeangène Vilmer 2013), led him to consider the state as the central player in international relations. But his skepticism and his relativism made him avoid considering the national interest, in a rigid sense, and power-seeking to be the essence of politics, as has been presented by the classical realists since Hans J. Morgenthau (Aron 1967b: 862; Montbrial 1985). His interest in the endogenous factors of political units, mainly his reflections on homo-heterogeneity and the legitimacy of political regimes and on democracy and totalitarianism, differentiates his thought from that of the neorealist Kenneth Waltz, whose area of study is the structure of the international system and relations between the units of the system, excluding all the factors internal to the state. In short, Aron's heritage, which we call *sociological liberalism*, goes beyond the two dominant paradigms of the discipline.

Unfortunately, the Aronian research program seems no longer to be judged on its own merits, and is often reduced to a Cold War theory or a naive rightist manifesto (Macleod and O'Meara 2007). Today, in France, the main approach in IR is explanatory and positivist. It takes part in the Durkheimian tradition. This "internationalist" approach was developed by other great founders: Marcel Mauss and Marcel Merle after him. Aron's sociology of international relations follows other trends and inspirations from the dominant school in France, founded by Marcel Merle just after World War II. A lawyer and sociologist, Merle used an orthodox Durkheimian vision of social life in which to set his analysis of international interactions, in a broad and not strictly political acceptation. It had a rich legacy, illustrated by the work of Bertrand Badie, Marie-Claude Smouts and Guillaume Devin, to name a few. Based on the inclusion of the role of non-state actors in the analysis of IR, it focused on the "international society", in which Aron did not believe. It is also different from the English liberal school of IR. Yet this other French school of IR, initiated by Aron, emerged in parallel to this dominant tradition and, for some specialists, pre-dates Merle's work (Battistella 2013). The development of this school, inspired by Weber and interpretative sociology, as well as the classics of French philosophical thought like Montesquieu and Tocqueville, will be the main concern of this chapter.

Even though, since the 1970s, a substantial literature has been published on Raymond Aron, his work and his theoretical approach to international relations, the tradition he initiated was progressively marginalized in the intellectual debate and the formation of new generations of researchers, likely because those contributions take often the characteristics of a tribute to the author, his high culture and ethical strength, and do not sufficiently underline his conceptual innovations. However, there are fewer works seeking to systematically reformulate the assumptions behind Aron's theory of international relations, and to renew its statements, results and hunches in order to continue this tradition. This comprehensive tradition, following the path of historical sociology opened by Weber, Oppenheimer and Troeltsch (Aron 1935: 45–79), is, however, an essential contribution to the IR discipline in France and abroad.[1] It is a different outlook than the explanatory and positivist French tradition of sociology of international relations, reviving the French classical liberal school of political and social thought (Meszaros 2017). It has a non-negligible utility to think war and peace in the light of their historical process and ideal-typical configurations.

How relevant is this French school of thought initiated by Aron to understand contemporary international relations? What are the fundamental elements on which we need to focus in order to renew this French school of sociological liberalism in IR?

In order to respond to these questions, this chapter intends to examine the intellectual roots of the French school of sociological liberalism created by Aron after World War II, on the conceptual framework he designed during his three-year academic sojourn in Germany. It also replaces the sociological liberalism in the French historical sociology tradition, loyal to its Aronian origins and able to catch up and converse with a thriving and influential Anglo-Saxon school. Finally, this chapter intends to show, by way of three items of food for thought, how sociological liberalism can be renewed in a research program and the usefulness of this approach to the IR discipline to understand the contemporary international reality.

The French IR sociological liberalism school

The French school of sociological liberalism in IR was born, intellectually, during Aron's postdoctoral stay in Germany between 1930 and 1933, when he discovered the concepts and theories developed by Weber and his fellows of the *Archiv für Sozialwissenschaft und Sozialpolitik*. This new way to understand social life, opposed on many subjects to the Durkheimian tradition, is based on interactions between individuals rather than on social groups, puts the emphasis on indetermination and freedom, and condemns social determinism. Aron was one of the first (together with Maurice Halbwachs) to introduce the works of German sociologists in French, notably those of George Simmel, Leopold Von Wiese, Ferdinand Tönnies, Alfred Vierkandt, Franz Oppenheimer, Max Scheler, Karl Mannheim and, above all, Max Weber, to whom he devoted a complete chapter (Aron 1935). His book, *German Sociology*, is much more than a simple "state of the art", despite its title. It is a theoretical construction, bringing together different authors and combining them in a scheme, while criticizing and rejecting others, like Marx and Mannheim. Aron mixed these new influences with the French tradition of thought and proceeded to a very fruitful synthesis between French *penseurs* of liberty and social life and the new school of *sozialwissenschaften*. Montesquieu, Tocqueville and Pareto[2] were introduced to Weber, Simmel and Tönnies to form a new tradition of thinking, both French and German, considering the individual as the fundamental atom of social life and of collective action. Refusing to reify social groups and to give them specifications per se, this gathering was the starting point of Aron's reflection, as it would be reasserted in his personal history of sociology, *Main Currents in Sociological Thought* (Aron 1967a).

More concretely, the French school of sociological liberalism in IR was born in the specific context of war and the aftermath of World War II that led Aron to consider strategic questions and develop his thinking on foreign politics, and also to produce a sociology of international relations, crafted from a sociology of the "Cold War", that is to say, a sociological approach to bipolarity (Aron 1963). The "Cold War", which he would rather call the "burning peace", was characterized by the reign and balance of terror, as well as a series of major international crises that had no possibility of direct confrontation between the two great powers. This paradox, identified by Aron from 1948, is summed up in the formula "impossible peace, improbable war". Aron was soon to write his first works on international relations, war and strategy, namely *Le Grand Schisme* (1948), more of a partisan book rather than a scientific one, *Les Guerres en chaîne* (1951), *La Coexistence pacifique, Essai d'analyse* (1953), *La Société industrielle et la Guerre* (1959). The numerous papers on "the theory and method of international relations", written in *Etudes politiques* and later *Les Sociétés industrielles*, also date from this period (Aron 1983: 299, 1972, 2005). His major work on international relations, *Peace and War*, and the publication of numerous newspaper articles written during and after World War II are his crowning achievement. As we will see, it can be seen as a "side project" of a much more ambitious project to reform the human sciences, recast around and unified by historical sociology. Moreover, Aron's major work, *Peace and War*, goes far beyond the limits of a treaty of diplomatic action, but rather encompasses reflections about the nature of interstate relations, conflict, clash of values and the essence of the political and power. It is a whole ontology of transpolitic interaction, or, put otherwise, international relations.

In spite of the originality of his thought and his work, Aron did not wish to create either a school or a place of worship (Riesman 1985). It happened naturally. "Master without a doctrine" (Baechler 1983: 64), passionate about debating, he opened a door for researchers who wished to subscribe to this intellectual and multidisciplinary tradition, generally during seminars which brought his "disciples" together (Jean Baechler, in his homage to Aron entitled *Maître et disciple*, reveals to us the way in which these seminars unfolded; see Baechler 1983).[3] Aron's historical sociology of international relations is a fundamental contribution to the IR discipline (Friedrichs 2001). It is not fundamental for realism, nor for the liberal English school tradition. Aron produced a theory of international relations which is original because it is a mixture of philosophy, as a way of forming concepts, sociology, which describes international life with a view to understanding its dynamics, and history, which gives a temporal view of the evolution of political forms and societies. We give the name "French sociological liberalism" to this specific conception of the theory of international relations. According to us, this international historical sociology, born with the publication in 1962 of *Peace and War*, is a variant of the French school of international relations sociology. It seems important today to develop a research program which would renew this "French sociological liberalism" paradigm.

This conception, unlike the Anglo-American acceptance of "sociological liberalism", is not based on the analysis of relations between people and non-state organizations, it does not conceive international relations as transnational relations, but it studies, from a state-centric perspective, the inner life of political units, the configuration of polarity of the international system and hits homo-heterogeneity based on political regimes. It includes the social life in the study of IR via its effects on the government of state. It also understands war as a sociological object and focuses on specific factors of power as nuclear weapons, economic levers, cultural and ideological influence. This Aronian tradition of sociological liberalism articulates three levels of analysis: a philosophical perspective that enables us to produce fundamental problematizations and create the essential concepts to analyze international relations objects; a sociological viewpoint permitting one to glimpse the regularities between facts and epochs beyond the singularities; the historical and monographic enquiries, dealing with the uniqueness of phenomena, focusing on the narration of actual events, whatever their size, and looking for the multiplicity of factors at work in the process (a single battle or election, the life of a party or an individual, the history of a country, of a century, or even of a civilization or of humanity (Aron 1963)).

This program is consequently, by definition, transdisciplinary and requires the researchers to be skilled in these three disciplines.[4] To make a complete and enriching historical sociology of international relations, it aims to mix the history of political units over the long term, sociological comparison tools to grasp the nature of interactions and social configurations of the global environment and, finally, philosophical conceptual rigor, necessary to adopt the best-approach angles to the problems implied by the complex nature of international relations. While the post-Cold War world experiences chaotic transformations, this method, based inherently on intersubjectivity, is necessary to understand the changes in the distribution of power on a global scale. It is also an essential reference to understand a world where the West is no longer hegemonic, but also that it wasn't always. Seen on a century or millennium scale, European civilization has not always been hegemonic. Before modernity, i.e., before the sixteenth century, Europe was not the richest or the most powerful part of the planet. It only gained supremacy over India in the eighteenth century, over China in middle of the nineteenth, and could only take over the Middle East after the collapse of Ottoman Empire in 1918. From the standpoint of historical sociology, which Aron conceived as the only pertinent basis on which to analyze global history and the daily evolution of international relations, the European hegemony was only recent, and, after all, just a parenthesis. As he wrote in his insightful essay *Dimensions of the Historical Consciousness*:

> From now on, historians of Asia are considering as a closed era the centuries that have passed from the landing of the first Portuguese ships on the coast of India to the departure of the last English and French troops in Malaysia and Madagascar.
>
> (Aron 1961)

There is no better demonstration that the theory he shaped is not limited to the analysis of the bipolar state of affairs. His work, concepts and research methods are designed to understand every single international system and the forces that keep one standing and bring another to decadence and corruption.

As Frederic Ramel noted, the influence of Weber was immediate on the debate on IR, and this is the legacy that Aron brought back to France:

> [Weber's] thought almost immediately penetrated the field of international relations. It represents one of the sources of realism which was making its mark after the Second World War and constitutes today a necessary place in the increasing importance of the history of the sociology of international relations.
>
> (Ramel 2006: 63)

Aron was more interested in the competition for power between states and found better tools to study it in Weber's political sociology. With its *agonal* dimension, Weber's sociology places the study of struggle, both inside and outside the state, at the center of social action. "He was not one of these sociologists, such as Durkheim, who believed that the military functions of the state belonged to the past and was fast disappearing [and] believed that conflicts would always remain between the great powers" (Aron 1967a: 562). In his political sociology, the monopoly of legitimate physical violence is in the hands of the state itself (Weber 1978). At the international level, this monopoly did not exist, which entails that interstate relations are characterized by permanent struggle. Conflict is therefore a constant of social life, not an occasional phenomenon caused by failure and decadence. In international relations, a system of law is insufficient to limit the conflicts which states are prone to. But, notwithstanding the anarchy which is characteristic of the international system, Weber does not vindicate realpolitik or Wilhelmian Machiavellianism. On the contrary, he criticizes it and considers that the national interest is the only form of objective rationality which can serve to organize the government's priorities, which are mainly those of survival (see especially Ramel 2006: 71–76). The reason for Aron's interest in the Weberian sociology of international relations can be understood by considering his own personal experience of the war. Man and his thoughts are the product of two separate contexts.

The first context is intellectual, being that of the debates ensuing from existentialism and communism. It lays the foundation of the ideological debate of the time, in which Aron took part as a commentator on Sartre and Marx, but also as a journalist and as an analyst of domestic politics. With his PhD dissertation on the philosophy of history, and the ambition to reformulate a theory of the social sciences, he fully entered into the academic and ideological debate of his time:

> The *Introduction to the Philosophy of History* only represented, in my mind, a chapter, the most formal, of historical knowledge theory. I was hoping, back in these days, to add to this introduction, first a theory of social sciences, and then more concrete theory of historical interpretations – interpretation of eras, civilizations, of the becoming of humanity.
>
> (Aron 1961: 33)

Reading his output before World War II, it is not an exaggeration to state that Aron had drawn up a blueprint to recast human sciences, rebuilt on a historicized rational actor, an individual choosing the best options for him according to his welfare *and* cultural yearnings. In Aron's view, human sciences form a system which has a core theory, a main department of research and different methods of inquiry. The core hypothesis of this research program combines a vision of *homo œconomicus*, strongly influenced by Pareto's work and what he calls the *rational actions* of man. But where Pareto saw non-rational actions, based on preferences rather than interest, Weber, and Aron after him, found another type of rationality: the value-oriented rationality, which enables man to gather means toward an end, i.e., to act. It is upon this philosophy of man and his actions that Aron wanted to build his own epistemological system. He dedicated his dissertation to treating a classical problem: the self-understanding of man and of his historical condition. Put another way, the question was, how can man understand human history as a whole, and elaborate a conception of his place and destination inside it? This investigation is, in itself, an answer to the existentialist doctrine. As a free and undetermined agent, or a "historical being", man cannot be seen as a simple agent "reproducing a universal pattern" (Aron 1938: 53–54). There is no "structure of history" that could enable us, humans, to understand the meaning and the direction of our history as a species. The remark targets the Marxist conception of history, and the part played in it by class conflict. It resumed the reflections of Weber on the "limits of historical objectivity", from which Aron derived the subtitle of his dissertation, and the work of Simmel on *The Problems of the Philosophy of History*, often cited in the dissertation. Weber condemned any naive researcher, like Leopold Ranke, who is "convinced that knowledge of historical reality must be or should be a copy 'without presupposition' of objective facts" (Weber 1904). Otherwise, he refutes any design or any universal model of social interaction that would explain every historical situation. For Marx, Egyptians and their slaves, Romans and the plebs, medieval lords and peasants or bourgeoisie and proletarians are all actualizing such a universal pattern, found in class conflict. According to the hypothesis of free, rational and historicized man, this is not only inaccurate, but blinds us and disables our capacity to understand dissimilar historical situations. It is these hypotheses that Aron appropriate and systematized to form his own view of historical and human sciences. "Studying politics is studying the actors, and therefore analyze their decisions, their goals, their means, their mental universe" (Aron 1983: 108). Loyal to his intellectual commitments, Aron would be Weberian until his death. This pledge to comprehensive sociology is a central point to understand his comprehension of international politics and IR. Trying to understand war and interstate relations, he brought with him the German apparatus of historical sociology that was totally neglected in France at that time. His mastering of sociological methods and of philosophical concepts, his vast historical knowledge and this original Weberian positioning contributed to give him a unique place in the French academic landscape.

Aron's sociological liberalism contribution to sociological history

Aron's IR theory is focused on states and state relations. But, one must add that he is not getting rid of ideas and representation. On the contrary, he brings back ideologies and beliefs into the core hypotheses of IR through the concepts of homogeneity and heterogeneity. Today, transnationalists express a main reproach about previous theories of states' behavior on the international stage: their incapacity to take into account the non-state actors. But is it accurate to address this critique of Aron's formalization?

In a depiction of the intellectual path that led him to write *Peace and War*, Aron lists a set of six fundamental questions a researcher in IR should ask himself when he studies an international situation, or as he puts it, "a diplomatic constellation". In order to respond to the transnationalist critic, it is interesting to respond to those six questions asked by Aron with a concrete case, often examined by Mearsheimer, the rise of China and its peaceful or violent implications for Southeast Asia.

The main purpose of these first three questions is, in a very Weberian approach, to reconstruct the *meaning* of acts and words of policy makers. A preliminary question tends to define the limits and the protagonists of the arena: "What are the boundaries of the diplomatic field we deal with?"[5]

This first question brings a specific problematic: are all the diplomatic issues connected to the others? Contrary to liberals, Aron suggests that globalization is not the baseline of all phenomena in the modern world (a position that surely helped neoliberal IR thinkers to reject Aron into "classical realism"). Some problems are strictly local and remain unaffected by the world structure, others are global. There are local problems between two states, regional issues, gathering problems of a multiplicity of states, and, finally, global matters, like nuclear weapons, affecting the whole world, or at least all the global powers. For instance, a border problem between Angola and the Democratic Republic of Congo can stay local and will not affect the African Union or the United Nations. The two states will find a solution according to their power relation. So what is the diplomatic view of the rise of China? It is mainly a regional problem, challenging all the states of Southeast Asia, which are to find a new role in a remodeled sub-continent. It is not yet a world problem, as the status of China as a global power can only be the outcome of the diplomatic struggle.

The second question aims to specify the true power relations into the revealed diplomatic category: "What is the shape of power relations within that arena?" Here we arrive at the problem of the way power relations act on the behavior of states. Is that rival state more powerful than mine? Can it make me accept and accomplish its will to do something or abandon one of my projects? As a good Clausewitzian and Weberian sociologist, Aron thinks power is a relation. It can be achieved, of course, by force, constraint and coercion, but also by prestige, charisma, moral adhesion and rational calculation. It opens a conceptualization like "soft power" all the way to attaining a goal without using military deterrence only. For China, the question is: when will it be sufficiently powerful to balance American power in the region and implement its hegemony?

The third question wants to know how these power relations express themselves, and what form violence would take if it occurs: "What is the mechanism of war to which the leaders refer more or less clearly in order to assess the importance of a given position or relationship?" We are now in the field of the military calculations of foreign policy makers. What happens if the situation degenerates with an escalation to the extremes? There would be no more dialogue and weapons would replace words: this is war. But power is not a measurable quantum when it comes to military struggle. It is a complex and delicate social organization of people and technologies of destruction put together to defeat an enemy. Even if a country is richer or stronger, it can fail to invade one of its neighbors or a remote country, because power needs to be projected and that projection entails a cost. Furthermore, this complex calculation can be wrong in the minds of policy makers, as we foresaw in Mearsheimer's depiction of World War II. For China, the calculation must focus on the possible reaction of other regional states and of their main ally, the United States. Is there any possibility that all the countries of the region will join an American coalition against China, in a classical *bandwagoning* move? Will this coalition be able to defeat China in the South China Sea? This is the calculation it has to make in order to define to what limits its "aggressive" (or "revisionist") behavior can go and when to stop, and not to risk a military confrontation with the United States.

Aron states very clearly that this first set of questions was not inspired by the Cold War, but rather by the European concert of nations of the nineteenth century and the first half of the twentieth (and therefore mostly by the vision of the two world wars as one single episode, "from Sarajevo to Hiroshima", as he states in *Les Guerres en Chaîne*, which has been called "the second Thirty Years War" by his successor Jean Baechler). Describing Aron's theory of IR as strictly restricted to the Cold War (as in Roche 2011b) does not fit with the project of the author. The next three questions are, in essence, "ideological-political". We get a little more realism and enter into the Weberian comprehensive method in IR.

The fourth question is asked to size up the level of heterogeneity in the conflict: "To what extent did states in conflict recognize one another, so that only borders and not the existence of the states themselves were at stake in the struggle?" In continuation of Papaligouras' work (Papaligouras 1941), this question states very clearly what critical approaches and constructivists will conceptualize much later: there is no power by itself. The power of an ally or a friend can be borne more easily than the power of an enemy. It is the famous example of Wendt: a gun is more threatening in the hand of one of my enemies than it is in the hand of a friend (Wendt 1996). For China, the answer to that question indicates the path its rise will take. Will its power be perceived as a threat by other regional states? After all, American hegemony came as a liberation for a long list of countries after German or Soviet domination. New conditions might arise and transform the perception of China by other East Asian states, opening the way to an acceptance, and even a desire, for a strong and powerful China. The realignment of Philippines' President Rodrigo Duterte in favor of a Chinese alliance could make it the first country to break with the United States and support an advantageous status with the new regional hegemon.

The fifth question intends to grasp the level of autonomy of international politics or its dependence on internal political problems and struggles: "What is the relation between the functioning of domestic politics and the decisions of statesmen?" Here, another fundamental theoretical standpoint separates Aron from realism. States are not black boxes. They are not neutral to the ideology of other states. But it is not only from one state to another that the connection is made. It is also between leaders and competing political units inside the states. As the internal political rules set the "opportunity structures" for parties and actors in a political struggle, the ideology and the alliances will interfere with foreign policy decisions. A simple example will make this clearer. If a government has the support of communists in the parliament, it will be very difficult for it to condemn a communist *coup d'état* in another state. The allied communists will threaten to leave the coalition and the government will have no other choice than to stay silent or to fall. Another example is the choice of Leon Blum's government not to intervene in the Spanish Civil War. The far right was, at that time, very powerful. It was "pacifist", as the majority of far right adherents were former soldiers of World War I. Choosing to go to war against Franco would have been a real gift to the far right and could perhaps bring it to power. The Blum government had its hands tied and could not act as it wanted because of the fragility of its majority in the National Assembly. In the case of China today, the point would be to know to what extent the Chinese government is free to pursue its goals or is prevented from doing so by internal complications. As there is no organized opposition and only fractions within the Communist Party of China, the freedom to act does not seem diminished by internal politics (see also Sartori 1976). However, an inquiry into the struggle inside the party and on the personal ties of Chinese leaders with foreign leaders would be necessary to give a definitive response.

Finally, the last question is a clear choice to move away from the realist paradigm. "What meaning did the latter give to peace, to war, and to relations among the states?" Aron does not speak about the behavior of *states*, but always about the behavior of people holding the highest positions in a state involved in conflict or in cooperation. From that perspective, war, peace, national interest or mistrust are questions of perception, and therefore of misperception (Jervis 1976). In a way, Aron helped to pave the way to theories based on the analysis of ideology and sense, "world visions" (*weltanschauung*), on political decisions. Constructivism is not far off, even if Aron always considered *interest* as the bedrock that explains the conduct of foreign policies in IR. But it is not an everlasting concept, a political *conatus*, which always encompasses the same items, as security, prestige or economic prosperity. It is a "moving and subjective" truth, surrounding varying perceived dangers and benefits. In the Chinese case the government could choose to go to war with some neighbors, like Taiwan, and, in the process, with the United States. But that would mean that they see war as the only way to get a "revision" of the terms of peace. Nevertheless, this last remark set another distinction in Aron's theory that was perhaps made by contemplation of the Cold War or by another historical situation. As peace is a passive state and war an active one, to pass from peace to war demands that one of the political units choose to go to war. That would mean that it is the best way to achieve its goals on the international stage. It is, at least to some extent, an optimistic way to think of IR, since two states or two great powers do not need to have the same vision of peace as their rivals. They just need to agree on the general term of it and find some interest in it, and agree that war would be a "bad deal" for everyone. For war not to occur, there is no need for complete homogeneity; limited heterogeneity is sufficient. If the powers are distant and not directly threatening each other (unlike France and Germany in the twentieth century, or like China and the United States today), an acceptable accommodation could be reached, as it was with the Soviet Union for 46 years. This is what Aron's historical sociology has to say on IR, along with his borrowings from German historical sociology, the Weberian school and the input of French classic political thinkers. The field of historical sociology since Aron has been considerably developed and nowadays constitutes a fertile ground for IR theory. Aron's sociological liberalism forms part of the mainstream of historical sociology.

Today, the historical sociology of international relations movement can be classified as an actual current of IR and a tool used by many researchers. The achievements of this informal school are numerous, and names like John M. Hobson, Stephen Hobden, Richard Lawson, Shmuel Eisenstadt, Randall Collins, Stathis Kalyvas, Richard Lachman, Michael Mann and Hendrik Spruyt are mentioned here to demonstrate the dynamism of this trend. Issues like world history (Spruyt 1996; Hobson 2012; Subrahmanyam 2014), the definition of and role played by "civilizations" (Baechler 2002, 2005; Eisenstadt 2006), the state and its way of acting on the international stage (Hobson 2000; Lachman 2010), the nature and the invariants of human violence (Collins 2008), infra-state conflict and guerilla warfare (Kalyvas 2015), interstate war (Dabila 2013), ideological opposition and clash of values (Meszaros 2007, 2008) and level of analysis in IR were profoundly renewed by the methods promoted by historical sociology.

Among these authors, one can command our attention a bit longer to illustrate the ways in which historical sociology understands IR today. The method of

Hendryk Spruyt, for instance, is a good example of the method extending Aron's set of questions in modern research. In his introduction to IR, *Global Horizons* (Spruyt 2009), the first task attributed to a theory is not to search for and define, once and for all, what is the most relevant level of analysis to study all political interaction between political units. The state (Morgenthau 1948), the structure of the international system (Waltz 1979), the perception of individuals, the intellectual atmosphere, the choices and failures of policy makers are all influences on the conduct of international affairs. Therefore, a theory of IR must conceptualize all of them, and allow identification of which is the most pertinent in a given situation. Accordingly to this conceptual assertion, he defines three basic levels of analysis: individuals and decision makers, states and their component parts (which implies a non-unitary definition of the state, which can also be found in Allison 1971; Mead 2002), and the structure of the international system. All of them contain incentives for political units to act in different ways and can modify the "opportunity structures" (we borrow this concept from Sartori 1976) on the international stage.

> Moving from the first level to the third level we aggregate politics at an increasing scale and move up in the degree of abstraction. Individual leaders make decisions, but they are part of political institutions within the state. States in turn form part of an international system. This system constrains and perhaps determines how states behave. The degree of structural determination differs as well across the various levels of analysis. Individuals must take the demands of the larger collectivity, the formal institutions in the state, into account. States in turn must heed the constraints and opportunities in the international system.
>
> (Spruyt 2009: 30)

This model is not just a remix of previous theories. It is a clear ambition to reach a synthesis, enabling analysis of various situations and the most effective variation explaining a major shift in the international system. It gives us a way to combine several types of approaches and methods, without privileging one above the others, like structural realism favors the configuration of the international system. Neither fully realist nor fully convinced by the liberal, Aron promotes this kind of multi-level epistemic model, enabling us to understand which parameters (decision makers, equilibrium within the state, changes in international system) contributed the most to unbalance a specific situation. This is what the historical sociology of IR model initiated by Aron allows us to do.

Food for thought for a renewed research program of a comprehensive theory of contemporary international relations

According to us, Aron's IR sociological liberalism is one fundamental source for the elaboration of a comprehensive theory of contemporary relations. Following on from the six motivating questions at the root of *Peace and War*, which were tackled above, we present three items of food for thought of Aron's sociological liberalism of IR that are essential to constitute a comprehensive theory of international relations. The first one is war and the ontological aspects linked to a sociological study of war. The second depends on the first one because it analyzes the configuration of the international system expressed in terms of polarity and homo-heterogeneity. The third is political violence as a fundamental aspect of relations between men and societies. In sum, international relations requires understanding war between states through the units' ideological conceptions, political regimes and the system's polarity, and finally to question political violence as a phenomenon inherent to men and societies.

The first food for thought with respect to Aron's IR sociological liberalism concerns war and its ontological consequences. According to the tradition of Weber and Clausewitz, Aron considers international relations and war as sociological objects. The specificity of these subjects is found in the difference which exists between the internal and external orders: society is characterized by the monopoly of legitimate physical violence; the international order is characterized, on the contrary, by the absence of this monopoly of coercion, that is to say, by the legality and legitimacy of resorting to armed violence by the different actors (Aron 1967b: 843–845). This distinction is of fundamental importance to the sociology of international relations because it defines the subject of study. The internal, the space where the monopolization of violence has led to the suppression of "the war of all against all", is the concern of political sociology. The external, the space where the absence of a monopoly of violence implies maintaining a permanent conflict of one state against another, is a matter for the sociology of international relations.

War is the central subject of this sociology. It exists at an international level, writes Kenneth Waltz, "because nothing can prevent it" (Waltz 1959: 188). Aron, unlike Durkheim, Mauss or Merle, does not consider it to be a *pathology* of the international system but a *normal* phenomenon. It is an invariable which structures the history of the international system. Even if it does not occur, the efforts of states to prevent it organize the international scene. War, therefore, is undeniably a historical fact and also a social reality, but of a particular type:

> International relations are driven by the alternatives of war or peace; evidently, war is an historic event of considerable importance, inherent to centuries' history, since there is no civilization which has not known war and even protracted wars of varying frequency; but this historical phenomenon seems not to be a social phenomenon at first sight or, if I can say, it has the unique character amongst the subjects of sociology to be at the same time both social and asocial. It is sociality because of a certain social relationship between those who fight, but simultaneously it is the very negation of the term social, because those who fight agree upon their enmity and the breakdown of social relations. Sorokin puts civil wars and foreign wars in the

same category, calling the phenomenon *breakdown of social relations*. In other words, in this quite classical perspective, war is more a dissolving of social ties than a social phenomenon itself.

(Aron 1963: 308)

The sociology of international relations must therefore study this particular social phenomenon: war. This specific sociology is all the more important in the nuclear age when the political costs of a conflict have profoundly changed and require a rethinking of the traditional scope of thought which has prevailed up to the present in the study of international relations:

Why am I so interested in military affairs? This started during the last war. I felt ashamed that no French intellectuals had reflected on war. And then, there is another reason which seems to me to be more important, and that is nuclear arms. Using nuclear arms is no longer warfare in the ordinary sense of the word. Nuclear warfare has become a subject of philosophical consideration. In fact, when using an arm so as not to deploy it effectively or where the arm becomes the way of avoiding the war, we leave the competence of military specialists and enter that of the political philosopher.

(Aron 2006: 906)

This philosophical reflection on the nature of war is complementary to a sociology of war, and concerns different forms of war during the Cold War (guerilla warfare, war of liberation, etc.) and the "concrete study of international relations" which, for Aron, is both historical and sociological (Aron 1967b: 852). A theory of international relations must contain the three dimensions of philosophy, sociology and history. The theory that Aron puts forward concerns the international system, that is to say, the entity constituted of political units having regular relations with each other and which are susceptible to being implicated in a general war (Aron 1962: 103). This theory, the aim of which is *praxeological*, puts the accent on three emblematic figures of international relations: the diplomat, the soldier and the strategist (in *Peace and War* Aron makes reference only to the diplomat and the soldier, but in the rest of his works he shows the importance of the strategist). Through these key actors, it is possible to separate, among general international phenomena, the specific diplomatic-strategic relationships between independent political units, in order to study them.

From an ontological point of view, war is not a relationship between one human and another, but a relationship between states (Aron 1962: 113); the international system which Aron studies is the *interstate system*, more precisely of a whole composed of political units (the states) which have "regular diplomatic relations" and which are susceptible to making war (Aron 1962: ii). Aron does not reject the idea of a *transnational society*, such as that described by Marcel Merle, evidenced by "commercial exchanges, migration of people, common beliefs, cross-border organizations and finally ceremonies or competitions open to members of all these units" (Aron 1962: 113).

On the other hand, he does not accept the idea of a *world society* or an *international society* which would encompass "the interstate system, the economic system, transnational movements, the different forms of exchange (of commerce in the wider eighteenth-century view) from civil societies to another, supranational institutions" (Aron 1962: viii). In short, such a *society* would include all the aspects of "international life" and would no longer have the characteristics of a society. Using the concept of society implies a coherent totality. Thus, Aron, contrary to Merle, uses the concept of a system "in a non-rigorous way" (Aron 1962: viii). He does not seek to produce a systemic analysis of international relations, nor to produce an explicative global theory of international phenomena, like Morton A. Kaplan.

For Aron, it is a meaningless task to try to produce a general theory of international relations (Aron 1962, 1967b). Just like Weber, he refuses all causal, deterministic and absolute explanations. His theory is part of a comprehensive logic, that is to say, one which permits the understanding or interpretation of international facts. He seeks to establish sociological typologies (a method using the ideal-type inspired by Weber and Tocqueville) using principles (in Montesquieu's sense of the word) rather than determining laws (Aron 1962: 179, 180). His method aims to understand the behavior of actors and make the meaning they give to their behavior more objective. This objectification is made possible thanks to the construction of concepts useful to analysis.

The research program we aim to develop will be based on this sociological perspective of war and diplomatic-strategic relationships. It will study the place of the state as the central actor of international relations even if non-state actors today are in competition with him. This sociological analysis of international relations is integrated in a wide perspective that includes a philosophical and historical approach in order to develop adapted concepts to question the contemporary path of states in *polities'* history.

The second food for thought of Aron's IR sociological liberalism is directly connected to his ontological perspective and expressed in terms of polarity. It highlights anarchy that provides insights into a fundamental problem: why is there a permanent quest for power, security and prestige on the international scene? The behavior of states is the result of the material configuration of these power relationships expressed in terms of polarity (monopolarity and multipolarity or, more precisely, bipolarity, oligopolarity and polypolarity) and in terms of homogeneity and heterogeneity according to the degree of legitimacy of the political regimes (these concepts were inspired by Panayis Papaligouras; see Papaligouras 1941; Aron 1962: 103, 1983: 302; Meszaros 2007, 2008). The homogeneous/heterogeneous duo reinforced the distinction friend/enemy, originally formulated by Carl Schmitt, and gives it a specific meaning (Schmitt 1992).

The concepts of homogeneity and heterogeneity hence invite us to view international relations from an original angle, focusing in particular on the role of ideas, norms and conceptualizations that actors create according to their environment. The concept of homogeneity and heterogeneity outlined by Papaligouras was used first by Aron and then by Kissinger as an important cultural variable, leading to the variable of polarity (Aron 1962, 1967b; Kissinger 1957, 1994). In the work of both authors heterogeneity results mainly from revolution and the formation of what Aron called "ideocracies". It is "the relatedness or, on the contrary, the hostility of established regimes in the states" which creates the important distinction between homogeneous systems and heterogeneous systems, a distinction that results from the idea that "the external behavior of states is not commanded only by the struggle of powers", goals being also partially determined by the nature of the regime and by ideology (Aron 1983: 452; Hoffmann 1983: 845ff.). The main concepts presented here, the polarity and the homo-heterogeneity that structure Aron's thought, are definitely sociological.

The research program we aim to develop is based on the reinterpretation of those main concepts used by Aron in *Peace and War*. One of the main axes of this research program consists in the analysis of the evolution of the international system from the end of the Cold War in terms of polarity. The concept of polarity has been well developed by Aron and enriched by his disciple Jean Baechler, who contributed to the clarification and improvement of some notions formulated by Aron. When Aron invokes "multipolar" systems, Baechler explains, in several of his works, that Aron refers in fact to "oligopolar" systems (Baechler 1999, 2002, 2005). The idea prevailed, but not the terminology. Most commentators nowadays refer to the evolution of a "multipolar" international system while they mean by that term an "oligopolar" system. The term "oligopolar" is undoubtedly more accurate, insofar as the term "multipolarity" allows an ambiguity between polypolarity and oligopolarity ("many" and "several"). The question is not trivial insofar as the properties of polypolar systems with many actors are not the same as those of oligopolar systems, which are composed of between five and 15 active players, the current major powers. Oligopolar systems are indeed remarkably stable, while a polypolar system is particularly unstable. The former is a positive sum game, where nobody is stronger than the coalition of all the others and therefore where everyone has an interest in collaborating with others to maintain the balance of power. A good example would be the European concert of nations between 1815 and 1914. The latter is a more like an unorganized crowd, where coalition costs are high and confidence in others low. The situation of Europe between the two world wars would be a good historical illustration, with a high benefit for the first one to attack (here, Germany).

In Aron's thought, a "homogeneous" oligopolar system is particularly stable, because a "heterogeneous" oligopolar system is a system whose stability is threatened not because of the number of players, but because of the heterogeneity of the actors composing the system (Aron 1962: 108ff.). In other words, a homogeneous oligopolar system may become unstable if and when a heterogeneous variable is introduced into the system. It is advisable to identify this heterogeneous dynamic, which can be of different kinds: for instance, very rapid growth of a trend within the system, changing the balance of power distribution between political units and leading a state to a "revisionist" policy with regard to the global equilibrium (as discussed by Schmitt's chapter in this book); the occurrence of a political or social revolution changing the power struggle and its perceptions; a political and religious conflict; an identity crisis, etc.

There are two main possibilities, the first one being the increase of heterogeneity through an increase in the number of actors. European political history, Aron's model, is a great illustration of this phenomenon. This is what happened with the successive national independence movements, from the Treaties of Westphalia to the Treaty of Versailles, or with successive EU enlargements, when it integrated Eastern European countries after the collapse of the Soviet empire that destabilized the European system and made it very difficult to adopt common rules (the enlargements of 2004, 2007 and 2013). This is also the case with the increase in the number of actors in the Middle East with the collapse of the Ottoman Empire. The second possibility is the transformation of stable oligopolar systems in unstable polypolar systems. Jean Baechler demonstrated that in the tribal world, when, for one reason or another, very stable oligopolar tribal systems are brought into contact with each other, usually by war, the result is the loss of oligopolar systems in favor of the formation of a polypolar system which is in constant war. This polypolar system goes through a phase of bipolarization to achieve a hegemonic domination, which inevitably turns into empire. In this second case, heterogenization does not result from the increasing number of actors, but from their differentiation, because of the destabilizing growth of a variable, whether economic, demographic, cultural, religious or ideological. This was the case when the European system faced the French Revolution, and in World Wars I and II with the multiplication of heterogeneous actors. It was also the case with the Japanese economic and cultural rise in the East Asian regional system in the first half of the twentieth century, or with the kindling of communism in Latin America in the 1960s. According to us, today, these two possibilities are occurring simultaneously: the heterogenization of the international system and the transformation of the former oligopolar system into a polypolar, very ideologized system is the consequence of the increase of the role and the number of actors with different natures, states and non-state actors, such as Daesh.

Aron's sociological liberalism could notably be added to the current debate on polarity, hegemonic powers and balancing politics. His approach associates the configuration of polarity, expressed in terms of power, and a sociologic analysis of political regimes' relations. His legacy permits engagement with a discussion of other approaches, such as Waltz's or Mearsheimer's conceptions that question balancing, buck-passing and bandwagoning (Waltz 1979; Mearsheimer 2001).

The third food for thought of Aron's IR sociological liberalism is human violence, and therefore political violence, but not just as a rational calculation of interest, nor a cold determination of the best behavior, putting affect and values aside. We often fight to defend values and not just to maintain our security. Regimes fight to defend similar regimes, sometimes when there is only the slightest incentive to do so. Sometimes, violence is totally against the national interest and states can renounce it. But, again, interest is just one of the parameters here. Also, because violence is unpredictable.

If we follow the analysis of Randall Collins, violence is not just a way like any other to resolve problems. Dealing with fear, danger and anger, it has a particular "situational dynamic" (Collins 2008: 7). War, just as any other method of using violence, needs an accumulation of tension. When it is released, the two contenders use all their "emotional energy" to reach their goals, and little room is left for calculation and deceit. Certainly, as organized violence, war tends to be rationalized by the minds of politicians and generals, and also by the political goals of war. But human passion sets aside these two ways of conducting war, as Clausewitz underlined when he chose these three elements to form the Holy Trinity of War (see Clausewitz 1989: Book VIII, ch. 6b). If international politics is conducted through war, he adds, it does not make something completely different out of it. It does not change its very nature. But war has its own particularities, its own "grammar", which influences, in return, the conduct of politics. There are two errors not to make. The first is to think that in war, only victory matters, and to give priority to strategic or, worst, tactical goals, and forget the political order they are supposed to serve. The second is to ignore the laws of war and imagine you can wage war without all the emotional energy violence needs to be efficient. War is "confrontational tension" (Collins 2008) and one has to follow the rules to defeat the enemy. A prince unwilling to go to war would be as weak as the unarmed prince Machiavelli described in his essay, because it would refuse the most basic rule of politics and international political confrontation.

Therefore, one cannot just sit and watch two foes bleed each other to death, as Mearsheimer stated. The greatest example of this is the fight between Byzantium and Persia in the seventh century, which exhausted the two empires and led to the Islamic conquest of the Middle East. But this event, just as the American hegemony over Western Europe, contained a certain amount of luck and was not strictly the calculation of the greater strategist. When dealing with Islamic conquest and the American takeover of Europe, ignoring the ideological settings of the configuration is just impossible. Human political violence is too complex to be reduced to a chess game.

In conclusion, we affirm that the thought of Raymond Aron has not delivered all its features and is still today at the heart of debates in IR theory between realism, liberalism, the English school and constructivism. We aimed to show that the renewal of Aron's scientific project, sociological liberalism, invites the development of an ambitious program of research that fits into the wave of historical sociology. In order to open the way to this research program, we also aimed to briefly present three items of food for thought: war as sociological object, the link between polarity and homo-heterogeneity and political violence as the basic unit of reflection on IR. These lines of thought are just some among others to explore. They show the pertinence of Aron's sociological liberalism for IR theory today, and invite researchers from different backgrounds to join the effort to renew his scientific project.

Notes

1 Stanley Hoffmann sometimes referred to Aron as "my master in historical sociology" (Hoffmann 2002: 6).
2 Although Italian, Pareto lived and taught in Switzerland and wrote most of his work in French (Aron 1937).
3 His name has been given to the Center of Sociological and Political Studies Raymond Aron (CESPRA).
4 On philosophy, sociology and history as the three disciplines of human sciences, see Baechler (2000).
5 All the questions are quoted from Aron's *Memoirs*, translated into English in 1990 by George Holoch (Aron 1990: 195).

References

Allison, G. (1971), *Essence of Decision*. New York: Little Brown.
Aron, R. (1935), *La sociologie allemande contemporaine*. Paris: Alcan.
Aron, R. (1937), "La sociologie de Pareto", *Zeitschrift für Sozialforschung*, vol. VI. Paris: F. Alcan, 489–521.
Aron, R. (1938), *Introduction à la philosophie de l'histoire: Essai sur les limites de l'objectivité historique*. Paris: Gallimard.
Aron, R. (1948), *Le Grand Schisme*. Paris: Gallimard.
Aron, R. (1951), *Les Guerres en chaîne*. Paris: Gallimard.
Aron, R. (1953), *La Coexistence pacifique: Essai d'analyse* (published under the pseudonym François Houtisse). Paris: Editions du Monde nouveau.
Aron, R. (1959), *La Société industrielle et la Guerre*. Paris: Plon.
Aron, R. (1961), *Dimensions de la conscience historique*. Paris: Plon.
Aron, R. (1962), *Paix et guerre entre les nations*. Paris: Calmann-Lévy.
Aron, R. (1963), "Une sociologie des relations internationales", *Revue française de sociologie*, 4:3, 307–320.
Aron, R. (1967a), *Les Étapes de la pensée sociologique*. Paris: Gallimard.
Aron, R. (1967b), "Qu'est-ce qu'une théorie des relations internationales?" *Revue française de science politique*, 17:5, 837–861.
Aron, R. (1972), *Etudes politiques*. Paris: Gallimard.
Aron, R. (1981), *Le Spectateur engagé (entretiens)*. Paris: Julliard.
Aron, R. (1983), *Mémoires: 50 ans de réflexion politique*. Paris: Julliard.
Aron, R. (1990), *Memoirs: Fifty Years of Political Reflections*. New York: Holmes & Meier.
Aron, R. (2005), *Les sociétés modernes*. Paris: Presses Universitaires de France.
Aron, R. (2006), "Autoportrait", *Commentaire*, 4:116, 903–908.
Baechler, J. (1983), "Maître et disciple", *Commentaire*, 1:28–29, 62–66.
Baechler, J. (1999), *Contrepoints et commentaires*. Paris: Calmann-Lévy.
Baechler, J. (2000), *Nature et Histoire*. Paris: PUF.
Baechler, J. (2002), *Esquisse d'une histoire universelle*. Paris: Fayard.
Baechler, J. (2003), *Aspects de la Mondialisation*. Paris: PUF.
Baechler, J. (2005), *Les morphologies sociales*. Paris: PUF.
Battistella, D. (2012a), "Raymond Aron: A Neoclassical Realist before the Term Existed?" in Toje, A. and Kunz, B. (eds.), *Neoclassical Realism in European Politics: Bringing Power Back in*. Manchester: Manchester University Press, 117–137.
Battistella, D. (2012b), "Raymond Aron, réaliste néoclassique", *Etudes internationales*, 43:3, 371–388.

Battistella, D. (2013), "La France", in Balzacq, T. and Ramel, F. (eds.), *Traité de relations internationales*. Paris: Presses de Science Po, 157–179.
Bourricaud, F. (1985), "Entre 1947 et 1950", *Commentaire*, 1:28–29, 32–34.
Canguilhem, G. (1985), *Le Normal et le pathologique*. Paris: PUF.
Châton, G. (2012), "Pour un 'machiavélisme postkantien': Raymond Aron, théoricien réaliste hétérodoxe", *Etudes internationales*, 43:3, 389–403.
Clausewitz, C. (1989), *On War*. Princeton, NJ: Princeton University Press.
Collins, R. (2008), *Violence: A Micro-sociological Theory*. Princeton, NJ: Princeton University Press.
Dabila, A. (2013), *L'affrontement Guerrier: Approche Sociologique de l'Engagement Martial*. PhD dissertation, Paris-Sorbonne University.
Eisenstadt, S. (2006), *The Great Revolutions and the Civilizations of Modernity*. Leiden: Brill.
Friedrichs, J. (2001), "International Relations Theory in France", *Journal of International Relations and Development*, 4:2, 118–137.
Frost, B.-P. (1997), "Resurrecting a Neglected Theorist: The Philosphical Foundations of Raymond Aron's Theory of International Relations", *Review of International Studies*, 23:2, 143–166.
Hassner, P. (2007), "Raymond Aron: Too Realistic to Be a Realist?", *Constellations*, 14:4, 498–505.
Hobson, J.M. (2000), *The State and International Relations*. Cambridge: Cambridge University Press.
Hobson, J.M. (2012), *The Eurocentric Conception of World Politics (1760–2010)*. Cambridge: Cambridge University Press.
Hoffmann, S. (1983), "Raymond Aron et la théorie des relations internationales", *Politique étrangère*, 4, 841–857.
Hoffmann, S. (2002), "Le XXIe Siècle a commencé", *Vingtième Siècle*, 76:4, 5–14.
Holeindre, J.-V. (2012), "Introduction: Raymond Aron, un classique de la pensée internationale", *Études internationales*, 43:3, 321–338.
Jeangène Vilmer, J.-B. (2013), "Pour un réalisme libéral en relations internationales", *Commentaire*, 141, 13–20.
Jervis, R. (1976), *Perception and Misperception in International Politics*. Princeton, NJ: Princeton University Press.
Kalyvas, S. (2015), *Civil Wars*. New York: Polity Press.
Kissinger, H. (1957), *A World Restored: Metternich, Castlereagh, and the Problems of Peace 1812–1822*. Boston, MA: Houghton, Mifflin.
Kissinger, H. (1994), *Diplomacy*. New York: Simon & Schuster.
Lachman, R. (2010), *States and Power*. Cambridge: Polity Press.
Macleod, A. and O'Meara, D. (2007), *Théorie des relations internationales: Contestations et résistances*. Montreal: Éditions Athéna.
Mead, W.R. (2002), *Special Providence*. London: Routledge.
Mearsheimer, J. (2001), *The Tragedy of Great Powers Politics*. New York: W.W. Norton & Company.
Meszaros, T. (2007), "Un apport philosophique marginalisé: le concept de société internationale chez Panayis Papaligouras", *Études internationales*, 38:1, 87–109.
Meszaros, T. (2008), "Système contre société: Deux concepts antithétiques? Quand la 'nouvelle vague' de l'École anglaise défie l'idée de société internationale", *Études internationales*, 39:3, 411–431.

Meszaros, T. (2017), "The French Tradition of Sociology of International Relations", *The American Sociologist*, 48:3–4, 297–341.
Montbrial, T. de (1985), "Aron et l'action politique", *Commentaire*, 1:28–29, 105–106.
Morgenthau, H. (1948), *Politics among Nations: The Struggle for Power and Peace*. New York: Knopf.
Papaligouras, P. (1941), *Théorie de la société internationale*. Geneva: Kundig.
Ramel, F. (2006), *Les fondateurs oubliés: Durkheim, Simmel, Weber, Mauss et les relations internationales*. Paris: Presses Universitaires de France.
Riesman, D. (1985), "L'héritage de Raymond Aron", *Commentaire*, 1:28–29, 131–133.
Roche, J.-J. (2011a), "Raymond Aron, un demi-siècle après Paix et guerre entre les nations (1re partie)", *Revue de défense nationale*, 736, 7–18.
Roche, J.-J. (2011b), "Raymond Aron, un demi-siècle après Paix et guerre entre les nations (2e partie)", *Revue de défense nationale*, 736, 7–18.
Sartori, G. (1976), *Parties and Party Systems: A Framework for Analysis*. Cambridge: Cambridge University Press.
Schmitt, C. (1992), *La notion de politique*. Paris: Flammarion.
Spruyt, H. (1996), *The Sovereign State and Its Competitors*. Princeton, NJ: Princeton University Press.
Spruyt, H. (2015), *Global Horizons: Introduction to International Relations*, 3rd edn. Toronto: University of Toronto Press (1st edn. 2009).
Subrahmanyam, S. (2014), *Aux Origines de l'Histoire Globale*. Paris: Fayard.
Waltz, K. (1959), *Man, the State, and War*. New York: Columbia University Press.
Waltz, K. (1979), *Theory of International Politics*. New York: McGraw-Hill.
Weber, M. (1904), "Objectivity of Social Science and Social Policy", *Archiv für Sozialwissenschaft und Sozialforschung*, 19:1, 22–87.
Weber, M. (1978), *Economy and Society*. Berkeley and Los Angeles: University of California Press.
Wendt, A. (1996), "Norms, Identity, Cultures in National Security", in Katzenstein, P. and Jepperson, R. (eds.), *The Culture of National Security*. New York: Columbia University Press, 33–75.

9 Raymond Aron and the ethics of current global affairs

Ariane Chebel d'Appollonia

The study of global affairs focuses on a complex set of dynamic and interrelated political, socioeconomic, technological, and cultural processes as an interdisciplinary field that transcends disciplinary boundaries. Questions relating to global affairs are alternatively analyzed through employing the concepts of "global society," "global distributive justice," "global governance," or "human security." The field, broadly defined, analyzes the roles of various actors (state and non-state), examines new political agendas that potentially frame world politics (such as the United Nations' Responsibility to Protect initiative, familiarly known as R2P), and studies the significance of emergent, novel crises and threats in a globally networked world (such as terrorism and migration).

This chapter will discuss the relevance of Raymond Aron's historical and philosophical approach to some relatively recent formulations in global affairs. It will develop three core arguments. First, Aron's theory of International Relations (IR) is not only still relevant despite the systemic changes that have occurred since the end of the Cold War, but in fact has taken on an increased significance. Indeed, his discussion of the legitimacy and legality of the use of force is notably prescient in the context of the ethical issues raised by recent humanitarian interventions. Second, Aron's work provides a helpful way to analyze the complexity of the world system based on a balanced synthesis of principled realism and realistic idealism. This synthesis can help avoid the flaws of both unrealistic realism and immoral moralism in addressing such issues as the "global war on terror," the management of migration flows, and violations of human rights and/or civil liberties (by democratic and non-democratic states). Finally, and in contrast to many scholars of ethics in IR, Aron's work offers a praxeology that transcends the distinction between conviction (deontology/rule-based political decisions) and responsibility (consequentialism/end-based political actions). His morality of prudence therefore has a sustained veracity in a modern context.

Aron's conceptualization of IR

What is the relevance of Raymond Aron's work in comprehending the current state of global affairs? Was he mainly a contextual, Cold War thinker or did he offer conceptual tools useful for addressing the main issues and threats we are facing in the second decade of the twenty-first century?

Answering these questions requires a brief presentation of his conceptual framework, most cogently presented in *Peace and War among Nations*, based on an historical and sociological analysis of a global system in the thermonuclear age. He argued that the specific features of interstate relations were then related to the extension, for the first time to the whole globe, of a single international system. This system was characterized by its heterogeneity, and dominated by the nuclear duopoly of the United States and the Soviet Union. Aron listed specifically important features of the Cold War era, such as the "multiplicity of autonomous centers of decision, and therefore the risk of war" (1962: 28), as well as the plurality of political ends among the actors. What constituted the distinctive feature of interstate relations, he argued, was the linkage between legitimacy or legality and the use of military force.

In the absence of an entity holding a monopoly over the legitimate use of violence, each state was obliged to provide for its own security, locked in a struggle that was driven as much by ideology as by the search for power. The systemic configuration (bipolar or multipolar) of forces thus depended on the kinship or hostility between the internal regimes of the different actors. Both the United States and the Soviet Union defined their respective national interest in ideological terms, fueling a conflict between capitalist and socialist camps. Aron dismissed the idea that the existence of weapons of mass destruction could effectively stabilize the international system because "the balance of deterrence is a psycho-technical equilibrium" (1962: 669). Hence, he analyzed extensively the ambivalent elements embedded within deterrence strategies, and listed concerns raised by both escalation and disarmament. A global war was unlikely, he argued, because the "purpose of these weapons is to destroy the positive intention – real or assumed – of the aggressor" (1976: 242). Peace was also unlikely for two main reasons. First, the nuclear revolution decentralized violence, as illustrated by the multiplicity of both limited wars among states as well as civil wars. Second, "states have not left, in their mutual relations, the state of nature" (1962: 19). As a result, "interstate relations present an original feature, which distinguishes them from all social relations: they take place under the shadow of war, they imply by essence the alternative between peace and war" (1962: 17).

The shadow of war stemmed, according to Aron, from this absence of a legitimate monopoly of power at the international level. He emphasized this crucial specificity of IR by noting "there is no equivalent of a tribunal in international society." The use of force by states was therefore considered both legal and legitimate – by the states themselves as well as by the United Nations: "The UN Charter explicitly recognizes the 'sovereign equality' of states, and diplomats have never succeeded in defining the 'international' *par excellence* – aggression" (1967: 191). In this Hobbesian state of nature, international society remained an asocial society whose laws were left to each actor's interpretation. Aron acknowledged the existence of "universal and formal rules"; yet, he also expressed serious doubts about the emergence of an international human rights community.

Like proponents of the Realist school of Aron's era (such as Hans Morgenthau, George Kennan, and Reinhold Niebuhr), he therefore pointed out the permanence of national ambition, the importance of a balance of power, and the impossibility of peace through law. He dismissed the idea that an "ethic of law" would pacify state competition through the spread of international law: "Since international law is conservative, since states have never fully accepted its obligation, since, further, no tribunal, judging in equity, recommends the necessary changes, the states that invoke the morality of law often pass for hypocrites rather than heroes" (1962: 609). The multiplicity of rival legal sovereign states was the main characteristic trait of an "anarchical order" in which states rejected "the authority of law, of morality, or of collective force" (1966a: 480). The result was a "precarious order or endemic disorder" based on the uncertainty of "peace through fear" (1966a: 490).

Aron thus expressed skepticism toward the cosmopolitan ideals advocated by liberal theorists who promoted what he considered as an "unrealistic idealism." He dismissed the idea of a European federation powerful enough to devalue the "fact of political sovereignties, the existence of distinct states which wish to be autonomous" (1962: 748). He qualified the idea of a world federation as a "Utopia" and remained skeptical of the possibility of a "genuine planetary community" and "human society" (1966a: 479). In contrast to any abstract reflection on politics that distanced itself from the reality of political life, Aron proposed to "establish concrete accessible objectives conforming to the secular law of IR and not to limitless and perhaps meaningless objectives such as 'a world safe for democracy' or 'a world from which power politics will have disappeared'" (1962: 584–585). Analyzing previous attempts to implement peace through law (such as the Kellogg–Briand Pact), Aron noted that "anyone imagining he was guaranteeing peace by outlawing war was like a doctor imagining he was curing diseases by declaring them contrary to the aspirations of humanity" (1962: 583). He opposed this naive conception of "idealist diplomacy" in many of his writings – notably in his study of von Clausewitz in which he criticized the "ideology of a fading away of sovereignties," as well as "a gradual pacification of international relations" through a "complex interdependence" and the emergence of "international regimes" (1976: 284).

Aron, however, dismissed theories of IR that reduced international politics to a struggle for power, as well as any theory of "national interest." Realism became unrealistic, he argued, when its proponents ignored reality's complexities. Furthermore, "the external behavior of states is not determined by the ratio of forces alone" (1962: 108). A "true realism" should acknowledge that "even in the relations between states, respect for ideas, aspirations to higher values and concern for obligations have been manifested" (1962: 609). Aron thus actually balanced a Machiavellian analysis of IR with a Kantian approach based on his philosophical conception of history. He expressed, in various ways, the permanent dialectics inescapably fueling the plurality of political ends: "On the one hand, is the necessity of progress and, on the other, is history as usual, and the drama of empires, of armies, of heroes" (1961: 270); "History is violent and our ideal peaceful" (1962: 578). While emphasizing the amorality of politics and the "state of nature" in IR, Aron therefore maintained his conviction in the prevalence of the "idea of reason."

Aron envisioned what a "universal state" should look like, although he never expressed any faith in the utility of international organizations. Such a state, he argued,

> could survive only by the effective monopoly of legitimate violence. It would have to possess enough weapons to prevent provincial groups from resorting to force or, at least, to prevent the extension of conflicts, if these groups conserved an army.
>
> (Aron 1966a: 485)

Transnational society, he added, "would thus be presented as the true international society, which supranational organizations would progressively regulate, military competition between states gradually losing its virulence and narrow its scope" (1967: 196). A universal state would thus require "the consent of the people and the states to surrender a portion of their autonomy that has been held essential over centuries" (1966a: 485). Aron listed a series of conditions for any organization of the "United Nations type" to be able to guarantee peace and security. The first was "that in case of unqualified aggression by a state, the Security Council be unanimous in recognizing the aggression and in designating it as such." The second was that the conflict submitted to the United Nations

> be juridically defined, that it lend itself to the formal legalism of the Charter so that the wrongs of the parties may be determined, not according to political expediency, but by reference to the letter of fundamental texts and concepts.
>
> (Aron 1954: 20)

And the third was the emergence of an effective "world conscience" so "the judgment of public opinion would suffice to prevent crime or to check the criminal" (1954: 21).

Yet, according to Aron, none of these conditions has ever been fulfilled in human history and had never been so far from fulfillment as during the Cold War era. The goal of a reconciled humanity should be pursued while nonetheless warning against any overt optimism. "There is no prohibition," he wrote

> against attempting to define international society on the basis of the state of peace instead of the risk of war ... I wish it would be so tomorrow. But considering the long history of complex societies, the theoretical definition I have chosen seems to me to be closer to reality, more in keeping with experience, more instructive, and more productive.
>
> (Aron 1967: 196)

Global affairs in the post-Cold War era

Aron provided an extremely accurate analysis of the international system during the Cold War. Is his conceptual framework still relevant today for the understanding of new actors, norms, and issues? He admitted, a few years after publishing *Peace and War among Nations*, that "the global system, as I described it, had already changed by the time my description was published" (1967: 198). He was aware that

> the course of international relations remains supremely historical in every meaning of this term: there are unceasing changes, the systems, which are multiple and fragile, suffer the effects of all the transformations, decisions taken by one man or a few set into motion millions of people and provoke irreversible mutations.
>
> (Aron 1972: 379)

He reiterated his belief in the importance of historical contingencies, notably in his last publication, *The Last Years of the Century* (1983). Since then, the international system has undergone significant changes.

Some of them confirm the relevance of Aron's conception of a "bellicose peace." As he predicted, neither the United States nor the Russian Federation that emerged from the ruins of the former Soviet Union has launched a global nuclear war. Yet, the world still faces the daunting threat of limited nuclear conflicts – a threat fueled by significant, seemingly inherent limitations to disarmament as well as the largely uncontrolled proliferation of weapons of mass destruction. Furthermore, Aron correctly argued that relative stability at the global level did not generate the same at the national level. According to Stanley Hoffmann, Aron captured the ambiguities of deterrence by pointing out that "the less the superpowers will be tempted to use the absolute weapon, the freer they will feel to use conventional weapons" (1985: 20).

The end of the Cold War did not enhance stability throughout the international system. Conventional violence actually escalated during the 1980s and early 1990s, albeit at the sub-national level. The decade or so following the end of the Cold War witnessed 118 conflicts, primarily civil wars, resulting in the deaths of approximately six million people (including two million children) (Smith 2004). This upsurge was most evident in Europe – primarily in the Balkans and the Caucasus – in the context of the disintegration of Yugoslavia and the Soviet Union, and in Africa. While the number of interstate conflicts therefore declined, the initial optimism about the end of the Cold War was quickly supplanted by a new pessimism in reaction to the spread of violence. This pessimism was reinforced by the resurgence of conflicts involving ethnic cleansing, as illustrated by the genocidal atrocities committed in Srebrenica and Rwanda. Wars of decolonization have been replaced by conflicts involving failed states – leading to a vacuum of authority. Today's failed states – such as Afghanistan, the Democratic Republic of Congo, and Somalia – lack the governance capacities required to assert authority within their own borders. They have come to be feared as "breeding grounds of instability, mass migration, and murder," as well as reservoirs and exporters of terror (Walt 2015).

The number of armed conflicts sharply declined after 1998, as well as numbers of people killed in conventional wars. Most conflicts today involve poor countries with armies lacking heavy conventional weapons. These low-intensity conflicts thus reduce direct casualties among soldiers. In addition, the United States and its allies often use precision-guided arms, such as drones, causing relatively few battle deaths (Human Security Center 2005). The numbers of "indirect deaths," however, have increased among civilians. These include "non-violence deaths that would not have occurred had there been no fighting" – such as deaths caused by disease, malnutrition, or a lack of access to humanitarian assistance. In some cases, such as Darfur, the ratio of indirect to direct deaths exceeds 10:1 (Human Security Center 2005: 7). The number of refugees and displaced persons increased from 16 million in 1980 to 40 million in 1992. In contrast, the number of forcibly displaced people reached 65.3 million in 2015 – with more than 33,000 a day on average forced to flee their homes as a result of conflict and persecution. Furthermore, the risk of conflict between the major powers remains high, involving either a possible direct confrontation (as illustrated by American and Chinese tensions in the South China Sea) or an indirect one (such as in Syria, where Washington and Moscow support their allies in a proxy war).

These developments validate Aron's pessimism about the emergence of a peaceful international society, as well as his concerns about the conjunction of hostility and violence in a post-Cold war era. As he noted, "in many respects, the duopoly is a less unpredictable situation than a conjuncture involving numerous actors. The situation was all the more stable as long as each of the duopolists exercised virtually uncontested power within its own camp" (1966a: 491).

Other changes in the international system since the end of the Cold War have, however, challenged Aron's state-centered approach. Three major trends are noticeable. First, the "global system" he described has actually indeed become globalized. According to the Commission on Global Governance, "never before has change come so rapidly, on such a global scale, and with such global visibility" (1995: 12). The globalization of technology, governance, and flows has increased the material unity of the world. A growing share of the world's economy today involves cross-border flows. Flows of goods, services, and capital amounted to $26 trillion in 2012 (equal to 36 percent of global GDP). More than 2.7 billion people were connected to the Internet that year – with a 280 percent increase in Internet traffic since 2005 (McKinsey 2014). In 2015, the number of international migrants worldwide – people residing in a country other than their country of birth – was the highest ever recorded, at 244 million (up from 154 million in 1990). The overall annual flow of remittances has nearly tripled since 2000 and now tops $500 billion. Evidence of globalization is affecting our daily lives – for better or worse – as illustrated by the spreading of democratic values, as well as the diffusion of uniformity in a "McWorld" forged by global markets (Barber 2004). Aron dismissed the "idea of world unity" because, he argued, Western civilization has spread only "a thin layer of uniform technology over the surface of all continents" (1954: 23). The layer is thicker than he expected, which, in turn, fuels the so-called "clash of civilizations" and anti-globalization movements.

Second, the international system remains a society of states. Yet international organizations, as well as non-state actors, are playing a growing role in the development of global governance. The international community is now populated with intergovernmental organizations (IGOs), nongovernmental organizations (NGOs), regional organizations, and other transnational actors such as foundations. Governance thus relates to a variety of phenomena such as global social movements; civil society; the changing regulatory capacity of states; public–private networks; transnational rule making; and forms of private authority (Dingwert and Patterg 2006). Furthermore, transnational issues (such as climate change, pandemic diseases, and terrorism) have blurred the distinction between internal and external threats, and thus between internal and external security. This increased interconnectedness among global issues has led to the decentralization of decision making. Global governance involves a multi-level system in which local, national, regional, and global processes are intertwined. James Rosenau summed up these processes by stating that "global governance is conceived to include systems of rule at all levels of human activity – from the family to international organization – in which the pursuit of goals through the exercise of control has transnational repercussions" (1995: 13). Aron's framework, based on the distinction between domestic and foreign policy among sovereign states, has subsequently been challenged in the current post-Westphalian order. According to Bryan-Paul Frost, for example, "one question that can be legitimately raised about Aron's point of departure is whether or not international relations can be so clearly separated from domestic politics" (1997: 154). Domestic actors, for example (such as anti-apartheid activists), have repeatedly worked through transnational social mobilization networks to persuade governments to adjust their foreign policies in order to promote universal values (Klotz 1995). The traditional approach of state-based sovereignty is thus contested as much "from below" (with the emergence of a global citizenry) as from "the top" (by attempting to create supranational regulations).

Third, the common goal of all the actors engaged in this "global society" is to strengthen the foundation of the world's political architecture, notably through the web of transnational information and action networks. Thus, as Amstutz suggests,

> even though the world lacks central government, it has governance nevertheless. The order and stability of the world derives not from chance or from the domination of one or two powerful states but from the voluntary actions of states – actions that are taken in light of widely accepted values, procedures, behavorial patterns and rules.
>
> (Amstutz 2008: 219)

Global governance is not based upon the authority to impose rules. Its most fundamental aspect relates to the spreading of norms, rules, and standards that should ideally structure both domestic and international activities. Examples of normative shifts include the notion of "human security" and the principle of R2P. Human security, a neologism that entered public discourse through the 1944 United Nations Development Program (UNDP) report, incorporates many more threats than traditional security. In addition to military conflicts, it relates to issues actually threatening the lives of millions of people, such as the remnants of proxy wars; large-scale displacement of civilian populations; environmental disasters; pandemic diseases; poverty and hunger; international terrorism; drug, arms, and people trafficking; and gross abuses of human rights (Annan 2000). The referent object of human security is the individual rather than the state, society, or community, as illustrated by the agenda of the Commission on Human Security (2003) as well as the UNDP (UNDP 1994). From this perspective, state sovereignty is no longer an uncontested norm because violations of human rights warrant at some point legitimate and/or legal intervention into the affairs of that state by others (Annan 1999; Krasner 1999). According to the International Commission on Intervention and State Sovereignty, sovereignty should be reconceived as "the duty to protect." States have the primary responsibility for protecting their own citizens from human-made catastrophe; yet, it shifts to the wider international community, regional, or global organizations when states can no longer fulfill that responsibility. The R2P principle does not give rise to a "right of intervention"; rather, "the principle of non-intervention yields to the international responsibility to protect" (ICISS 2001). At the UN world summit in 2005, member states endorsed this notion of international responsibility when "the rights of individual humans trump the sovereignty of the thuggish states in which they live" (Weiss 2016: 23).

Global governance is extending its reach by persuading sovereign states to comply with the basic norms of transnational legal accountability on a voluntary basis. This is illustrated, for example, by the creation of institutions dealing with human rights protection such as the Permanent Court of Justice, the International Court of Justice, and the International Criminal Court. Political and legal preconditions for a global criminal justice system are admittedly embryonic. Advocates of global governance, however, are actively engaged in the creation of an international human rights regime, as well as a global criminal justice system. In addition, there has been the rapid expansion of conflict prevention, peace making, and post-conflict peace-building activities since the early 1990s. The main objective of these operations has been to prevent the recurrence or expansion of armed conflict – as part of a "comprehensive approach" emphasized by the UN Security Council "through the promotion of economic growth, poverty eradication, sustainable development, national reconciliation, good governance, democracy, the rule of law, as well as respect for, and protection of, human rights" (Resolution 1674, 2006).

Aron's contribution to the ethics of global affairs

The paradigm shift advocated by policy proponents of global governance has mirrored intellectual currents among scholars of IR. The consensus among them since the 1990s has been that the world was changing and hence IR approaches have to change accordingly. The Copenhagen School, for example, critiqued the utility of the old militarized and state-centered view of security. Barry Buzan, Ole Wæver, and Jaap de Wilde conceptualized a wider agenda for security studies, involving non-military as well as military threats, and states and non-state actors (Buzan *et al*., 1998). The multiplication of complex crises in a globally networked world has increased interest in specific spheres of international ethics, notably just war theory, human rights, and global justice (Donnelly 2003; Finnemore 2003).

Does Aron's conceptualization make sense of the current ethical issues in a global international system? Answering this question requires a focus on the praxeology he developed, both in the last section of *Peace and War*, as well as in other studies (such as *Introduction to the Philosophy of History*). Aron did offer a normative analysis of the ethical foundation of statecraft based on his work on the moral foundation of historical knowledge. This approach combines the Machiavellian problem of legitimate means and the Kantian problem of universal peace. It can be defined as a hybrid position incorporating both principled realism and realistic idealism. Politics cannot exclude morality, because "even in relations among states, the respect of ideas, the aspiration to values, the concern for obligations have been manifested. Rarely have the communities behaved as if they were not obliged to anything towards one another" (1962: 596). Politics should not it be reduced to morality either because "never did values or common interests command the conduct of actors in great circumstances" (1962: 719). This normative analysis remains relevant, not despite, but because of the systemic changes that have occurred since the end of the Cold War.

Aron's intellectual enterprise in re-evaluating the ethical bases of international politics can fully comprehend the ethical dilemmas inherent to global governance. His "true realism" – based on the "antinomy of force and juridical norms" (1962: 605) – avoids the flaws of both neo-realism and cosmopolitanism. The neo-realist perspective that emerged during the 1980s, largely under Kenneth Waltz's influence (1979), displayed some interest in the ethical dimensions of IR. Yet, most neo-realists (such as Arnold Wolfers, Robert Tucker, and Kenneth Thompson) conceived of morality as a set of negative constraints on foreign policy. That is,

> morality limits the means that can be employed in the pursuit of national ends and constrains the selection of ends themselves. Morality according to the neo-realists does not impose any positive duties of charity or magnanimity when dealing with foreigners.
>
> (Recchia 2007: 544)

As a result, neo-realism remains extremely vague in defining the balance between morality and efficiency, as well as clarifying when emergency conditions favoring intervention apply. Proponents of this rather amorphous "ethics of lesser evil" thus oppose or endorse humanitarian interventions for reasons that are not related to moral obligations.

By contrast, cosmopolitans like Charles Beitz and Marshall Cohen have provided a radical alternative approach to realism by developing a global morality based on the rights of persons. According to Beitz, territorial boundaries are not morally significant: "since boundaries are not coextensive with the scope of social cooperation, they do not mark the limits of social obligation" (1979: 151). The moral claims of individuals can thus challenge the autonomy of states, since the rights of states depends on the rights of persons. Like Beitz, Cohen insisted that universal moral rules do apply to international relations, and the behavior of states should be judged accordingly (1985). Cosmopolitans, however, tend to dismiss the conditions applicable to the effective protection of rights – such as a sustainable institutional reconstruction in the case of peace-building operations. Cosmopolitanism, like traditional idealism, can thus promote unrealistic policies under the guise of moral crusades.

Aron's praxeology provides a more nuanced approach, based on a liberal conception of realism. Unlike neo-realism, Aron's liberal realism does not regard morality as a negative constraint that states can dismiss in the absence of a supreme emergency. Unlike cosmopolitanism, it emphasizes that the possibilities for moral behavior require a realistic evaluation of the balance of power, as well as certain institutional and social prerequisites for sustainable pacification. Furthermore, Aron stressed the danger of the instrumental use of morality, when ethical justifications intervene *ex post* to provide a justification for actions – what Morgenthau described as "a process of rationalization of irrational, selfish motives lurking behind any human decision in the sphere of politics" (1946: 155). During the US military intervention in Iraq, for example, moral rhetoric dominated. For the Bush administration, security concerns (with reference to WMDs), as well as democratic arguments (with the objective of toppling a tyrannical regime) legitimated the intervention based on "just cause" and "right intervention." Aron would have probably disagreed. Yet, unlike Morgenthau, he would not have argued that all moral claims made to explain certain actions are inevitably hypocritical.

Aron, in contrast, asserted the complexity of politics, the "plurality of ends" that characterized most issues in current global affairs. Any ethics of immigration, for example, is complex. There are strong arguments favoring both open and closed borders that address ethical questions: Do states have a moral obligation to let in different categories of migrants? Do states have a moral obligation to exclude migrants in order to protect the interests of their citizens, or to at least select only some categories of migrants? What criteria of selection would be morally legitimate? These questions, Veit Bader argued, illustrate the "unresolved tension between individual and collective rights, between a universalist, inclusionary, liberal tradition stressing the natural rights of all human beings irrespective of ascriptive criteria, including nationality, and a more particularist, exclusionary republican tradition" (2005: 333). Cosmopolitans favor open borders. This approach, according to the contextualized morality advocated by Aron, is neither feasible nor fair in terms of the domestic obligations of states toward their citizens. Particularist arguments in favor of closed borders are often tainted with unethical considerations, such as the preservation of ethnic/racial/cultural national identity from an ethnocentric perspective. Aron's praxeology offers a more nuanced approach by suggesting a problem-driven rather than a theory-driven analysis. Both freedom of movement and right to entry are not absolute principles; yet, a closed border policy should respect minimal obligations following humanitarianism and distributive justice. In order to "establish concrete accessible objectives" (1962: 584), it is safe to assume that Aron would suggest collecting credible empirical evidence on people flows; on the diversity of migrants; and the costs and benefits of immigration. This objective knowledge can help identify the broad causal factors of migration while avoiding the "inexorable determinism" of single-factor explanations (1962: 279). It also helps determine the range of political options available to different actors (such as sending countries, receiving countries, international organizations, or NGOs). These options are informed by both moral and political principles according to principled realism. Myron Weiner, for example, argued that immigration policies are "not a matter of general moral principles but of politically defined national interests and values" (1996: 192). National interests, however, are intended to protect national claims and global needs, the interests of domestic society and global humanitarian care (Hoffmann 1981).

Aron's preference for a synthesis between neo-realism and cosmopolitanism provides useful guidelines for the ethical evaluation of other aspects of global governance such as humanitarian interventions. These interventions raise key questions: What level of rights violation justifies military interventions? Which states/institutions possess the authority and/or legitimacy to intervene? What should be the goals of humanitarian interventions (protecting civilians, arresting perpetrators of crimes, regime change)? What is the most effective policy compatible with the moral good? What are the probabilities of promoting democracy and stable governance abroad by means of military intervention? Scholars debating the contribution of Michael Walzer in *Just and Unjust Wars* (1979) have redefined the just war theory by listing tropes to judge humanitarian interventions. As noted by Andrew Valls,

> almost no one maintains the extreme position that state sovereignty is entitled to no consideration or, at the other extreme, that no considerations can justify violating a state's sovereignty. The debate, then, is about where the line is to be drawn, when and how intervention is justified.
> (Valls 2000: xvii)

Aron's praxeology actually helps drawing the line by rejecting the notion that the morality of humanitarian interventions should be evaluated in terms of threat to national interest. Some US neo-realists, for example, supported the intervention in Kosovo not because of gross human rights violations but rather because they perceived the situation in the Balkans as threatening US national interests. They opposed other interventions, such as the attempt in 1991–1992 by the United Nations to protect Shiite Muslims in Iraq (see Recchia 2007 for a review of these positions). Such flexibility in defining vital national interest independently from the suffering of vulnerable populations actually perverts the distinction between legal and legitimate interventions. It also leads to double moral standards, as illustrated by inconsistencies in US foreign policy. The United States, for example, justified the 1994 intervention in Haiti as ensuring protection of civilians and a peaceful transfer of power; yet, while genocide was taking place in Darfur in 2004, the United States denied that the international community had the obligation to intervene – in violation of the spirit of the Genocide Convention.

Conversely, Aron's praxeology provides clear guidelines in order to avoid the temptation of crusading interventionism. The multiplication of peacekeeping operations is a positive development in the international system. There are several examples of overall successful multilateral interventions, such as in Mozambique (1992–1994) and Sierra Leone (1999–2005). Yet, as illustrated by the failed US intervention in Somalia in 1993, actions in support of human rights can turn into a humanitarian disaster. Purely humanitarian reasons for intervention are insufficient. Humanitarian intervention is legitimate if it fulfills basic criteria: when its actual aim is to protect people's fundamental rights; the type of intervention it involves is appropriate to meet this objective (*jus in bello*); there is reasonable chance of success; and the post-conflict situation is properly handled (*jus post bellum*). Furthermore, intervening states have to be skilled in dealing with the complexities of local situations into which they send their troops. An ethical perspective thus needs not simply to call for intervention but also to consider a large range of variables, as well as counter-arguments such as improper motives for intervention, undue costs imposed on intervening states, and resistance to intervention from some of the members of the country subject to intervention.

Securing humanity in the twenty-first century

Aron was quite cognizant of the "passions, follies, ideas and violences of the century" (1962: 587). Obviously, Bryan-Paul Frost noted, "we cannot turn to Aron's corpus directly for answers to political problems that plague our century" (2006: 527). There is no "Aronian school" either but scholars have addressed the ambivalence of global affairs in a similar way. Liberal realists, such as Hedley Bull (1977), acknowledge the realities of competition among states but did so by strengthening the importance of values and norms. They focus on the social and cultural dimensions of interstate relations that should limit international violence. Stanley Hoffmann summarized the main goal of liberal realism:

Ethics cannot hope to establish the nirvana of a world government in the short run; it can aim only at moralizing state behavior, on the one hand, and, on the other, at enlarging in a variety of ways what could be called the cosmopolitan sphere of international affairs.

(Hoffman 1998: 45)

Liberal realists, like Aron, "navigate a middle course between conservative versions of realism and ambitious visions for transforming the international system" (Bell 2010: 103). Some of the "English school" scholars, such as R.J. Vincent (1986) and James Mayall (2000), are often viewed as supporting an Aronian-inspired analysis of the "international society" based on the "liberalism of fear" conceptualized by Judith Shklar (1989).

What makes Aron unique, however, relates to his "ethics of wisdom." Aron constantly asserted, in his multiple theoretical books and empirical articles, the necessity for policy makers to be aware of the complexities of politics. His normative praxeology informs a theory of action – a praxis overcoming the Weberian opposition between ethics of conviction and ethics of responsibility. Aron suggested a "reasonable compromise" between the two: "every politician has to resolve the antinomy of an ethic of conviction and an ethic of responsibility for the consequences of applying political means to achieve one's end" (1971: 86). Aron provided relevant tools that strategies of ethical decision-making should include. These strategies necessitate the calculation of both means and ends by combining consequentialism (ends-based action) and deontology (rule-based action). The former assumes that the morality of an action is judged by the results that are achieved rather than motives. Yet, given the indeterminacy of politics, consequentialism can engender negative feedback, as illustrated by the use of extra-legal detention centers (Guantanamo) and torture in fighting transnational terrorism. Pierre Hassner noted that Aron rightly emphasized the "dialectic of subversion and repression, the fact that one may destroy terrorists but their main tactic is to bring more repression in order to mobilize potential supporters" (2007: 504). The latter assumes that the morality of a decision has to be judged by its inherent rightness rather than its outcomes. However, it remains to be proved that political leaders have always the capacity to identify appropriate moral principles and behave accordingly – especially in the current context of "ontological insecurity" and "permanent state of exception" (Agamben). Good intentions can also lead to negative outcomes, such as the cholera epidemic spread by UN blue helmets in Haiti.

Aron argued that neither approach is sufficient. He suggested instead the practice of *prudence*, a notion inherited from the Aristotelian conception of practical wisdom and the Thomistic acceptation of prudent statecraft. Prudence requires seeking the implementation of common goods by weighting different alternatives, translating ethical intentions into realistic actions, and evaluating the potential outcomes on the basic of objective knowledge, as well as socio-historical circumstances. Aron's ethics of wisdom is by definition casuistic, thus it does not allow for generalization (Hassner 2007; Cozette 2004). We don't know what he would have suggested to policy leaders facing new types of war, new enemies, but also new opportunities to promote a "liberal peace" based on war-adverse norms and human rights. Are we looking at a "utopian moment of possibility" (Winter 2008) when new ideas change the world? Or are we engaged in a spiral of violence, fueled by global poverty, natural disasters, and human-made catastrophes? An Aronian-inspired praxis is more relevant than ever for those who try to address these questions. Aron warned us that "the dangers are no longer the same, but they have not disappeared ... The adventure is still far from this final state" (1966a: 502). He added:

> History has more imagination than wise men. It has thus far refused to choose between collective suicide and the abdication of states. It has gradually brought a certain order out of the anarchy common to all international systems, an order favoring the limitation of armed conflicts.
>
> (Aron 1966a: 485)

References

Amstutz, M. (2008), *International Ethics: Concepts, Theories and Cases in Global Politics*. New York: Rowman & Littlefield.
Annan, K. (1999), "Two Concepts of Sovereignty," *The Economist*, September 18.
Annan, K. (2000), *Report of the Work of the Organization*. Official Records of the fifty-fifth session of the General Assembly, Supplement no. 1 (A/55/1) of August 30, 2000.
Aron, R. (1954), "Limits to the Powers of the United Nations," *Annals of the American Academy of Political and Social Science*, 296, 20–26.
Aron, R. (1961), *Dimensions de la conscience historique*. Paris: Plon.
Aron, R. (1962), *Paix et guerre entre les nations*. Paris: Calmann-Lévy.
Aron, R. (1966a), "The Anarchical Order of Power," *Daedalus*, 95:2, 479–502.
Aron, R. (1966b), *La sociologie allemande contemporaine*. Paris: Quadrige (1st edn. published 1935).
Aron, R. (1967), "What Is a Theory of International Relations?" *Journal of International Affairs*, 21:2, 185–206.
Aron, R. (1971), "Max Weber and Power Politics," in Stammer, O. (ed.), *Max Weber and Sociology Today*. Oxford: Blackwell, 83–101.
Aron, R. (1972), *Etudes politique*. Paris: Gallimard.
Aron, R. (1976), *Penser la guerre, Clauzewitz*. Vol. 2: *L'âge planétaire*. Paris: Gallimard.
Aron, R. (1983), *Les dernières années du siècle*. Paris: Julliard.
Bader, V. (2005), "The Ethics of Immigration," *Constellations*, 12:5, 331–361.
Barber, B. (2004), "Jihad vs. McWorld" (originally published in *Times Books*, 1995) in Lechner, F.J. and Boli, J. (eds.), *The Globalization Reader*. Malden, MA: Blackwell Publishing.
Beitz, C. (1979), *Political Theory and International Relations*. Princeton, NJ: Princeton University Press.
Bell, D. (2010), *Ethics and World Politics*. Oxford: Oxford University Press.
Bull, H. (1977), *The Anarchical Society: A Study of Order in World Politics*. New York: Columbia University Press.

Buzan, B., Wæver, O., and de Wilde, J. (1998), *Security: A New Framework for Analysis.* Boulder, CO: Lynne Rienner Publishers.
Cohen, M. (1985), "Moral Skepticism and International Relations," in Beits, C. et al. (eds.), *International Ethics.* Princeton, NJ: Princeton University Press.
Commission on Global Governance. (1995), *Our Global Neighborhood.* New York: Oxford University Press.
Commission on Human Security. (2003), *Human Security Now: The Human Security Commission Report.* Available at www.humansecurity-chs.org.
Cozette, M. (2004), "Realistic Realism? American Political Realism, Clausewitz and Raymond Aron on the Means and Ends in International Politics," *Journal of Strategic Studies,* 27:3, 428–453.
Davis, R.M. (2008), "An Uncertain Trumpet: Reason, Anarchy and Cold War Diplomacy in the Thought of Raymond Aron," *Review of International Studies,* 34:4, 645–668.
Dingwerth, K., and Patterg, P. (2006), "Global Governance as a Perspective on World Politics," *Global Governance,* 12, 185–203.
Donnelly, J. (2003), *Universal Human Rights in Theory and Practice.* Ithaca, NY: Cornell University Press.
Finnemore, M. (2003), *The Purpose of Intervention: Changing Beliefs about the Use of Force.* Ithaca, NY: Cornell University Press.
Frost, B.-P. (1997), "Resurrecting a Neglected Theorist: The Philosophical Foundations of Raymond Aron's Theory of International Relations," *Review of International Studies,* 23, 143–166.
Frost, B.-P. (2006), "Better Late Than Never: Raymond's Aron Theory of International Relations and Its Prospects in the Twenty First Century," *Politics & Policy,* 34:3, 506–531.
Hassner, P. (2007), "Raymond Aron: Too Realistic to Be a Realist?" *Constellations,* 14:4, 498–505.
Hoffmann, S. (1981), *Duties Beyond Borders: On the Limits and Possibilities of Ethical International Politics.* Syracuse, NY: Syracuse University Press.
Hoffmann, S. (1985), "Raymond Aron and the Theory of International Relations," *International Studies Quarterly,* 19:1, 13–27.
Hoffmann, S. (1998), *World Disorders: Troubled Peace in the Post Cold War Era.* New York: Rowman & Littlefield.
Human Security Center. (2005), *Human Security Report.* New York: Oxford University Press.
International Commission on Intervention and State Sovereignty. (2001), *Responsibility to Protect.* Available at http://responsibilitytoprotect.org/ICISS%20Report.pdf.
Klotz, A. (1995), *Norms in International Relations: The Struggle Against Apartheid.* Ithaca, NY: Cornell University Press.
Krasner, S. (1999), *Sovereignty: Organized Hypocrisy.* Princeton, NJ: Princeton University Press.
McKinsey Global Institute. (2014), *Global Flows in a Digital Age.* Available at www.mckinsey.com.
Mayall, J. (2000), *World Politics: Progress and Its Limits.* Cambridge: Polity.
Morgenthau, H. (1946), *Scientific Man versus Power Politics.* Chicago, IL: Chicago University Press.
Recchia, S. (2007), "Restraining Imperial Hubris: The Ethical Bases of Realist International Relations Theory," *Constellations,* 14:4, 531–556.
Rosenau, J. (1995), "Governance in the Twenty First Century," *Global Governance,* 1:1, 13–43.

Shklar, J. (1989), "The Liberalism of Fear," in Rosenblum, N. (ed.), *Liberalism and the Moral Life*. Cambridge, MA: Harvard University Press, 21–38.

Smith, D. (2004), *Trends and Causes of Armed Conflicts*. Berghof Research Center for Constructive Conflict Management.

United Nations Development Program. (1994), *New Dimensions of Human Security: Human Development Report*. New York: Oxford University Press.

Valls, A. (ed.) (2000), *Ethics in International Affairs*. New York: Rowman & Littlefield.

Vincent, R. (1986), *Human Rights and International Relations*. Cambridge: Cambridge University Press.

Walt, S. (2015), "New Twist on an Old Story," *Foreign Affairs*, November–December.

Waltz, K. (1979), *Theory of International Politics*. New York: McGraw-Hill.

Weiner, M. (1996), "Ethics, National Sovereignty and the Control of Immigration," *International Migration Review*, 30.

Weiss, T. (2016), *Humanitarian Intervention: Ideas in Action*. Malden, MA: Polity Press.

Winter, J. (2008), *Dreams of Peace and Freedom: Utopian Moments in the 20th Century*. New Haven, CT: Yale University Press.

10 The diplomat, the soldier, and the spy

Toward a new taxonomy in International Relations

Olivier Chopin

In *Peace and War*, Aron describes the effort to take into account "normative implications [that] are inherent in every theory" as well as the anticipation of the moral consequences of our actions: he elaborates on the "antinomies of diplomatic-strategic conduct" that imply the need for what he calls a praxeology. Referring to a "dialectics of Peace and War" derived from his meditation on Clausewitz's philosophy and specific to the Cold War context, Aron narrows down foreign policy analysis to two existential figures, the *Diplomat* and the *Soldier*. In the aftermath of 9/11 and in the context of a return of conflict in international relations, the distinction between peace and war is becoming blurred, for example, through the mechanisms of threat inflation (Thrall and Cramer 2009; Kaufmann 2004). This chapter argues that, seminal as it is, Aron's taxonomy should be corrected, and his representation enhanced by the adjunction of a new function, a third "character". We suggest that the Spy should join the Diplomat and the Soldier.

Since 2011, intelligence has become more visible as an important contributor to the decision-making process, through two main dynamics: centralization and normalization. But as intelligence becomes more central and more normal, it paradoxically becomes more problematic. Aron's praxeology is a powerful tool to embrace both the practical and moral complexities of current intelligence policies led by Western democracies. What role could intelligence play in Aron's vision of foreign policy conduct? And what do we learn from Aron in order to deal with the ethical paradoxes of today's use (and misuses, or even abuses) of intelligence and clandestine activities?

Aron used to say that international political issues are indeed political questions. And we should never forget their political dimension: an actual encounter of conflicting interests, values, and opinions. Like political issues, international issues have to be interpreted, debated, and are not easy to formulate scientifically. Aron as a turbulent friend of Simone de Beauvoir and Sartre, Aron as a historian, and Aron as a philosopher have been studied and his legacy kept alive by followers and commentators (Bachelier 2007; Mahoney 1992). But Aron as an International Relations (IR) thinker has been progressively ignored or rejected by scholars (see Schmitt's Introduction to this volume). We share with other contributors in this book the belief that because Aron is a political thinker and

180   *Olivier Chopin*

because he was interested in the philosophy of history, many insights can be gained from studying his writings about international relations, restoring his position in the theory of IR as well as considering him as a mentor to speculate about current issues.

Intelligence in Aron's *Peace and War*

Daniel Mahoney and Brian Anderson notice in their introduction to the new edition of *Peace and War* that, following the "atrocities of September 11 … politics has returned vengefully, making the liberal optimism of the 1990s appear naïve". And, they claim, "the great French liberal Raymond Aron would not have been surprised at the stubborn persistence of politics" (Mahoney and Anderson 2003: xi). That is true. But maybe Aron would have been surprised at the new central role liberal regimes let intelligence play *publicly and openly* in the realms of war, foreign policy, international security, as well as domestic security.

One of the first academic definitions of intelligence came at the time of the creation of the CIA, and was given by Sherman Kent in his book *Strategic Intelligence for American World Policy*. Intelligence can be defined as

> a kind of knowledge ("What intelligence have you turned up on the situation in Columbia?"), … the type of organization which produces the knowledge ("Intelligence was able to give the operating people exactly what they wanted") [and] the activity pursued by the intelligence organization ("The [intelligence] work behind that planning must have been intense").
>
> (Kent 1965: xxiii)

According to Aron, there are three sources of power (see also Chapter 3): territory and resources (both of which can be quantified and measured) and the "collective capacity for action of a state" which "depends on spiritual resources that resist all quantification" (Mahoney and Anderson 2003: xii). In his own understanding, where would Aron have placed intelligence? Could intelligence products or intelligence organizations be seen as part of a state's resources? Or the activity as a facet of the capacity for action? We will never know for sure, as Aron has written so little, even close to nothing, on intelligence.

Aron does not entirely pass over intelligence in *Peace and War*, as there are several mentions of events or institutions related to it. But he does not address it as an issue, or even a parameter, in itself. And clearly the few appearances of the theme suggest that Aron sees intelligence primarily as a matter of espionage and clandestine operations and not as "strategic intelligence", the "functional" tool part of a broader decision-making process that Kent defines and places at the heart of a state's foreign policy.

Aron uses once, and only once, the formula "strategic intelligence" in the "Final Note (Rational Strategy and Reasonable Policy)" that closes *Peace and War*. But it is close to a *faux ami* and there is a subtle nuance that may be lost in the English translation here. Aron explains:

It is true only that, according to the time and the circumstance, combat, strategic intelligence or debate dominate international relations. Between Cortez's Spaniards and the Aztecs no debate was possible. Against the Soviet divisions, no intelligence would have saved the Hungarians. When the atom bombs fell on Hiroshima and Nagasaki, the Japanese could only suffer. Strategic intelligence and the effort to persuade are reduced to impotence only at the extreme moments of the combat, when the warriors' muscles are strained, when swords clash against shields, or when bombs or shells fall on soldiers or cities.

(Aron 2003: 771–772)

In the original edition in French, Aron does not use the word "*renseignement*", which is the translation for "strategic intelligence", but he twice uses the words "*intelligence stratégique*" and writes that "*aucune intelligence n'aurait sauvé les Hongrois*". So maybe Aron is playing with words, knowing very well that intelligence in English refers to *renseignement* in French. But why not use the word, then? One possible interpretation is that Aron deliberately does not want us to consider intelligence in the narrow functional and organizational sense of strategic intelligence as defined by Kent and all the intelligence studies after him. He may rather have in mind the broader idea of the Ancients' *metis*, the mythological embodiment of prudence which became in the common language the quality that combines wisdom and cunning, or what the French language defines as an "*intelligence rusée*" (for a genealogy of *metis* in strategic thinking and a historical reconstruction of the relation between ruse and force, see Holeindre 2017).

The specific practices of espionage are mentioned twice in *Peace and War*. At the very end of chapter 7, "On Space" (which opens the second part of the book, "Sociology"), Aron mentions briefly the American spy-plane U2, along with interception missiles and imagery satellites (Aron 2003: 208). In the second section of chapter 17 ("Persuasion and Subversion, *or* The Blocs and the Non-Aligned Nations"), dedicated to the economic diplomacy of rubles and dollars, Aron explains that economic aid, either in the field of civil industry or defense armament, is not a credible way for Soviet regimes to develop clandestine espionage networks, and that intelligence activities are always separated from the main local party organization (Aron 2003: 515–516). Those are the only two mentions of spies, or collection, or information networks or clandestine activities. It proves that Aron does not ignore the existence of such things, and does not discard them as irrelevant, even if he clearly does not integrate them directly in his reflection. They are just elements of a context, not the central part of a process.

Nevertheless, Aron gives more consideration to another set of activities attached to intelligence organizations. The third section of chapter 17 is dedicated to "The Dialectics of Subversion". And at the core of this dialectics lie what intelligence people call "covert operations" and "political action", i.e., the clandestine and active part of parallel and secret diplomacy (in addition to this specifically dedicated section, mentions of subversion and mutual influence from the two blocs run through the entire book: chapter 4, section 5; chapter 17, section 4; chapter 18, sections 2 and 4; chapter 22, section 4). Subversion is systemic, not an anomaly. Both blocs use it, if differently. "In the absence of a common desire for stability, the constant effort of persuasion and subversion derives from the heterogeneity of the system" (Aron 2003: 522–523). And the Third World is the natural political space for this indirect *conflictualité*:

> The balance-sheet of heterogeneity and dialectic of subversion are different in the relations of the two blocs with the third world, which lies open to the propaganda of the two blocs, to the infiltrations of men and ideas coming from both ... As for the state effecting the subversion, it must possess agents or an organization capable of transforming rebellion into revolt or revolt into revolution, of directing the revolution in the path most consistent with its interests or with its ambitions.
>
> (Aron 2003: 525)

Interestingly, he also mentions:

> Radio propaganda addressed to whole peoples, which played a spectacular and successful role against the Third Reich, *has become a normal institution* ... [and] the Soviet regimes ... regard Western radio propaganda as a subversive activity and treat it as such [by jamming].
>
> (Aron 2003: 523, emphasis added)

In the area of subversion, one of the two players is more inclined to "these *subsidiary actions*" and to run those "*parallel organizations*", and maybe more efficient at it:

> The campaigns against German rearmament, against the atom bomb, in favor of Franco-Soviet friendship, are only three of the innumerable examples of the technique – let us call it *infiltration* – by which Soviet policy attempts to win sympathizers or adherents to its cause in milieu which would not subscribe to the Communist cause presented as such.
>
> (Aron 2003: 524, emphasis added)

If the Soviets are more efficient at covert activities and political action, this derives from the nature of the regime:

> Now, at least one of the two [super powers] would seem better adapted to the nature and rules of this conflict, which is more political than military, more clandestine than open, more violent than peaceful, [and] whether it is a matter of ideology or of organization, the Soviet camp is equipped for subversion.
>
> (Aron 2003: 525)

One should not be mistaken, the Soviets are not the only ones who play the ("Great") game:

> the balance-sheet of heterogeneity in Europe is more even than most observers are inclined to believe, at least in the sphere of psycho-political warfare. In fact, the presence of the West between the Kremlin and the Soviet citizen is quite as real and perhaps more effective than the presence of the Soviet Union between the White House or Westminster on the one hand and the American or British citizen on the other.
>
> (Aron 2003: 524)

And of course,

> the American, too, through the intermediary of the Central Intelligence Agency, have tried their hand at subversion. It was the CIA which undermined the regime, in Guatemala, of Colonel Arbenz, who thought to be a Communist or a Communist Sympathizer. It was the CIA which encouraged the Cuban refugees and organized the lamentable Bay of Pigs invasion attempt. But subversive actions controlled by secret services differ in nature from the same actions utilizing the believers of a faith and the militants of a party.
>
> (Aron 2003: 525)

It is worth noting that the CIA is the only intelligence service to be explicitly mentioned by Aron in his book. Neither Russia's KGB (which is once referred to as the "Russian secret police" without being named in chapter 15, section 2) nor the French SDECE (which preceded the DGSE) or British MI6 are cited.

But even if Aron dedicates a few pages to subversion and, implicitly, to the secret organizations that run those operations, those "secret wars" have little effect on the system itself, and may have little effect in the long run:

> For the time being, after fifteen years of the cold war and of the dialectic of persuasion-subversion, the Soviet citizen appears quite as little inclined to revolt against the so-called Communist regime as the American citizen against the so-called capitalist-democratic regime.
>
> (Aron 2003: 524)

Clearly, if Aron says little about intelligence collection and nothing about intelligence analysis or its participation in the "decision-making process", even the question of subversion, if it is not secondary, remains largely epiphenomenal.

Praxeology, prudence, and uncertainty

Aron was thinking in the context of the Cold War, of bipolarity. Every move, every attempt to end the Cold War contained the risk of leading to disequilibrium and ultimately to catastrophe, to nuclear holocaust. Two catastrophes had already occurred: what would a "second Second World War" be? It echoed Arendt's anxious claim that humanity was moving beyond politics in the nuclear age (Arendt 2014): politics was ending with the prospect of mutually assured destruction (MAD). Humanity could be destroyed: it meant a reversed, an inverted cosmopolitism (humanity as a whole, gathered in the promise of destruction, obviously led to the contrary of Kantian-type cosmopolitism). In a way, all of Aron's philosophy was intended to restore the condition of possibility of politics. Praxeology and the call for a *morality of prudence* were Aron's attempts to avoid that existential and political dead end the Cold War represented. We would like to show that even if humanity found a way out of that dead end and if the Cold War is behind us, the two recommendations, praxeology and the morality of prudence, remain relevant, for example, and especially, in the area of intelligence and decision making.

Aron's praxeology could usefully be recalled by many observers of intelligence who show a certain concern that if intelligence activities and organizations have no boundaries or regulation, they will certainly become something rogue and unrestricted, although they should be contained in certain limitations (Born and Caparini 2007; Betts 2009; Treverton 2009). This concern could find some support in Aron's conception of praxeology. Praxeology is the title of the fourth part of *Peace and War*, and the subtitle is "The Antinomies of Diplomatic-Strategic Conduct". In a way, praxeology is the finalization, the completion of an intellectual process that passes through three steps, Theory, Sociology, and History (the other parts of the book). They are at some level requirements to develop a proper praxeology. "*A la fin, il faut que la pensée rencontre l'action*" ("At the end of the day, thinking [or mind] must meet action"). The teleological implication of the formula "*à la fin*" ("at the end of the day") is very important. As Roy Pierce puts it: "Aron's greatest contribution to contemporary political thought is his effort to link science to choice, political sociology to political decisions" (Pierce 1966: 238).

Praxeology means two different things, two different kind of duality. Praxeology means a particular way to connect normative theory and political practice on the one hand, and it is an intellectual method, a methodology in its own right, on the other hand. The genealogy of Aron's vision of praxeology goes back to Immanuel Kant and is of course in tension with the Marxist definition of that word. Another way to put it: praxeology has two dimensions. A theory without any practical intention, or destination, is a "pure theory", something nearly rejected by Kant himself in his *opuscule* (Kant 1793). The problem, according to Aron, is that "lacking a single goal of diplomatic behavior, the rational analysis of international relations cannot be developed into an inclusive theory"; and he adds that at the minimum any theory has to be completed by a sociological approach, as "theory reveals the intelligible texture of a social ensemble; sociology shows how the determinants (space, number, resources) and the subjects (nations, regimes, civilizations), of international relations vary" (Aron 2003: 17). Reed Davis describes praxeology as "that difficult, contentious area in which theory, ethics and action converge" (Davis 2009: 24). He later remarks that "it is surprisingly difficult to understand exactly what Aron meant by the word *theory* ... Theory, as Aron used the term, is both a level and a moment of analysis" (Davis 2009: 87). Likewise, action without any theory is not a practice but pure technics, a "technology", something mechanical. Without any dimension of normativity, the consequences and the outcomes of political action may lead to unrestricted violence, an action without boundaries nor any kind of regulation.

Reed Davis, after Brian Anderson, places Aron in the "Prudence tradition of international politics" (Anderson 1997; Coll 1993; Davis 2009: 112). Aron's "morality of prudence" may be still relevant today in the realm of intelligence studies as it places at its core the problem of uncertainty, which is said to become the main challenge for intelligence analysts as it is for policy makers (Fukuyama 2008). The "morality of prudence" is a variation of the ethics of responsibility defined by Max Weber (Weber 1994). Aron tries to put back Weber's ethics of responsibility "at its center" or "at the center", after the term has been radicalized and put too far "on the right" by Carl Schmitt through his "decisionism" (Schmitt 2004, 2006). Aron's praxeology is a rectification of wrong interpretations of Weber's decisionism.

The link in Aron's thinking between philosophy of action and philosophy of history is clear when we acknowledge it, but strangely Aron's thoughts on IR (action) are less prestigious in the French tradition than his historical contribution (Bachelier 1996). "Men make history, but they ignore the kind of history they make." That formula is linked to the notion of "*Illusions rétrospectives de la nécessité*" ("the retrospective illusions of necessity"). Because events happened in a certain way does not mean they were supposed to happen that way (see Schmitt's Introduction to this volume). At the very moment of decision making, the concrete situation of the decision maker is characterized by only one word: *uncertainty*. In the context of strategic intelligence, such an "Aronian" approach of prudence, by placing an emphasis on the ethical injunction contained in the idea of prudence, could be a relevant addition to the literature on uncertainty and anticipation, which often remain largely functional and technical (Stalcup 2015).

The Diplomat, the Soldier, and the dialectics of war and peace

As we are about to question whether Aron would nowadays still describe foreign policy only through the Diplomat and the Soldier, or if he would feel the need to place between them a third character (the Spy), we first have to understand what those two archetypes symbolize. Or, to put it differently, we need to introduce the dialectics of war and peace.

When he first introduces those two characters, Aron uses the notion of symbolization: "Inter-state relations are expressed in and by specific actions, those of individuals whom I shall call symbolic, the *diplomat* and the *soldier*" (Aron 2003: 5). We could as well define the Diplomat and the Soldier as the allegorical "ideal-typizations" of public diplomacy and of strategy/military action. We consider here that there is a relation between Aron's use of an allegorical (in Aron's words, symbolic) *style* and what Reed Davis calls a categorical *framework* in his description of Aron's method: "comprehensive interpretations of the human condition that establish the basic distinctions and logical relations that are believed to inhere in reality" (Davis 2009: 25).

The diplomat decides between war and peace. His ethos is the preservation of peace. The Soldier refers to another duality: victory or defeat. His only goal is victory. His duality is not purely derived from the duality of war and peace. To gain a better peace you need to win the war. Entering war with the perspective of losing is an absurdity coming from the people, a moral fault coming from the leader. We have seen how praxeology is the instrument to link principles and consequences: if the statesman is only a man of principles and ignores the consequences of his decisions, or if the man who acts does not derive his action from a set of principles, then action will result in war and defeat. Antinomies lie at the core of the issue of the diplomatic-strategic conduct: in the area of foreign policy more than in any other sector of politics and policy making, the tension between norms, values, principles, standards, and consequences of action leads to unsolvable contradictions that will concretely take the shape of violence or even war. Can we avoid, or at least limit, the consequences of those antinomies? Is war avoidable? Is true peace reachable?

Peace is a regulative ideal ("*ideal régulateur*") of IR. Aron plays with the regulative idea ("*idée régulatrice*") in Kant. Those are ideas without which other ideas cannot be conceived, and are derived from the transcendental idealities, time and space (Kant 1781, 1784, 1797). Peace is the ideal without which no international action can be considered, envisioned, or conducted. Even enemies, when they enter war, consider peace as the ultimate result of their actions. You quit a state of peace to enter war because you expect or hope for a better peace: more stable, more just, more to your advantage, longer. Even the more realist of the realists, the most rigorous disciples of Thomas Hobbes and Machiavelli can understand peace as the ultimate destination of humanity. They do not believe that it is a concrete possibility, that actual peace is at hand, that a pacification of the world can be reached and even less achieved. But they cannot ignore that, theoretically and "morally", peace is the ultimate end of history.

Does Aron regard peace, as Kant puts it, only as a "Sweet Dream made by Philosophers"? According to Aron, war is the practical human horizon for the political leader.

> The behavior of the diplomat-strategist, in effect, is specifically dominated by the risk of war, confronting adversaries in an incessant rivalry in which each side reserves the right to resort to the *ultima ratio*, that is, to violence.... Let us confine ourselves to stating that diplomatic-strategic behavior does not have an obvious objective, but that the risk of war obliges it to calculate forces of means.
>
> (Aron 2003: 17)

Even if I do want peace, even if I want to keep it, to restore it, to build it, war lies on the "horizon of action". Every decision, every action can lead to war, can be a path to war. Even more so if we are not aware of that possibility, if we forget that potentiality. So, in short: for Aron, peace is the regulative ideal of IR but war remains the inescapable horizon of our actions.

For Aron, the idea that any kind of conflict can degenerate in pure war is a heritage from Carl Schmitt. The illusion of peace as the horizon for political action is inherited from Machiavelli. Aron's views about Machiavelli's legacy is a complex issue (Aron 1993). In *Peace and War*, Aron mentions very briefly the "dispute over machiavellianism or of *raison d'état*" (Aron 2003: 783): he seems to ironize gently on Eric Weil's reading of Friedrich Meinecke's classical *Die Idee der Staatsräson* (Aron 2003: 780–781), but without developing it. As Machiavelli puts it in the famous statement from chapter 14 in the *Prince*: "A ruler, then, should have no other objective and no other concern, nor occupy himself with anything else except war and its methods and practices, for this pertains only to those who rule" (Machiavelli 2008). Peace is more dangerous than war for the Prince because peace is a state of shared illusion. War is more clear, a state of *clairvoyance*: you cannot ignore war when you are at war. You cannot forget peace when you are at war. You crave for it more and more every day. You forget war more and more every day when you are at peace. That illusion is particularly true for the *Popolo*. The *Grandi* remember better because of the permanent dissent between them. In the famous chapter 25 about *Virtù* and *Fortuna*, the rivers are symbols for foreign invasion armies (Machiavelli 2008). The Prince has to become the one who prepares for war in peaceful times.

In the context of the complex organizations and bureaucracy that characterize modern states and governments, intelligence services precisely fulfill the task of bringing foreknowledge (*clairvoyance*), remaining vigilant, protecting from the illusions of peace.

The Spy: redefining intelligence in a post-9/11 context

The dialectics of peace and war are a good way to understand today's use of intelligence (What may be the role of intelligence in connection with diplomacy on one side and the use of military force on the other side? How can intelligence help, or be part of, the definition and the conduct of the diplomatic-strategic policy?). A fruitful approach is to interrogate the links between one of the most seminal intelligence theory books (or at least an effort to theorize about intelligence), Michael Herman's *Intelligence Power in Peace and War*, which echoes the title of Aron's own IR theorization (Herman 1996). Herman was head of GCHQ and Vice-Chairman of the UK Joint Intelligence Committee (JIC); he has known professionally both the British and the American national intelligence systems, and, in addition to being a former practitioner, he is a scholar and runs the Oxford Intelligence Group at Nuffield College in Oxford. The contemporary effort in the literature on Intelligence Studies is to make connections between IR theories and theory of intelligence, which are two scientific areas that rarely connect (Andrew 2004). A useful entry point is the two books by Aron and Herman, as they help us understand that those two academic literatures, though they are very different, share a common preoccupation, or at least stand in the same position regarding their environment: the preoccupation for politics from which social and international issues are supposed to be understood.

Herman writes that for intelligence activities,

> perhaps in some ways it is like in medicine; doctors in general practice are said to spend most of their time on things that affect patients' quality of life, but occasionally their role is life-saving. Intelligence has something of the same variation.
>
> (Herman 1996: 154)

Peace and war are two different contexts in which the same activity produces different effects. And more than being two opposite states, peace and war are the two ends of a continuum. In peacetime, the difference between diplomatic and intelligence activities lies in the nature of the means through which they conduct their business: visible and acknowledged versus secret and clandestine: "The central feature of intelligence collection is collecting information without its target's consent or cooperation, and often without its knowledge. States give their consent to the existence of diplomats and diplomatic reporting, but not to intelligence sources" (Herman 1996: 119). In wartime, there is no conceptual difference between intelligence and military activities; intelligence is simply part of the conduct of operations: "War provides the best laboratory for intelligence. Victory is a clear objective; intelligence has an unambiguous role of understanding the enemy; it has a higher priority than in peace and attracts more talent." Still, "generalizations about wartime effects are ... not easy. Obviously intelligence alone does not make for victory without force to use it" (Herman 1996: 145). The duality of war and peace is a real intellectual tool in Herman's reflection on intelligence. And the functional roles of public diplomacy and military power in foreign policy are clearly separated even if they can be combined or related one to the other.

But for Herman the duality is only one of context. He does not think of intelligence as an activity related to some *dialectics* of war and peace. And intelligence is not presented in his book as a third dimension of the decision-making process, alongside diplomacy and the use of force. It is rather an extension or a part of them:

> In war [intelligence] assists the effective use of force. Sometimes in war (and in counter-terrorism) it goes further and transforms the ways in which the action takes place. In peace its effects are often in diplomatic execution rather than the making of foreign policy. In both war and peace intelligence's consistent impact are its cumulative, relatively unsurprising contributions to effectiveness and influence. Overlaying any regular patterns there is serendipity or luck.
>
> (Herman 1996: 155)

Herman nevertheless acknowledges the specificity of international terrorism as a threat leading to a confusion between war and peace:

> parts of nominal peace are simply less violent versions of war, and intelligence there has extensions of its wartime power for the application of force. Thus it is central to counter-terrorism and negates terrorism's characteristics of invisibility and surprise. Defeating terrorism usually depends on intelligence success and not the force available.
>
> (Herman 1996: 153)

But even in that case intelligence remains a simple tool for foreign policy making: "tactical intelligence support adds to certainty and confidence in foreign policy execution; ... it gives immediacy, practicality and focus to existing general conclusions" (Herman 1996: 153). The following sections are an attempt to adapt Herman's reasoning to the current security context where terrorism would be seen as the major threat, or at least the most defining and pressing one for foreign policy. Since Herman wrote his seminal essay, the distinction between war and peace has become less clear-cut. And furthermore, by inserting Herman's formalizations into Aron's intellectual frameworks of the dialectics of the diplomatic-strategic conduct and of the dialectics of war and peace, we will show how intelligence is no longer conceived simply as a part of military planning or as an alternative support to public diplomacy, and we will speculate on how intelligence becomes a factor in its own right in the making of foreign policy.

Since 2001, a new actor has emerged in addition to the two functions Aron envisioned and it has become mixed with diplomacy and strategy within the decision-making process: the intelligence communities (central intelligence machineries (UK), *architectures nationales de renseignement*, national intelligence systems). There is a new trend in intelligence that can be defined with two words: centralization and normalization, both within government machineries and in the general public sphere. This movement is accompanied by a complete transformation of what is expected from national intelligence systems. They become more central, more normal, and more problematic at the same time. The very meaning of intelligence is transforming nowadays (Irondelle and Chopin 2013).

Intelligence is more and more central both in the decision-making process and in the public sphere (Jeffreys-Jones 2003; Tucker 2014): especially certain aspects of intelligence activities such as secret rendition and detention programs, torture as a tool for Humint, militarized unmanned aerial vehicles and targeted killings, interception of communications, special forces, etc. Action is the finality of intelligence: intelligence's primary role/function is to support action. We now have a new way of thinking about intelligence, of describing intelligence, which was not possible at the time Raymond Aron and Michael Herman were writing.

Intelligence issues are considered in the United States and United Kingdom as political science objects. They can be theorized and discussed scientifically. And at the same time they are not considered abstractly. They are practical issues.

Why do intelligence organizations do what they do? How do they perceive and define what they do? Intelligence organizations are bureaucracies, with rules, doctrines, authorizations, appropriations, etc. They rely on procedures. Complexity and bureaucracy once again refer to Max Weber (Weber 1978, 1994).

Here we have to make a distinction between the *logics of intelligence* (Why do intelligence organizations do what they do?) and the *problematic of intelligence* (Why is there a problem there, how do we perceive the problem?). Why does the use of intelligence and covert action or clandestine activities represent a problem, an issue for democratic regimes and liberal societies? Why has intelligence become a more "normal" topic in government and public life? It is considered as a new magic tool, a magic wand: we can do more with less. And no decision in foreign policy seems to be taken without consulting the intelligence communities. This happens inside the decision-making process, most of the time secretly in that respect. But it also happens publicly: the intelligence organizations are increasingly considered as some kind of certification tool for "threats" (Agrell and Treverton 2015). For instance, every year or so the Office of the Director of National Intelligence (ODNI) will release a report titled "The Worldwide Threat Assessment of the US Intelligence Community". They can also be used as tools to counteract, to disrupt, or to prevent decisions or actions. It becomes normal, usual, even casual to talk about intelligence production, about intelligence activities, about assessments that come out of the intelligence processes. In a way, the public perception of people working in the intelligence sector tends more and more to conform to the self-perception of intelligence officers since the 1970s (Brunet 1997). This normalization process comes from a kind of imposition, of mental projection, in the public sphere of the self-perception of the actual spies (Dewerpe 1994; Chopin and Oudet 2016).

Returning to the dialectics of war and peace, the intelligence analyst or officer has two missions: in times of peace, his mission is not to prepare for war but to wage it anyway. We will use the Spy here as the allegorical "ideal-typization" of the intelligence officer or intelligence analyst. The Spy keeps on waging war in times of peace: secret wars, invisible wars, silent wars. It is a direct application of Machiavelli's command. Peace is, at one and the same time, true and an illusion. It is strategically irrelevant. This secret war, the Spy's war, does not necessarily lead to the other war, real war, true war. Intelligence can even be one of the tools in the hands of the Diplomat to accomplish his ethos, to preserve peace. Intelligence can be the realm of mutual confidence between enemies. But intelligence and covert action are simultaneously instruments of another form of diplomacy, a real diplomacy in its own right but "parallel", based on an inversion of the dialectics of war and peace. We trade with our allies and with the enemies of our allies. If intelligence is considered as another form of diplomacy, then it is the equivalent of a form of schizophrenia (but only when you realize it, when it is known, publicly acknowledged). But this inversion of the determinations of war and peace is the very logics of this kind of activity. The Spy is the one who inverts the usual positions of peace and war. It is a form of transgression: peace in war and war in peace.

Intelligence and security

In what respect is the Spy new and different than the Diplomat and the Soldier? The Spy would be a challenge to characterize as some intelligence activities relate to (secret) diplomacy when others relate to (covert) military action. Where does the ultimate specificity of intelligence that would substantiate the correction of Aron's taxonomy lie? First, the core of the "functionalist" approach of intelligence that Anglo-American Intelligence Studies has developed is represented by analysis and the production of strategic knowledge as an essential step in the decision-making process; then in the issue of uncertainty that is characteristic of the securitization context (Fingar 2011).

Aron chooses to open the "Final Note" of *Peace and War* with a long quotation from the economist Oskar Morgenstern and to engage with him in a strong debate about the operationalization of political science, constitutions, and game theory. Aron's judgment of Morgenstern is severe: "This quotation reveals the mixture of rigor and confusion, of profundity and naïveté characteristic of certain scientific minds at grip with problems external to their discipline, especially political problems" (Aron 2003: 768). One of the passages of Morgenstern's long quotation was about

> the problem of decision-making under uncertainty, where the uncertainty is not the simple, well understood kind to be dealt with by the probability theory, but is of the highly complex nature arising from the strategic move of the opponent, who labors under the same difficulty.
> (Aron 2003: 767–768)

Aron does not answer precisely on uncertainty, but does engage in an argument about probability and game theory in the following pages.

So we do not know whether for Aron "the problem of decision-making under uncertainty" raised by Morgenstern should be considered as rigorous and profound or, on the contrary, a confused and naive problem. But it is one of the "shared beliefs" of international relations and foreign policy analysis academic communities that uncertainty in the post-9/11 context is now of an even "higher complex nature": intelligence organizations are in the process of being centralized and normalized in governments' global decision-making processes (Chopin 2017) because they are seen as tools to reduce uncertainty: "Managing uncertainty is essential to making foreign policy ... A critical function of the intelligence community is to help policy-makers ..., especially when they depend on factors that are uncertain and complex" (Friedman and Zeckhauser 2012). Even if these tools prove to have many structural limitations (Bajolet 2014; Jackson 2010).

It is a truism to say that nowadays all types of security are interconnected. Even in the context of the Cold War Aron would not disconnect collective security and national security. But, now more than ever, international security issues are envisioned in a continuum with domestic or "homeland" security. The injunction to protect, from the global perspective of Responsibility to Protect

(R2P) to the national obligations of "protecting the homeland", obliges the statesman to reassess all dimensions of foreign policy through the lenses of security, while the dialectics of war and peace, and the "obligations" imposed on us by the insurmountable "antinomies of action", remain entirely pre-eminent (Aron 2003: 787). The Spy is the allegorical embodiment of security that links diplomacy and the use of force in a new way. Intelligence is the tool and at the same time the *sign* of this redefinition (Chopin and Oudet 2016).

Aron helps us think about intelligence issues in the contemporary world by adding new perspectives to a very functionalist and technical framework for analyzing intelligence activities and organizations. Aron wrote very little about intelligence during the Cold War and it is impossible to infer what he would have said about current intelligence issues and the challenges intelligence services face today. Aron nevertheless can contribute to our thinking about those issues if we refer to some of his ideas and concepts: reading Aron today with the literature on intelligence in mind can be at the same time challenging and rewarding. The dual nature of praxeology, combining a theory-and-practice methodological dimension and an element of normativity, can provide an alternative and more complex approach to the topics of democratic control of intelligence activities, or of the "ethics of intelligence", which both rely on conformity to standards. The practice of, and obstacles to, intelligence analysis are two of the major subtopics of Intelligence Studies. They share with Aron's morality of prudence the fundamental and unsolvable problem of uncertainty. The dialectics of war and peace can prevent us from taking for granted that the *duality* of war and peace is not relevant any more when intelligence should deal only with *threats*. Aron's allegorical theorization of diplomatic-strategic conduct can prove to be a relevant intellectual tool to address the current interface of public diplomacy, military power, and intelligence under the categorical, unavoidable, and imperious rise of a political imperative: security.

Aron was under the impression that "in certain respect, because of the worldwide extension of the diplomatic field and the invention of thermonuclear weapons, the present circumstances are unique and unprecedented" (Aron 2003: 17–18). We would talk of globalization now, and of global war-mind or jihadism more than nuclear war, but the feeling is still the same. What may be unique and unprecedented is how the "intelligence stratégique" has been given as a specific responsibility to the Spy, when for Aron that quality, that ability, was shared by the Diplomat and the Soldier. If the intelligence analysts, officers, and leaders are to join "the experts, the minister of state or the philosopher – that is, those who advise, decide or act" (Aron 2003: 14), then they should undertake the same professional duties Aron expects of them:

> The political thinker who ignores the problem of war fails two key interrelated duties of his calling: that of advising the statesman (and, in a democratic context, educating the citizen); and that of mirroring as accurately, as "scientifically" as possible, the reality of the political world.
>
> (Mahoney and Anderson 2003: xi)

They should also take on the moral duties Aron urges us never to forget: "Let us try not to fail either of the obligations ordained for each of us: not to run away from a belligerent history, not to betray the ideal ..., the day when peace has become possible – supposing it ever will" (Aron 2003: 787).

References

Agrell, W., and Treverton, G. (2015), *National Intelligence and Science: Beyond the Great Divide in Analysis and Policy*. Oxford: Oxford University Press.

Anderson, B. (1997), *Raymond Aron and the Recovery of the Political*. Lanham, MD: Rowman & Littlefield.

Andrew, C. (2004), "Intelligence, International Relations and 'Under-theorisation'", *Intelligence and National Security*, 19:2, 170–184.

Arendt, H. (2014), *Qu'est-ce que la politique?*. Paris: Seuil.

Aron, R. (1974), *The Imperial Republic: The United States and the World 1945–1973*. New York: Little Brown & Company.

Aron, R. (1978), *Politics and History: Selected Essays by Raymond Aron*. New York: The Free Press.

Aron, R. (1993), *Machiavel et les tyrannies modernes*. Paris: Editions de Fallois.

Aron, R. (2003), *Peace and War: A Theory of International Relations*. New Brunswick, NJ: Transactions Publishers.

Bachelier, C. (1996), *Raymond Aron: Une Histoire du XXe siècle – Anthologie*. Paris: Plon.

Bachelier, C. (2007), *Raymond Aron*. Paris: CulturesFrance.

Bajolet, B. (2014), "La DGSE, outil de réduction de l'incertitude?", *Revue Défense Nationale*, 766, 27–31.

Betts, R. (2009), *Enemies of Intelligence: Knowledge and Power in American National Security*. New York: Columbia University Press.

Born, H., and Caparini, M. (2007), *Democratic Control of Intelligence: Containing Rogue Elephants*. London: Routledge.

Brunet, J.P. (1997), "Les langages du secret: Des mots pour (ne pas) le dire", *Le Renseignement – IHESI Cahiers de la Sécurité intérieure*, 30, 87–101.

Chopin, O. (2017), "Intelligence Reform and the Transformation of the State: The End of a French Exception", *Journal of Strategic Studies*, 40:4, 532–553.

Chopin, O., and Oudet, B. (2016), *Renseignement et sécurité*. Paris: Armand Colin.

Coll, A. (1993), "Prudence and Foreign Policy", in Cromatie, M. (ed.), *Might and Right after the Cold War*. Lanham, MD: Rowman & Littlefield.

Davis, R.M. (2009), *A Politics of Understanding: The International Thought of Raymond Aron*. Baton Rouge, LA: Louisiana State University Press.

Dewerpe, A. (1994), *Espion: Une anthropologie historique du secret d'État contemporain*. Paris: Gallimard.

Fingar, T. (2011), *Reducing Uncertainty: Intelligence Analysis and National Security*. Stanford, CA: Stanford Security Studies.

Friedman, J., and Zeckhauser, R. (2012), "Assessing Uncertainty in Intelligence", *Intelligence and National Security*, 27:6, 824–847.

Fukuyama, F. (2008), *Blindside: How to Anticipate Forcing Events and Wild Cards in Global Politics*. Washington, DC: Brookings Institution Press.

Herman, M. (1996), *Intelligence Power in Peace and War*. Cambridge: Cambridge University Press.

Holeindre, J.V. (2017), *La ruse et la force: Une autre histoire de la stratégie*. Paris: Perrin.

Irondelle, B., and Chopin, O. (2013), "Comparaison franco-britannique de la recherche sur les services de renseignement", *Criminologie*, 46:2, 15–42.

Jackson, P. (2010), "On Uncertainty and the Limits of Intelligence", in Johnson, L. (ed.), *The Oxford Handbook of National Security Intelligence*. Oxford: Oxford University Press.

Jeffreys-Jones, R. (2003), *The CIA and American Democracy*, 3rd edn. New Haven, CT: Yale University Press.

Kaufmann, C. (2004), "Threat Inflation and the Failure of the Marketplace of Ideas: The Selling of the Iraq War", *International Security*, 29:1, 5–48.

Kant, I. (1781), *Critique of Pure Reason*.

Kant, I. (1784), *Idea for a Universal History with a Cosmopolitan Purpose*.

Kant, I. (1793), *On the Common Saying: This May Be True in Theory But It Does Not Apply in Practice*.

Kant, I. (1797), "Part 1: The Doctrine of Right", in *Metaphysics of Morals*.

Kent, S. (1965), *Strategic Intelligence for American World Policy*. Hamden, CT: Archon Books (first published 1949 by Princeton University Press).

Machiavelli, N. (2008), *The Prince*. Ed. Skinner, Q. and Price, R. Cambridge: Cambridge University Press.

Mahoney, D. (1992), *The Liberal Political Science of Raymond Aron*. Lanham, MD: Rowman & Littlefield.

Mahoney, D., and Anderson, B. (2003), "Introduction to the Transaction Edition", in Aron, R., *Peace and War: A Theory of International Relations*. New Brunswick, NJ: Transaction Publishers.

Pierce, R. (1966), *Contemporary French Political Thought*. New York: Oxford University Press.

Raynaud, P. (1988), *Max Weber et les dilemmes de la raison moderne*. Paris: Presses Universitaires de France.

Schmitt, C. (2004), *Political Theology: Four Chapters on the Concept of Sovereignty*. Chicago, IL: University of Chicago Press.

Schmitt, C. (2006), *The Concept of the Political*. Chicago, IL: University of Chicago Press.

Stalcup, M. (2015), "Policing Uncertainty: On Suspicious Activity Reporting", in Saminian-Darash, L. and Rabinow, P. (eds.), *Modes of Uncertainty: Anthropological Cases*. Chicago, IL: Chicago University Press, 69–87.

Thrall, T., and Cramer, J. (2009), *American Foreign Policy and the Politics of Fear: Threat Inflation since 9/11*. New York: Routledge.

Treverton, G. (2009), *Intelligence for an Age of Terror*. Cambridge: Cambridge University Press.

Tucker, D. (2014), *The End of Intelligence: Espionage and State Power in the Information Age*. Stanford, CA: Stanford University Press.

Weber, M. (1978), *Economy and Society*. Oakland, CA: University of California Press.

Weber, M. (1994), *Political Writings*. Cambridge: Cambridge University Press.

Index

9/11 (September 11) 180; *see also* post-9/11

Adenauer, K. 120
Ailleret, C. 94, 97–98, 101–102
Allison, G. 107, 153
American 16, 183; analysts 104, 107; anti-American dimension of Franco-German understanding 101; coalition against China 150; colleagues of Aron 128–129; democracy 123; determination to fight 123; deterrence capabilities 5; economic liberalism 116; Euro-American values 139; foreign policy 138–140; hegemony 151, 159; ideological systems 128; ideology 131, 138; industrial society 133; imperialism 129; military retreat 105; modernization theory 128, 130, 134; national intelligence systems 187; neoconservatives 120; policy in Vietnam 76; political elite 117; Political Science Association 53; power balance 150; pro-American 4; social sciences 100; social scientists 129; spy-plane U2, 181; strategic school 108; strategic thought 95; takeover of Europe 159; technology 134; tensions with China 168; territory beyond reach of SS-20, 121; University of Paris 89n1; values 135; Western political values 10; World Policy 180
Americans 29, 107
Amstutz, M. 169
Anderson, B.C. 72, 180, 185, 192
Andropov, Yuri 122
Anglo-American: acceptance of sociological liberalism 146; Intelligence Studies 191
Annan, K. 170
Arendt, H. 94, 184

Aristotelian 9, 18; conception of practical wisdom 175; ethos 78; interpretation of Aron 88, 89n2; neo-Aristotelian 9; phronesis 79
Aristotelianism 20
Aristotle 2, 10, 20–21, 79, 82; Middle Way (*in medio stat virtus*) 143
armed conflicts 75, 168, 170, 176
arms control 99, 104–106; negotiations 107; talks and agreements 102
arms race 57, 105
Aron, R. 7–8, 14–31, 34–38, 41–46, 48–51, 57–62, 64–66, 70–89, 93–96, 100–106, 108, 108n1, 111–113, 114–123, 126–127, 130–140, 142–149, 154–157, 160n2, 160n5, 166–167, 176, 181–187, 191–193
Aron, R. Peace and War among Nations 2, 9–11, 53, 57, 59, 79, 164, 167
Aron, R. Peace and War: A Theory of International Relations 14–17, 21, 27, 30–31, 51, 87, 100, 104, 119–121, 123, 145–146, 149, 154–155, 157, 171, 179–181, 184, 187, 191
Aronian 80, 82, 144, 174; approach 185; inspired 175–176; inspired views of Rao 137; practical philosophy 89n2; research program 143; tradition of sociological liberalism 146
Aron's IR theory 21, 53–54, 57, 61, 93, 144–145, 150, 152, 163; classical foundations 9, 16
Audier, S. 2, 9

Bachelier, C. 179, 185
Baechler, J. 145, 150, 152, 157–158, 160n4
balance of power 60, 66, 102, 104, 106, 116–117, 157, 165, 172

Index

balance of terror 99, 107, 145
Barkin, J.S. 54–56, 70
Battistella, D. 2, 53, 60, 142–143
Baverez, N. 3, 71, 75, 83, 88, 112
Beaufre, General André 94–95, 100–103, 108
Beitz, C. 172
Bell, D. 54, 127, 130, 175
Berlin 3, 74, 89, 112, 115; Blockade 96; status 104
bipolar 147; configuration of forces 164; equilibrium 30; systems 20–21, 30, 61; world of superpowers 28
bipolarity 145, 156, 183
bipolarization 158
Bonfreschi, L. 111, 114
Breiner, P. 7, 76
British: analysts 98–99; ambassador in Paris 121; citizen 183; forces 4; government publications 112–113; MI6, 183; military policy 99; national intelligence system 187; strategic model 102; strategist 83
Brodie, B. 95–96, 108
Bull, H. 2, 53, 70, 142, 174
Buzan, B. 171

Camus, Albert 4
Canguilhem, G. 3, 8–10, 34, 36–50, 51n1, 65, 142
Castex, Admiral Raoul 96
Central Intelligence Agency (CIA) 180, 183
Chatenet, P. 120, 124n2
Châton, G. 2–3, 9, 79, 89n1, 143
China 96, 130, 132, 135, 146, 150–152; Communist Party of 151; Indochina 76; industrial output 133; rise of 149; South China Sea 150, 168
Chinese 107, 131; alliance 151; government 151–152; tensions in South China Sea 168
Chopin, O. 9, 11, 189–192
Churchill, Winston 103, 105, 114, 120
classical realism 55, 149
classical realist 1, 56, 79, 86, 143; liberal 73; mainstream 70; neo-classical 60
Clausewitz, C. von 5, 10, 30–31, 60–61, 83, 93–95, 98, 102–103, 106–107, 109n3, 120, 122–123, 142, 150, 154, 159, 165, 179
Clausewitzian: character of international politics 30; neo-Clausewitzian nuclear analysts 103; sociologist 150; synthesis 106, 109n3

Cohen, M. 172
Cold War 28, 66, 116, 120, 123, 145, 150, 152; context 179, 183, 191; cultural 127; decline in political intensity 129; different forms of war during 155; early years of 111; emerging 27; end of 87, 157, 163, 167–168, 183; era 19, 164, 166, 171; French/transatlantic strategic debate 94; ideological conflict 107; intelligence during 192; international system during 167; liberals 128; opposition to nuclear weapons during 75; political dead end 184; post-Cold War era 167–168; post-Cold War world 146; test of will 121–122; theory 143
Cold Warrior 1, 12
Colen, J. 2, 73
Coll, A. 79, 185
Collège de France 5, 103
Collins, R. 152, 159
Colloques de Rheinfelden 130, 133–134
Colquhoun, R. 3, 32n1, 32n2, 33
Commission on Global Governance 168
Commission on Human Security 170
communism 5, 88, 119, 147; Aron's fight against 71; kindling in Latin America 158; Stalinist 116
communist 183; cause 182; coup d'état 151; expansion by force 140; French party 113; ideology 115, 129; movement 4; North Vietnamese ideology 140; Polish former 95; regimes 121, 183; temptation facing recently decolonized countries 127, 137
Communist Party of China 151
communists 137, 151
Congress for Culture Freedom (CCF) 126–131, 134, 136, 138–140
constructivism 1, 53–55, 64, 70, 152, 159; see also realist-constructivism
constructivist 54–56, 60, 63, 151; proto- 70, 78; see also realist-constructivist
convergence 54, 100, 138, 185; global industrial 131; negative 129; political 129; systems 128–129; theory 128–130; West-Soviet Union 127
Cooper, B. 109n3
Courtin, René 114
Cozette, M. 86, 176
Cuba 137; Cuban Missile Crisis 104–105; Cuban refugees 183

Dabila, A. 9–11, 152
Dahrendorf, R. 128

Index 197

Davis, R.M. 2, 8–10, 17, 32n3, 34, 65, 71, 88, 184–186
de Beauvoir, Simone 121, 179
découplage 99, 106
defense strategy 97
de Gaulle, Charles 4, 7, 116–117, 120, 123, 129; *force de frappe* 93; Free French movement 95; military policy 99; nuclear weapons 104; *Rassemblement du Peuple Français* (RPF) party 101, 113; speech at *Ecole Militaire* 99; withdrawal from NATO 102; *see also* Gaullist (s)
Delbrück, H. 95, 102, 113, 120
d'Estaing, Giscard 102–103
détente 102, 106, 130
DGSE (preceded by SDECE) 183

EEC 118–120
Eisenstadt, S. 152
English school 58, 70, 85, 142, 145, 159, 175
espionage 180–181; *see also* intelligence, spy/spies
ethic/ethics 81; Aron's 88, 175; of consequences 78; contemporary normative 76, 78; of conviction 7, 70, 73–78, 84, 88, 175; of global affairs 171; of immigration 172; of intelligence 192; international 9, 71, 171; in IR 163; Kantian 88; of law 165; legal deontological 80; of lesser evil 172; place in Social Science 80; of prudence 8; of responsibility 7, 70–71, 73, 76–79, 84, 175, 185; of restrained warfare 81; situational or contextual 82; of ultimate ends 73; virtue 78–79, 88; war 83; of wisdom 175
Euromissiles 105–106, 121
Europe 3, 11, 14, 25, 51, 61, 106, 115, 117, 127, 132–133, 135, 138, 146, 183; nineteenth century 103; American takeover of 159; Aron's views on 120, 123; between the two world wars 157; central 29; Concert of 86; conflicts 167; conventional forces 100; Council of 114; decline of 96, 116; defence of 118; *In Defence of Decadent* 121–122; differences in regime types 63; Eastern 29, 105, 116, 119, 121; Hitler's 113, 119; international system 58; invasion of 96; Napoleon's drive to rule 64; peace settlement 102, 104; politically united 111; post-war 131; power vacuum 114; rise of Nazism 74; strategic autonomy of 99; united 112; US commitment in 116; vision of 113; Western 28, 99, 107, 114, 118, 121, 126–127, 129, 159; withdrawal of Jupiter IRBMs 105
European Defence Community (EDC) 101, 118
existentialism 50, 147; existentialist doctrine 148

Fabre-Luce, A. 112, 119, 124n1
Foch, F. 83
Fodor, J. 37
force *see* use of force/recourse to force
foreign policy 18, 67, 81, 111, 117, 169, 180, 185–186; analysis 66, 179, 191; conduct of 56, 59, 61, 179; decisions 151, 190; makers 150; making 188–189, 191; misguided 129; motives 64; negative constraints on 171; objective 63; primacy of 118; reassess 192; Swiss independent 26; theory of 9, 54–57, 59–60, 142; US 5, 129, 131, 138–140, 174
France 7, 32n2, 35, 64, 81, 108, 152; against Algerian independence 133; Aron in 2–3, 53, 96, 130; Atlantic alliance 117; *Collège de* 5, 103; convergence 129; defeat of 112; diplomatic initiatives 98; empty chair in the EEC 120; expert on nuclear matters 97; Fifth Republic 119; historical sociology 149; imperial and Mediterranean power 118; intellectual civil war 99; IR approach 143–144, 147; liberation 123; military influence 102; military policy 99; military superiority 101; nuclear debate 100; nuclear test 83; post-World War II era 14; reconciliation with Germany 112–114, 117, 123; revolutionary 64, **65**; Rostow's thought 135
Franco-German reconciliation 101–102
Franco-Russian agreements 66; friendship 182
Freedman, L. 60
Free French 4; economist René Courtin 114; journal (*La France Libre*) 112; movement 95
French 1–2, 97, 160; academic landscape 149; author 66–67; citizens 133; colonels 107; communist party 113; *corps de bataille* 102; decline since

French *continued*
  Napoleon 95; governing elite 128; government 121; involvement in European battle 102; Jews 3, 123; journal *Nouvelle Revue Française* 126; Left 129; liberal 180; Marxism 128, 130; *national agrégation* committee 34; National Assembly 118; parliament 118; philosopher 71, 111, 119; political elite 114; political field 5; politics 4, 93, 108; power 98; predominance 101; reconciliation with Germany 113; *renseignement* 181; Revolution 63, 94, 158; scholar 7; school of IR 143–146; science 35; SDECE 183; sociological liberalism 145–146; statesmen 64; strategic equation 95; strategists 100, 106, 108; tradition 185; translation 8; troops 147; withdrawal from NATO 101; writers 112
French debates 5, 9; nuclear *Grand Débat* 109n2; strategic 11, 93–94
French intellectuals/intelligentsia 3, 35, 121, 155; community 14; elite 112
French military: policy 101; posture 102; thinkers and players 98
French nuclear atomic force 99; deterrent 5, 11; doctrine 100; *Grand Débat* 109n2; thinking 108
French strategic 95; arena 103; culture 108; debates 11, 93–94, 105; official thinking 102; policy 101; problem 102; school 108
French thinkers 1, 94; classic political 152; military 98
French tradition of thought 144–145; liberal 71; military 98; nuclear 108; official strategic 102; philosophical 143
Frost, B.P. 2, 9–11, 53, 82, 142, 169, 174
Fukuyama, F. 21, 185

Gallois, P. 94–95, 97–103, 105–106, 108
Gaullist (s) 4, 129; journal 116; military policy 101; movement 117; RPF 114
genocide 75, 84, 174; genocidal atrocities 167
German 101; Aron's speeches in 114–115; Aron's visit 3, 74; Bundeswehr (West German) 118; civilians and cities bombed 81, 115; domination 151; historical sociology 149, 152; *Machtpolitik* (power politics) 87; new tradition of thinking 145; *Ostpolitik* 106; people 16, 105; philosophy 14; power revival 114; reconciliation with France 101–102, 113; Reich 113; sociologists 7, 144; students in Frankfurt 115; troops 75; version of the Monroe doctrine 113; writer Clausewitz 103
German rearmament 97, 101; campaigns against 182
Germans 16, 115
Germany 14, 64, **65**, 88, 118, 135, 152, 157; Aron's stay in 3, 14, 88, 112, 114, 144; East 116; Federal Republic of 118, 121; French relation to 95, 102, 112; Nazi 105, 112; obtain atomic weapons 101; policies of appeasement toward 74; rearmament 97, 101; reconciliation with France 123; reconciliation with France 112–114, 117; unity with Italy 133; war with 3; war capability 109n4; Western 106, 121; *see also* Third Reich
Girard, R. 105–107
Guilhot, N. 54, 72
Gutting, G. 45

Halévy, E. 71, 112
Hall, J. 139
Hassner, P. 2, 84, 86–87, 142, 175–176
Herman, M. 187–189
Herz, J. 73, 86
historical sociology 3, 144–146, 149, 152–153, 159, 160n1
Hitler, A. 7, 14, 74–75, 80, 105, 113, 119, 142; Hitlerism 95; *see also* Nazi
Hobbes, Thomas 81, 186
Hobbesian natural rivalry 97; situation 23; state of nature 86, 164; structure of international relations 103
Hobson, J.M. 152
Hoffmann, S. 2, 53, 71, 78–79, 88, 157, 160n1, 167, 173–174
Holeindre, J.V. 2, 143, 181
human rights 81, 84, 116, 122, 170–171, 176; activists 75; international community 165; requirements in Helsinki Final Act 121; violations 163, 170, 174
Human Security Center 168
Hungarian revolution 99, 119
Hungarians 181

Ikenberry, G.J. 63
immigration 172–173
India 130, 132–133, 135, 137, 146–147; Aron's argument about 136; social-economic situation 131

Indian 133; academics 137; economist Rao 136; intellectuals 129; leaders 132
instability 21, 168; of deterrence 101; structural 99
intelligence 11, 179–180; analysts 185, 190, 192; Anglo-American Studies 191; collection 183, 188; communities 189–191; issues 189, 192; organizations 180–181, 184, 190–191; Oxford Intelligence Group 187; services 183, 187, 192; strategic 180–181, 185; *stratégique* 192; studies 181, 185, 187, 191–192; tactical support 189; UK 189; US Community 190
intelligence activities 188, 191; aspects of 189; boundaries or regulation 184; democratic control of 192; framework for analyzing 192; normal to talk about 190; separated from main local party organization 181
Intelligence Power in Peace and War 187
intercontinental ballistic missiles (ICBM) 98–99; SS-20 medium-range 106, 121
International Commission on Intervention and State Sovereignty 170
international ethics 9, 71, 171
international politics 149; Aron's analysis of 15; bellicose character 20; changed nature of 31; Clausewitzian character 30; conducted through war 159; debates 3; ethical bases of 171; influence of norms, values and culture 62; level of autonomy 151; power as defining feature of 55; prudence tradition of 185; reduction to struggle for power 165; study of 58; System and Process in 53; theory of 55–57, 59, 66
International Relations (IR) 70, 142, 179; *see also* theory of international relations (IR)
inter-war: dreams 71; period 19, 74
Iron Curtain 96, 116, 118

Jackson, P.T. 8, 54, 191
Jaspers, K. 44, 94, 105
Jeangène Vilmer, J.B. 2, 9, 11–12, 54, 143
Jewish 3, 123
Jews: European 122; French 3
jihadism 107, 192
Johnson, L.B. 140; administration 129
Joint Intelligence Committee (JIC) 187; *see also* United Kingdom
Jupiter IRBM missile 98, 105

Kahn, H. 82, 102, 104

Kalyvas, S. 152
Kant, I. 2, 9, 36, 38, 46–47, 70, 79, 86, 88–89, 142, 184, 186
Kantian 18–19, 71, 86, 88; analysis of IR 165; asocial society 85; interpretation 89n2; liberalism 89; post-Hegelian 89; premise 38; problem 18, 79, 84, 171; thesis 45; training 8; type cosmopolitanism 184
Kantianism 18, 20; neo-Kantianism 14, 33
Kaplan, F. 53, 108
Kaplan, M.A. 142, 156
Kennedy, J.F. 101, 105, 107, 137, 140; administration 99–100, 129
Kent, S. 180–181
Khrushchev, N. 129, 137
Kissinger, H. 66, 131, 157
Kojève, A. 21
Korean War 96, 105

Lachman, R. 152
La France Libre 4, 95, 112, 119
Latin America 127, 137; communism in 158; states 137
Le Figaro 4, 93, 98–99, 108, 111, 129–130, 132, 135, 137
legitimacy 18, 80, 154; to intervene 173; lacked political 114; of political regimes 143, 156; principles of 20, 24, 27, 64; retroactive 39; of the use of force 163–164
liberal 70–71, 121, 153; capitalism 134; conceptions of Aron 142–143, 172; concerns 9, 63; conservative 122; democracies 5, 71, 83, 134; disciple of Machiavelli 89; English school of IR 143, 145; French classical school 144; French thought 71; institutions 133, 139; jurist 114; peace 176; political category 126; regimes 180; societies 71, 190; theorists 165; thinkers 14; tradition 133, 172; universalism 130; values 9, 54, 71, 81, 84, 139; West 130
liberalism 1, 54, 70–71, 88, 159; American economic 116; application of 133; of fear 175; Kantian 89; neo-liberalism 53; political 112, 116; *see also* sociological liberalism
liberal realism 71, 143, 172, 174
liberal realists 72–73, 78, 86–87, 174–175
liberals 149; Cold War 128; neoconservative 72; nineteenth-century 9, 46
Liberté de l'esprit 116

200 Index

Liddell Hart, B.H. 83
Loth, W. 129
Louis XIV 64

Maastricht Treaty 122
Machiavelli, N. 2, 4, 9, 70, 79–80, 83, 87, 89, 93–94, 102, 159, 186–187
Machiavellian 19; analysis of IR 165; conflictual pluralism 85; problem 18, 79, 171
Machiavellianism 18, 20, 71, 83; absolute 80–82, 84; anti 81; dispute over 187; moderate 81, 84; post-Kantian 79, 89; quarrel of 80; Wilhelmian 147
Mahoney, D. 2, 9, 78, 82, 88, 108, 179–180, 192
Malia, M. 130
Malis, C. 9, 11, 83, 103
Malraux, André 4, 95
Manent, P. 2, 9, 33, 51, 88
Maritain, J. 80–81
Mauriac, C. 116–117
McKinsey Global Institute 168
Mearsheimer, J. 149–150, 158–159
Mesure, S. 2, 9, 33–34, 45–46
Meszaros, T. 9–11, 144, 152, 156
migrants 168, 172–173
migration 155, 163, 168, 173; *see also* immigration
Milne, D. 134, 137
missile (s): Cuban Crisis 104; Euromissile 105–106, 121; interception 181; IRBM 98; on board 98; Pershing 122; SS-20, 121; *see also* intercontinental ballistic missiles (ICBM)
Montesquieu 10, 15–18, 82, 94, 135, 143, 145, 156
Morgenstern, Oskar 191
Morgenthau, H. 12, 17, 53, 76, 79, 86, 143, 153, 165, 172
Mounier, Emmanuel 4
Mouric, J. 9, 11, 97, 114
Multi-Lateral Force (MLF) 101
multipolar 11; configuration of forces 164; systems 20–21, 30, 61, 157
multipolarity 156–157

Nabokov, N. 127
Napoléon 63–64, 80, 95, 113, 123; Napoleonic wars 63, 94
NATO 98; crisis 99; French withdrawal 101–102, 120; heads of State 106; integration of Bundeswehr 118; internal relations 102; members 62; New Approach Group 97; Nuclear Planning Group 102; Soviet Union SS-20 threat 121
Nazi 75; Germany 105, 112; great space 113; threat 111–112
Nazism 74, 88
neo-Kantian: rationalism 88; training 88
neo-realism 53, 56, 171–173
neo-realist: perspective 171; scholars 57
Neumann, I.B. 58
neutralism 28; armed 101–102
neutrality 28; axiological 7–8; European 116; reunification in exchange for 115
Nouvelle Revue Française 126
nuclear 94; age 29, 107, 143, 155, 164, 184; arms 155; bombs 19, 29; conflicts, limited 167; crisis 104–105; decision-making process 101; deterrence 3, 75, 82, 99, 107, 120; deterrent, French 5, 11; diplomacy 104, 108; doctrine, French 100; duopoly 164; European defense 101; European force 97; force 19; holocaust 184; matters 94, 97, 108n1; models 104; national strike force 99–100; neo-Clausewitzian analysts 103; powers, multiplication of 100; proliferation 106; revolution 98, 164; secrets 100; states 104; strategy 5, 9, 28, 93, 98, 100, 102–103; strategy crisis 99; submarines 98; test 83; thinking 97, 108; threat 22; warfare 155; warheads 98
nuclear debate 82, 99; *Grand Débat* 109n2; strategic 93
Nuclear Planning Group 101–102
nuclear/thermonuclear weapons 19–20, 27–29, 31, 75, 94–95, 97–98, 101, 103–107, 109n3, 146, 149, 192
nuclear war 84, 109n3, 155, 192; global 167; limited 29; unfindable (*guerre introuvable*) 104, 107

Office of the Director of National Intelligence (ODNI) 190
oligopolarity 11, 156–157
oligopolar systems 157–158
Oxford Intelligence Group 187

pacifism 74–75
pacifist 3, 74–75, 112, 151; ideals 111; movement 106; neo-Kantian 88
Papaligouras, P. 151, 156
peace and war 16, 30–31, 104, 164, 179, 187–188, 190; *see also* war and peace/ war or peace

Peace and War among Nations 2, 9–11, 14–15, 17, 21, 27, 53, 57, 59, 79, 100, 104, 120, 155, 164, 167, 180, 191
Pershing missiles 106, 122
Pierce, R. 184
Pipes, R. 120, 130
Poirier, Lucien 94, 100, 108
politics 7, 14, 47, 55, 62, 107, 111, 142, 153, 184, 186, 188; abstract reflection on 165; amongst Nations 53; amorality of 166; Aron's approach to 143; balancing 158; basic rule of 159; comparative 1, 10, 21; complexities of 172, 175; of compromise 77, 83; determined by struggle for power 71–72; domestic 81, 147, 151, 169; duality of 88; end of 80; foreign 145; French 4, 93, 108; game of 74; global 28; importance of 3, 7; internal 61, 151; interstate 2; involved in 113; irreducible to morality 82, 171; led to war 75; persistence of 180; primacy of 1, 11, 25, 93–94, 108; of reason 83; relationship with morality 73; of strength 59; studying 149; subordination of the military to 103; totalitarian amplification of 94; of Understanding 2, 32n3; use of (nuclear) force in 19; vocation for 8, 77; war is the continuation of 103, 106; weighing of consequences 79; world 163; *see also* international politics, power politics
polypolarity 11, 156–157
polypolar systems 157–158
Pope: John Paul II 107; Polish 122
post-9/11, 179; intelligence 187; uncertainty 9/11, 191
post-Cold War era 167–168; world experiences 146
post-Kantian Machiavellianism 71, 79, 89
post-Kantian machiavellist 11
post-war 113; Europe or United States 131; speculations 96
Pouliot, V. 57, 66
power politics 1, 53–54, 56, 59; disappeared 18, 165; end of 21; nationalist connotation of Machtpolitik 87; rejection of 22; tradition of 117

Ramel, F. 2, 147
Rao, V.K.R.V. 129, 136–137
Rassemblement du Peuple Français (RPF) 4, 101, 113–114
Raynaud, P. 32n4, 89, 89n2

realism 1, 12, 54, 70, 82, 86, 88–89, 142, 145, 150–151, 159; become unrealistic 165; classical 55–56, 149; conservative versions of 175; defensive and offensive 64; false 72, 84; hard-core 80; ice-cold 5; liberal 71, 143, 172, 174; pessimistic 120; political 33, 73, 79, 112, 123; principled 163, 171, 173; sources of 147; structural 2, 55, 61, 64, 153; true 165, 171; *see also* neo-realism
realist 53, 71, 73, 84, 87, 142–143, 151, 153, 186; attitude 88; Cold Warrior 12; criticism 81; disciple of Kant 89; with Kantian aspirations 86; liberal 70, 72, 78; neo-classical 60; observers 75; research 54; school 165; scientific 8; thinking 55; traditional understanding 62; understanding of human nature 56; *see also* neo-realist, realist-constructivism, realist-constructivist
realist-constructivism 54–56, 66
realist-constructivist 54–56, 70
realists 54–56, 76, 84–85, 87, 89, 186; classical 73, 79, 86, 143; liberal 86–87, 174–175; mainstream 53; neo- 57, 171, 174; progressive 71
rearmament campaigns against German 182; European 97; German 97, 101; moral 121; of Western Europe 118
Recchia, S. 171, 174
reconciliation 48, 50, 107; among differences of value 126; Franco-German 101–102, 112–114, 117, 123; national 170
Red Army 96, 105
reunification 102, 115; hypothetical 118
Roche, J.-J. 142, 150
Rougeron, Camille 94–95
Rousseau, J.-J. 81, 108
Russia **65**, 96, 129–130, 183
Russian 119; bombings of Aleppo 83; dissident Solzhenitsyn 121; Federation 167; Franco-Russian agreements 66; secret police (KGB) 183

SALT I 102, 104
SALT II 102, 106
Sartori, G. 151, 153
Sartre, Jean-Paul 3–4, 36, 74, 88, 121, 147, 179
Scheuerman, W.E. 71, 73, 86
Schmitt, C. 32n4, 113, 156, 185, 187
Schmitt, O. 9–10, 70, 78, 85, 89n1, 142, 157, 179, 185

Schuman, R. 120; Schuman Plan 117–118
Shils, E. 127
sociological liberalism 143–144; Aronian IR 146, 149, 152–154, 156, 158–159; French school of 144–146
Solidarnosc 122
Solzhenitsyn, Alexander 121
Sorbonne Trilogy 28, 128, 132
Soutou, G.-H. 108n1, 129
Soviet 114, 128; A-bomb 96; aggression 97; citizen 183; covert activities 182; divisions 181; domination 106, 116, 151; empire, collapse of 158; Franco-Soviet friendship 182; imperialism 119; industrial society 133; invasion of Western Europe 28; power 99; regimes 96–98, 181–182; Society 130; Sovietized France 117; spies 100; threat 102, 113–114, 117–118; world 131; yoke 121; zone 117; zone of influence 29; *see also* Russian
sovietism, expansion of 116
sovietisation: of Central and Eastern Europe 119; of East European regimes 96; of East Germany 116; non-Sovietization of South Vietnam 78
Soviets 29, 98, 102, 107, 182–183
Soviet Union 5, 29, 96, 103, 109n4, 130, 138, 152, 164, 183; collapse/ disintegration of 122, 167; convergence with the West 127; development of nuclear weapons 97; France's great design towards 120; French intellectuals support 121; French Left disillusioned 129; industrial output 133; liberation of Third World from colonization 137; losing the cultural Cold War 127; political transformations 129; SS-20, 121; strategic military superiority 104; *see also* Russia
Spanish Civil War 151
Spruyt, H. 152–153
spy/spies 9, 11, 179, 181, 185, 187, 190–192; American spy-plane U2, 181; self-perception of 190; Soviet 100
SS-20, 106, 121
stability 20, 24, 43, 167, 169, 182; of Aron's thought on Europe 123; automatic nuclear 100; international 67; quest for 104; threatened 157; *see also* instability
Stalin, Joseph 80, 105, 114–115; Battle of Stalingrad 113; death of 118; Stalinist communism 116

Stewart, I. 33–34
superpowers 28–29; accomplices in international system 129; alliance against total war 99; freezing nuclear competition between 104; monopoly of the bomb 116; temptation to use absolute weapon 167
Szymonzyk, S. 95

theory of international relations (IR) 17, 55, 58, 70, 146, 153, 180; Aron's 21, 54, 57, 93, 144–145, 150, 163; comprehensive 154; general 17, 70, 156; Peace and War 14, 119; scientific 67n1; three dimensions 155; US quest for 53
thermonuclear: age 164; bombs 19, 29; explosive power 98; threat 22; weapons 19, 27–28, 192; *see also* nuclear/ thermonuclear weapons
Third Reich 96, 113, 119, 182
Third World War 96
Thucydides 64, 93, 102, 114
Tocqueville, A. de 2, 9, 71, 93–94, 102, 142–143, 145, 156
Treverton, G. 184, 190
Tucker, R.C. 53, 171

unipolar 11; unipolarity 61
United Kingdom (UK) 4, 100, 139, 189; English liberal school of IR 143, 145; industrial nineteenth- century 131; intelligence communities 189; Joint Intelligence Committee (JIC) 187; MI6, 183; *see also* British
United Nations Development Program (UNDP) 170
United States (US) 29, 31, 32n2, 116, 131, 133–134; alliance management 62; arms control 106; atomic bombs 96; based IR specialists 53; best interests 137; bicentennial 123; break with 151; and China 150, 152; Cold War liberals 128; commitment in Europe 116; conflict with Soviet Union 97; *découplage* risks 99, 121; demobilization of the military 96; financial assistance 134; foreign policy 5, 131, 174; industrial rise 135; investment in decolonized countries 127; isolationism 116; liberal Leviathan 63; national interests threatened 174; neo-realists 174; nexus of military/ strategic thought 95; nuclear policy 164, 167; policy of nuclear secrets 100; political decision-making process 95;

proposed international control of atomic energy 96; reception of Aron's thinking 61, 100–101; security guarantee 99; strategists 108; system 109n2; systems convergence debates 128–130; technical edge on nuclear weapon 95; theory of (IR) 53; trajectory of development 138; use of precision-guided arms 168; Vietnam War 140; *see also* American
United States (US) intelligence 189; Community Worldwide Threat Assessment 190
United States (US) interventions: failed, in Somalia 174; in Haiti 174; military, in Iraq 172
US president Kennedy, J.F. 101, 105, 107, 137, 140; administration 99–100, 129
US president Truman, H.S. 105; administration 98; Point Four Program 131, 138
US presidents: Carter, J. 106; Eisenhower, D.D. 99; Johnson, L.B. 129, 140; Roosevelt, T. 103, 105
use of force/recourse to force 18–19, 24, 71, 85, 188, 192; asked to forgo 27; defending 84; legitimacy and legality of 163–164; nuclear 19

Valls, A. 173
Vietnam: American policy 76; disaster 106; War 76, 102, 138–140
Vietnamese people 140; North 140; South 78, 140

Walesa, Lech 122
Waltz, K. 2, 10, 55, 66, 67n1, 106, 143, 153–154, 158, 171
Walzer, M. 81, 173
war (s) 2–5, 8, 15, 19, 21, 28, 74, 85, 93, 103, 106, 108, 109n3, 112, 116, 145, 154–155, 158, 176, 180, 186–187, 189; by accident 105; capability of Germany 109n4; cause of 22; choosing to go to 151–152; civil 96, 99, 107, 114, 154, 164, 167; consequences of 83; continuation of policy by other means 30–31, 106; conventional 75, 168; crimes 75; declared 35; of decolonization 167; development as destiny (*la guerre-destin*) 97; economic causes of 22; end to 101, 113; ethics 83; European 112; extreme situations 78; fear of 74; general 96, 155; human propensity for 51; hyperbolic 96–97, 107; impact of nuclear weapons 98; intelligence 188; internecine 119; interstate 152; just 84, 173; laws of 159; of liberation 113, 155; limited 82, 100, 120, 164; made by passions 107; mechanism of 150; Napoleonic 63, 94; nationalist 95; need to be limited 82; North Vietnamese efforts 140; outlawing 84, 165; personal experience of 147; political goals 159; popular 104, 107; possibility of 1, 25, 57–58, 123; potential eruption of 59; problem of 192; proxy 168, 170; Religious 94; revolutionary 104, 107; risk of 58, 75, 164, 166, 186; risk of prolonging 84; secret 183, 190; shadow of 108, 164; as sociological object 146, 154, 159; sociological perspective of 156; state of 81, 86; on terror, global 163; theory of 17, 83, 94, 103; think 94, 144; total 82–83, 95–96, 99, 120; twentieth-century 22; understand 31, 149, 154; weapon of 80; world 37, 84, 95, 150, 157–158; *see also* nuclear war, peace and war
war and peace/war or peace 31, 144, 154; alternatives of 21, 27; dialectics of 185, 188–190, 192; duality of 186, 188
Weber, M. 3, 6–9, 33, 42, 47–50, 59, 73–74, 76–78, 83, 87–88, 116, 142–145, 147–148, 154, 156, 185, 190
Weberian 66, 149; concepts 7; opposition 175; school 152; sociologist 150; sociology of international relations 147
Wendt, A. 151
World War I (First World War) 63–64, 111, 117, 151
World War II (Second World War) 14, 29, 88, 127, 150, 184; before 148; during 16, 81, 93, 103, 105; end of 106; fate of European Jews during 122; post-World War II 14, 27, 29, 95, 117, 143–145, 147; totalitarian ideology triggered 113

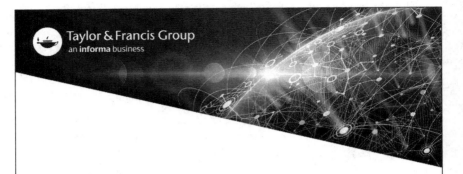